BLOWING UP UKRAINE

BLOWING UP UKRAINE

UKRAINE

THE RETURN OF RUSSIAN TERROR AND
THE THREAT OF WORLD WAR III

YURI FELSHTINSKY
MICHAEL STANCHEV

GIBSON SQUARE

Also by Yuri Felshtinsky

Blowing up Russia
The Secret Plot to Bring back KGB Terror

with Alexander Litvinenko

The Age of Assassins
How Putin Poisons Elections

with Vladimir Pribylovsky

This first edition first published by Gibson Square in 2022.

email: rights@gibsonsquare.com
website: www.gibsonsquare.com

CONTENTS

THE RETURN OF RUSSIAN TERROR AND THE THREAT OF WORLD WAR III

What is to be done?

Ukraine – The First Battle of World War III?

On February 24, 2022, Russia's territorial army invaded neighbor Ukraine without cause, warning, or the slightest concealment. The world was shocked by this hostile act. Overnight, Russia shattered over three decades of peace in Europe after the collapse of the USSR's "evil empire". The naked aggression in the backyard of three other nuclear powers suddenly made World War III seem like a genuine possibility and this was reflected in media headlines.

But the invasion came as no surprise to us. In the wake of Russia's sly earlier attack on Crimea, I published an article arguing that Putin had just written a new chapter in an old conflict with colossal ramifications. Michael Stanchev – Head of the History Department at Kharkiv's Karazin National University and an expert in Ukrainian diplomatic history – and I – a historian of Russia and its secret services – both felt that Europe had been pushed into a situation not seen since 1939, when Stalin and Hitler between them determined the fate of the world. To write this book we pooled our research and contacts – my known and anonymous intelligence sources in Russia and Ukraine, and interviews with key players such as oligarch Yulia Tymoshenko, and Stanchev's detailed knowledge of Ukrainian history and impeccable grasp of its historical sources and contacts in Ukraine's Foreign Office – to set out through which steps the Kremlin is becoming a threat to global stability and has been plotting the rebirth of the Russian empire over twenty years. Early on, we predicted – in print – the date of the invasion based on the six-year planning cycles of the Russian army (without anticipating the pandemic).

As we detail below, Russia's first violent coup against Ukraine took place as early as 1999 when then-Russian Prime Minister Putin and his intimates in the KGB-FSB surreptitiously tried to take Russia and Ukraine at the same time. Ever since, like circling vultures, they have tried again and again to resurrect the Russian Empire as their power and, importantly, wealth grew. From 2008, Putin's totalitarian leadership reached a level where he could comfortably use methods abroad that the rest of the world label as crimes against humanity (but the Duma carefully sanctions as legal through sweeping national laws). It is no coincidence that Russia attacks whenever gas and other mineral prices reach record highs. Oil and gas are the fuel on which Russia's aggression runs; Putin's first war crime (the unprovoked attack on neighbor Georgia in August 2008) followed five years of uninterrupted record gas prices.

Even Ukraine's population is unfamiliar with its own history and place in the world – almost as much as most beyond its borders are. Recent national history was simply ignored by Ukraine's often corrupt leaders – a case of censorship by omission and embarrassment – and there is also Putin's relentless rhetoric in Russian – many Ukrainians are bilingual in that language – that there is no such nation as Ukraine and that therefore none should one exist. Ukraine's jagged story of independence had not yet been told, let alone taught, in the way we set out here – creating a much needed antidote to Russian propaganda.

Whether Ukraine's state officials and oligarchs always deserve our sympathy, we leave for the reader to decide – though as a nation Ukrainians have been beyond heroic. Even eastern Ukraine, its most Russian-friendly part, was not as easily cowed by Putin as Russia's population is (and was) by the Kremlin. We take the reader through Ukraine from its origins as a people, its history of tension and conflict with Russia. Ukrainian politics remain shrouded in backroom mystery, but we unpick many key events. State-sponsored murders; electoral fraud; nepotism and corruption so intense and internecine that it makes even Putin's cronyism seem like mundanely well-organized looting of Russia's wealth. Against this stand its many popular revolutions – Maidans – supported by Ukrainian youths, students and small businesses resisting corruption and pro-Russian, self-serving oligarchs and state officials.

One could dismiss Ukraine's extraordinary and complex evolution of democracy as ultimately irrelevant to the world at large. But this would be a mistake. We uncover the patterns of behavior with which Russia intends to treat the rest of the world if given the chance. In addition, we show how over two decades of mounting frustration, Putin has become obsessed with Ukraine – comparable to Stalin's mania about Poland.

There is a school of thought that condemns Putin and his rhetoric or that of his Kremlin underlings as "the ravings of madmen" who talk, and so act, irrationally (or that thinks the Kremlin is merely acting out after "provocation" by the EU/NATO seeking closer ties). Vladimir Zhirinovsky, for example, the recently-deceased Duma leader of a party founded by the KGB in Russia's puppet parliament, repeatedly and publicly threatened Poland with an atomic bomb; Dmitry Rogozin, Deputy Prime Minister in charge of the defense industry, constantly threatens eastern Europe and especially Moldova with a military attack. But this is really how Putin's inner circle see the world and have done since at least 1999, as we aim to make clear with this book. Their methods may have become more extreme, but their plan has never changed. It pays to take what Putin officials say literally, as they mean it.

Even before the 2022 invasion, Ukraine's victimhood of – and complicity in – Russian corruption is relevant to the world at large. Its occurrence might not be so obvious in the West, but the difference is one of degree, not kind. Roman Abramovich, Alexei Miller, Igor Sechin: powerful allies of Putin have chains of influence, which stretch back to the upper echelons of the Russian political establishment. As soon as one associated person is granted influence abroad, has their name chiseled on the side of a significant building, Putin's agenda begins trickling in. In the US, the UK, Germany, France, and all the other countries favored by its oligarchs, we have seen it with those sucked into the Kremlin's vortex of Russian billions, contracts and unfettered power.

Furthermore, Ukraine has become important on a whole new scale. Since Putin became Russia's President we no longer have direct insight into the political process in Russia. Examining Russia's decades of lethal meddling with Ukraine's officials shows us how his regime really functions. One thing will become clear: Putin's greed for power, land and spoils is as consistent as it ever was. Already he is threatening to switch off the gas supply to Europe as he has done and still does with Ukraine. Russia will extract payments that will fatten the Kremlin's war chest. Yet even this pales in significance with the fact that, unlike Hitler, Vladimir Putin has nuclear arms. Russia's Foreign Minister, Sergei Lavrov, called the risk of nuclear war "serious" in April 2022.

Our story shows that Russia is not infallible. There have been moments of sheer luck, such as Ukraine's Presidential candidate Viktor Yushchenko surviving his poisoning in 2004. Putin also makes crude mistakes. There was the Russian Buk missile that shot down of Malaysia Airlines Flight MH17 with almost 300 passengers, another FSB plot that failed to influence Ukrainian politics by a hair. Ukraine's officials have made few mistakes in recent years – a welcome change from the past. President Volodymyr Zelensky's (elected with close to 75 percent of votes, including all eastern regions near Russia) only error has been to ask the US for the lifting of sanctions against Roman Abramovich. It is the least of coincidences that he was Russia's "peace" negotiator during talks with Ukraine in Istanbul, and it is significant that he was poisoned there and was treated in Turkey rather than Moscow. According to Boris Berezovsky's 2012 court filings (in a case he lost), half of Abramovich's wealth is held in trust for Putin and he is his presentable Western face. Regardless, given their closeness, any sanctions against him hurt Putin directly.

As I am writing this, Russian Federation's Army Forces are firing missile and bomb strikes over the Ukrainian city of Kharkiv, the home of my co-author Michael Stanchev and Ukraine's most Russophile of cities. This destruction and sowing of death is the Kremlin's punishment of the city's Russian-speakers after they stood up to Russia's advances to impose Kremlin rule in the town after the annexation of Crimea.

"The situation is terrible," he writes. "We are bombed every single day. They clearly decided to starve the entire city until we capitulate. Last night, I slept on the floor because of the air missile or bomb strikes that hit close to our building. Thank God, my wife and I are alive. Our children are asking us to leave, but I do not have a car and it is extremely dangerous now to drive on the roads of Ukraine." Not much later I received a message from our Ukrainian publisher saying that their printer in Kharkiv was bombed and this book won't be available in Ukraine as planned. This couldn't be more symbolic of Putin's intentions. We are extremely glad, therefore, that this edition will be followed by editions in other languages.

The invasions of Georgia (2008) and of Crimea (2014) were two moments when the West could have halted Putin with little effort. Each further instance of prevarication will make it more difficult, however, to stop Russia's aggression in its tracks. The capture of Crimea gave Putin two key strategic advantages in the 2022 invasion he was planning. First, it made the coast of Ukraine defenseless against relentless shelling from Russian warships. This gives Russia the upper hand in the war. Second, Crimean taxes flowed for eight years into Russia's war chest instead of Ukraine's. As Ukraine has a standing army but no navy to speak of, unless there is an allied peace-keeping fleet that prevents the shelling of coastal cities such as Mariupol and restores the balance of military power between Russia and Ukraine, the latter will not be able to hold on to its Black Sea and Sea of Azov territories from Russia to Moldova, or indeed seaport Odessa. Regardless of the "victories" Ukraine's army may win with the help of Western weapons in its interior, this loss of coastline is what Putin is really after. It will complete another stage in his "Operation Novorossiya", discussed in the final part of this book, that is itself part of a longstanding poker game aimed at slowly boring holes through the NATO alliance. A united military response by allies in the Black Sea will shock Russia as it is used to being able to bully its neigbors as it wishes.

More likely than not, the next step in the Kremlin's script is that tactical nuclear weapons will be deployed "by" the "independent" Donbas republics in Luhansk and Donetzk. Sealed off by Russian troops, as they now are, they will miraculously be able to design, test and produce their "own" nuclear warheads, which are of course merely a fig leaf for Russian nuclear arms stationed just across its own territorial border. What is to stop these "independent" republics from launching a nuclear war head at Kyiv or a nuclear missile straying "because of the wind direction" on or near the Polish border? Evidently Luhansk and Donetzk are merely be "protecting" themselves against Ukrainian aggression when they fire such a missile, Putin would claim. Finding out the forensic truth of such a strike will take years, as it did with the Russian Buk missile mentioned earlier that brought down flight MH17 from "insurgent" Donetsk four months after Crimea's annexation. To untangle a response to an actual nuclear bomb will be a lot more difficult than helping the Ukrainian population win its war of emancipation from Russia – rather than merely fighting Russia's land grabs – a window that is closing with each month of war that passes.

One look at Belarus clarifies that the nuclear stage of Operation Novorossiya has started. Unlike Ukraine, the Kremlin has successfully turned Belarus into a vazal state. Its President Alexander Lukashenko, neighbor to Ukraine and NATO members Poland, Latvia and Lithuania, rescinded his country's non-nuclear status on 27 February 2022, three days after Russia's invasion of eastern Ukraine and recognition of the two "people's" republics in Donbas as "independent" states. Both Belarus and Ukraine signed the Treaty of Non-Proliferation of Nuclear Weapons after the USSR fell apart, and handed over their Soviet nuclear warheads to the Russian Federation. Belarus never dismantled its nuclear infrastructure and can now re-arm "itself" with long-range nuclear weapons as a "sovereign" nation.

These three proxy locations from which to launch nuclear weapons are the perfect basis for a lethal global blackmail: give Putin what he wants, or there will be nuclear war. Russia's breathless announcement that the conveniently renamed "Satan II" intercontinental ballistic missiles will be operable from the Autumn 2022 is part of the blackmail. It is bluff at this stage, but it is no coincidence that this very public intimidation coincides with the very public war on Ukraine. With Putin's words, it is only a matter of time before they are much more than that. In Ukraine he is creating the momentum from which he can say, "we are reluctant to do this but we are forced to use them unless you surrender". Belarusians or people in Donbas may be killed in retaliation – as Russian soldiers are in the current attacks on Ukraine soil, not to mention Ukrainians since 2014 – but once that nuclear precedent is established, the clock cannot be dialled back.

If southern Ukraine falls, Putin will have a corridor to Transnistria, Moldova's western border with Ukraine. This is the next stage in Operation Novorossiya where Russia plans to use Ukraine's strength against itself. From there Putin can take minute Moldova and attack Ukraine from the west while picking away at NATO countries, waiting patiently like a spider in its web for a moment of weakness to swoop. The hard lesson from this book is that Putin needs to be resisted decisively when one can; yet that this is never easy for democracies, highly-imperfect ones like Ukraine included. Putin will simply come back stronger at one's own expense. At the moment tactical nuclear weapons are still not an operational part of Russia's equation. When they are it will be too late.

Yuri Felshtinsky, April 2022

INTRODUCTION

I previously wrote two books that turned out to be ahead of their time. The first one, *Blowing Up Russia,* I wrote with Alexander Litvinenko, former lieutenant-colonel of the KGB/FSB. At the time, it drew attention in the still free Russian-speaking media and an extract was published in *Novaya Gazeta* in Moscow. The book's publication, however, was banned by the Russian government – the first known case of such censorship since Solzhenitsyn's *Gulag Archipelago* in 1973.

In *Blowing Up Russia,* Litvinenko and I wrote how the Federal Security Service (FSB) successfully sabotaged democratic reforms in the country, and how the First Chechen War (1994-1996) was skillfully instigated through terrorist acts organized by Russia's special services. We chronicled the terrorist apartment bombings which took place in several Russian cities in September of 1999 and revealed in our book that the Russian security services were also behind these attacks, which brought about the Second Chechen War (1999-2009). The goal of security services at that time was to bring their own man, Vladimir Putin, to power. The West had great difficulty believing that this was an accurate description of what had happened in the "democratic" country of Boris Yeltsin, Russia's President from 1991 to 1999.

Five years passed, and in November 2006, Alexander Litvinenko died by poisoning in London. The reasons for this murder and its history are a separate story. But it was after Litvinenko was killed with a rare, deadly, almost untraceable radioactive substance (Polonium 210) produced only in Russian State laboratories, that Western public opinion, not only in Britain and the US, but all over the world, shifted to considering the historical truth of *Blowing up Russia*. In 2007, the book was published in translation in twenty countries from Europe to the US, Brazil to Japan.

The other book that turned out to be ahead of its time was *The Age of Assassins* which I wrote with Vladimir Pribylovsky, a Russian historian, journalist and 1990s Duma candidate.[1] Vladimir was 59 when he unexpectedly died alone in his Moscow flat on 13 January, 2016, shortly after the announcement that the verdict of the year-long independent, forensic Litvinenko Public Inquiry by a British judge would be published on 21 January, 2016 – the judge damningly concluded that Litvinenko's assassination was "probably approved" by Putin; MI6 concluded that *Blowing up Russia* had been a red line.

The Age of Assassins showed how for 10 years, from the collapse of the USSR in 1991 to 2000, the KGB (renamed "FSB"), kept trying to seize power over Russia, including control over the country's vast natural resources, financial system and economy, and how the first two attempts – in August of 1991 (the so-called "August Putsch") and in March of 1996 (the plot by General Alexander Korzhakov, head of Yeltsin's Security Service) – failed. As a result of these two failures, the KGB/FSB radically changed its tactics. Rather than seizing power through a coup, putsch or conspiracy, it now aimed for political power through ostensibly legal means, that is through nationwide democratic elections. There was really only one office that needed to be won: the Presidency of the Russian Federation held by Boris Yeltsin. It was a simple but effective plan. In exchange for full immunity from any prosecution upon relinquishing power, President Yeltsin was offered three potential candidates he could name as his successor: Yevgeny Primakov, a former KGB agent and former director of Russia's foreign intelligence; Sergei Stepashin, former director of counter intelligence and one of the masterminds behind the First Chechen War; and Vladimir Putin, Director of the FSB.

In effect, whomever Yeltsin chose, power would end up in the hands of the secret service. Putin got lucky. Yeltsin turned down Primakov, who was in a hurry to oust Yeltsin before his term expired by colluding with the anti-

Yeltsin-faction in Parliament. Yeltsin also turned down Stepashin, who conspired (or so it appeared to the Yeltsin's Chief of Staff and confidante, Alexander Voloshin) with Yuri Luzhkov, the Mayor of Moscow, who was himself hoping to become Prime Minister or President of Russia one day. Putin, a relative nobody and not a member of the *nomenklatura* (the USSR elite), was the last on the list. It was he whom Yeltsin picked by default.

In August of 1999, Putin was promoted by Yeltsin from the post of Director of the FSB to the post of the Prime Minister of Russia. And in September, the terrorist apartment bombings took place, which killed more *false flag* than 300 people and launched the Second Chechen War. On December 31, 1999, Yeltsin resigned as agreed, making Putin "Acting President" of Russia even before the national elections that were due to take place on March 26, 2000. On 6 February, the Russian army occupied the Chechen capital Grozny, which cast Putin as the victorious leader, and a month later, he won the election, receiving just over 50 percent of the vote (if the official figures are to be believed).

tyrant's reforms

Upon taking office, Putin radically changed Russia's system of government. He reformed the upper house of Parliament, the Federation Council, eliminated the autonomy and elections of regional governors. He proclaimed the so-called "vertical of power" and returned to the Soviet system of strict central control via the Kremlin, took control of the mainstream media and gradually eliminated freedom of speech, controlled elections at all levels and reshaped Parliament so that it became no more than a rubber stamp for Kremlin power.

Putin was also lucky in another way. The beginning of his rise to power coincided with a rise in raw material and mineral prices to historically unprecedented levels. This led to the rise in the level of prosperity in the country as he allowed the market economy to develop and flourish. Behind the scenes, Putin formulated a code or the rules of engagement that the elite had to accept under his rule. This code was very straightforward. Those who planned to compete for power with the Kremlin were to be finished off (economically and, where necessary, even physically). Those who only wanted to get rich were eventually allowed to become members of the "Corporation". This parallel organization to the state was headed by Vladimir Putin as the chairman of its board of directors. The composition of this "Corporation" and the number of shares owned by each of its members remained a strict state secret, which could only be guessed by those on the outside of this small group of 200 to 300 shareholders.

From the moment Putin came to power in 2000, he began to appoint to the highest government positions former and current employees of the security services, or people who were known (or there were good reasons to believe) to be agents of the special services. Technically speaking, Putin did not violate any laws by doing so. But the net result was that, within a few years, Russia found itself literally in the hands of the FSB. Former KGB officers held not only top government jobs but were also on the boards of directors of major companies or even led some of Russia's largest economic conglomerates, primarily in the natural resources and financial sectors.

Outside of Russia, it was believed that Putin's evident desire to usurp total state power stemmed from greed to enrich himself and those around him. But, as long as Russia's leading kleptocrat cleaved to the rule of law internationally and did not cast his dictatorial net beyond the borders of the Russian Federation, the US and Europe were not prepared to see him as a threat in the way that the Western world viewed with deep fear some of his predecessors – Lenin, Stalin, Khrushchev, or Brezhnev. In fact, Putin seemed to be the most progressive, the most predictable and even the most pro-American Russian leader that foreign governments had ever had to deal with. Together with Mikhail Gorbachev and Boris Yeltsin, Putin seemed like a leader with whom one could have sensible, if not friendly, business ties. Western media also treated Putin with the benefit of doubt, treating him, and those around him, as if they were decent men instead of people in the habit of ordering the death of opponents.

As we explained in *The Age of Assassins*, this was a naïve point of view. One of the goals in writing the book was to reveal to the public the insidious, gradual and intentional poisoning of democracy in Russia – with assassinations to "manage" elections where necessary. But Putin's reliability still seemed defensible at the time to many experts, even when their point of view was dealt a death blow when Russian troops began military action against Georgia, Russia's neighbor in the Caucasus, in August 2008.

The background of the Russian-Georgian conflict is convoluted and complex, and the Russian media, engaged in a disinformation war, did much to outfox the worldwide public media. Apart from being the birthplace of Joseph Stalin and his security chief Lavrenti Beria, Georgia as a country was one of those states that few people outside of its borders understood, never mind the historical complexity of the Georgian mini-territories of Abkhazia and South Ossetia. Western public was unable to make sense of the fine-grained sectarian antagonism in the south Caucasus, with people sometimes peacefully coexisting and sometimes warring with each other.

When in the same month of the attack it became clear that the Russian army had no plans to enter Georgia's capital Tbilisi and seize the whole of Georgia, Western powers breathed a sigh of relief and shelved their geo-graphical maps and expert briefings. The world moved on. Abkhazia and South Ossetia, where Russian troops remained, held referendums and declared "independence", "recognized" only by occupier Russia. Georgia broke off diplomatic relations with Russia in protest, but no one else did. The Russian-Georgian conflict gradually faded and was forgotten.

This was the context in which *The Age of Assassins* was published, a collective biography of Russia under Putin and the KGB, where Putin worked all his life. Though it warned against complacency where others saw a well-behaved kleptocracy, in 2008, one could still not compare Putin to Hitler or Stalin. Not because he was born in a different country, but because everyone thought – or rather hoped – it was important to Putin that he remained an influential member of the club of Western countries: despite the gangsterism of the September 1999 apartment bombings in Moscow, despite the second Chechnyan war, despite the suppression of freedom in Russia since 2000, despite the 2008 war against tiny neighbor Georgia.

In March 2014 with the annexation of Ukraine's Crimea, however, Putin crossed the Rubicon. He removed himself from the European and global community and made clear that the country's corporate financial interests took second place to Russia's national, or rather nationalist and geopolitical interests as he sees them. And Putin sees his Russia as a new empire, rising from the ruins of the past. Why? Because it used to be there.

Unfortunately, Putin knows very little of history, and it is no accident that German Chancellor Angela Merkel (who knows her history well) said that the Russian President lives in a different world. She did not mean that Putin has lost his mind. She meant that Putin operates with concepts from the nineteenth century and from the first half of the twentieth century when everyone thought in terms of territorial conquest and the unification of nations – in other words, in terms of the ideas long-outdated elsewhere in the Western world.

Russia fought a war in the Crimea in 1853-1856, and lost. In 2014, resuming the same war, Putin acted from a position of strength, just as Hitler did in his time when he started invading neighbors. But Hitler relied on a coalition with Italy and Japan, and from August 1939 – on an alliance with Stalin; yet, he still lost. Putin Russia's capture of the Crimea was in absolute isolation. It was not supported by any country (except a couple of African countries). Even China confined itself to polite neutrality.

The analogy between March of 1938, when Hitler first seized Austria and then, in September of that year, the Sudetenland, and Putin, who occupied Crimea in March of 2014, will be discussed at the end of the book. But the question is not whether Putin is another "Hitler" or "Stalin' or whether he is following in their blood-soaked footsteps. The question is what to do and what to expect for all of us who know the history of Hitlerism. If Hitler had stopped in March or September of 1938, or even in March of 1939, after occupying Czechoslovakia, he would have gone down in German history as a towering political figure and would have remained in the memory of the German people as the Führer who united ethnic Germans within the borders of the new German empire. But he did not stop, because Germans had to be "saved" and "united" throughout Europe. On 1 September 1939, he began military action against Poland, not realizing that he was starting a war that would go down in history as World War II. When he embarked on his Polish campaign he really did not want, or plan to, fight a major war.

Putin won't stop either. Like Hitler, Putin cannot stop. Russians are not "oppressed", as he calls it, in Ukraine, nor is it run by "Nazis". There are other countries like Ukraine with Russians. Ukraine will not be the end of the nationalist and imperialist aspirations of the Russian President for life. "Lifelong" because under the new Russian Constitution, Putin is entitled to remain President: first it was until 2018; then until the next Presidential Election; and then also to be reelected for another six years, until 2024 (by the end of which time he would have reached Stalin's age).

Seeing the haunting analogy, knowing the history of World War II, looking back at 1938, what could and should Western democracies have done then differently in order to put a stop to Hitler's thirst for expansion for the sake of expansion? Start a war with Germany in 1938? Make global anti-German agreements and isolate Germany by imposing all sorts of sanctions? Or, wait, do nothing and hope that the storm would blow over?

In 1938, Europe chose the latter option: to wait and do nothing. A year and a half later, having given up the remnants of Czechoslovakia, it was still caught up in the war that Hitler had started, and Hitler didn't even give anyone the option of surrendering. We know how Hitler, Germany and the Germans ended up – in defeat, in a ruined country, and with the Nuremberg Trials.

"Nuremberg Trials" of Putin lie ahead and they should be held in Sevastopol, Crimea's largest city with a population of 350,000 people. We should call out the names of its future defendants (at least some of them) now: Russian Foreign Minister Sergey Lavrov, serving since 2004 under Putin as his Von Ribbentrop (who was hanged by the verdict of the Nuremberg Tribunal); Russian Defense Minister since 2012, Sergey Shoigu; the political and ideological author of the "Capture Ukraine" project, Vyacheslav Surkov; former FSB director and Security Council Secretary since 2008, Nikolai Patrushev, who is responsible for force and punitive operations in the war with Ukraine; the Russian fascist Dmitry Rogozin; the medieval obscurantist-nationalist, Alexander Prokhanov; Russian television CEO and freedom suppressor, Konstantin Ernst; and those who remain behind the scenes: KGB/FSB generals Sergei and Viktor Ivanov and Igor Sechin. These are all the members of the Russian parliament and the Federation Council who first sanctioned the introduction of Russian troops into Ukraine, then the annexation of Crimea.

We will also remember at that moment: the silence of Anatoly Chubais, an obsequious minister who never objected to anything to his superiors; the embarrassing half-true statements of Alexander Voloshin, one of the creators of Putin's totalitarian "vertical of power"; Vladimir Pozner, who was allowed to comment on Western television networks – just as he was in the early 1980s when the Soviet army marched into Afghanistan – explaining in his perfect English and without blushing that the Crimea was but a "limited exercise" and a "liberation."

In March 2022, Western democracies faced a hard choice. They were exactly in the same position as in 1938: start a war with Putin? Make global anti-Russian agreements and isolate Russia by imposing all sorts of sanctions? Or wait and do nothing?

One thing is clear. Russia is unable to wage it on its own against the rest of the world. The likely result of this war will be the collapse of the Russian Federation, against which the collapse of the Soviet Union in 1991 would seem like a modest rehearsal. I am far from thinking that Russia today has enough internal strength to stop the impending catastrophe. Putin is the aggressor and warmonger. This war will bring shame, ruin, and death to Russia. The Ukrainians proved during the EuroMaidan that they are willing to die for their freedom. It is not obvious that Russians are willing to do the same for Putin's imperial ambitions.

Yuri Felshtinsky

1

A Thousand Year Wait

From a historical point of view, Ukraine has been unlucky. Being at the center of Europe, it was caught between four different layers of civilization – western and eastern, northern and southern. For Ukraine, this has become, if not a tragedy, then an eternal problem. From the very beginning of its existence, the peoples who inhabited this territory had to fight back from both western and eastern neighbors. It was attacked from the north by Scandinavian tribes; from the south by the Crimean Tatars and Turks. Ukraine was constantly in search of allies to survive. But the fact that Ukraine was the heart of Europe left a strategic chance to become an area of peace, not conflict, and a bridge of understanding and partnership between civilizations different in mentality and culture, religion and tradition.

Ukraine's problem was also that it was constantly part of another state or a foreign empire. Even though it lies at the heart of Europe, it has never had a well-known history either to itself as a nation or internationally to other European nations. Only "on the third attempt" of becoming a nation state – after Bohdan Khmelnytsky in 1654; Mykhailo Hrushevsky in 1917; and the collapse of the USSR in 1991 – did Ukraine finally gain its independence.

What then is Ukraine now that it is a nation state rather than an administrative region of another country? It may come as a surprise that it is one of the largest states in eastern Europe and geographically the second

European state after Russia (603.5 thousand square kilometers), comparable in size to France and Germany. Ukraine's population is roughly similar in size to Spain's and ranks just below thirtieth in the world, but is on a downward trajectory, falling from 51 million to around 44 million in 2020. It is unevenly distributed across the country. The eastern industrial regions (Donetsk, Luhansk, Dnipropetrovsk, and Kharkiv), closest to Russia, and the Carpathian regions (Lviv, Ivano-Frankivsk, and Chernovtsy), furthest away from Russia, are the most densely populated. Relatively sparsely populated are some areas of the Ukrainian Carpathians, Polesia, and southern regions (Volyn, Zhitomir and Kherson).

Ukraine has been inhabited by different peoples since ancient times. Today Ukrainians, Russians, Belarusians, Jews, Poles, Tatars, Bulgarians, and others — more than a hundred nationalities coexist on this land. Ukrainians are the titular ethnicity, making up the majority of the country's population — about 78 percent in almost all regions except Crimea. Russians are the second largest group in Ukraine — about 18 percent and live mostly in the eastern and southern regions of the country which are closest to Crimea and the Black Sea. Then come the Belarusians, Moldovans, Crimean Tatars, and Bulgarians. The Orthodox population is predominant (88 percent). Numerous attempts to unite and create a single local church have been unsuccessful, however.[2] The total number of Catholics in the country is around 4.8 million people. Muslims live mainly in Crimea (Crimean Tatars) and according to various sources number from 500 thousand to 2 million people. Crimea has around 2.3 million inhabitants, 65 percent of which are ethnically Russian.

Geographically, Ukraine has a multitude of neighbors. It is bordered to the south by the Sea of Azov and the Black Sea, to the west by Poland, Slovakia, Hungary, Romania, and Moldova, and to the north and northeast by Belarus and Russia. The biggest land border between Ukraine and Russia and Belarus is just over 3 thousand kilometers. The sea borders with Russia are 1,355 kilometers long, but they are still unresolved. The geographical center of Europe (according to measurements taken by both the military department of Austria-Hungary in 1887, and — by Soviet scientists after World War II — is located in the territory of modern Ukraine, near the town of Rakhiv in Zakarpattia region.

Even though Ukraine has only existed as an independent nation state for close to three decades, the history of its people is unique. After the collapse of the Soviet Union, Ukraine became the third nuclear power after the United States and Russia. Instead of vying to maintain that position, Ukraine showed the world that a could and should give up nuclear weapons and concentrate on peaceful co-existence when it renounced them in 1994.

Culturally, Ukraine is the country of the legendary soccer coach Valery Lobanovsky, the famous footballers Oleg Blokhin and Andrey Shevchenko, but also, no less famous, poets and writers Taras Shevchenko and Ivan Franko, Lesya Ukrainka, philosopher Grigory Skovoroda, and very young poets, writers, scientists, and ambitious politicians of the new generation. Ukraine can also be rightfully proud of its scientists, Nobel laureates – physiologist Ilya Mechnikov, physicist Landau and economist Simon Kuznets, engineer Evgeny Paton, surgeon Nikolai Amosov and many others.

What is "Ukraine"?

To understand better why the events taking place in Ukraine have such significance, it is necessary to have a grasp of the long history of its people. It is not only the land of Yaroslav the Wise but also of the "free Cossacks," led by Hetman Bohdan Khmelnytsky and his army, who were not afraid to challenge the Turkish Sultans, and Ukrainian Hetmans Peter Sagaidachny and Ivan Mazepa.

The very name "Ukraine" has its own historical explanation. The term is first mentioned in the Ipatievskaya Chronicle in 1187, and according to some scholars, comes from the Old Russian word "periphery", which originally was applied to the border lands of Kyivan Rus, then the Polish state, and later the Russian Empire. This was the interpretation of the term used by historians. Until the end of the thirteenth century, this term is found in chronicles and meant a different "Ukraine": the lands adjacent to the "Lyakh" from Volyn in the basin of the left bank (Ukraine to the right of the Dnipro river) along the middle course of the Southern Bug, and the north-eastern part of Galich land and the so-called Pereyaslav land (part of Kyiv and Chernihiv land). In the sixteenth century, the term "Ukraine" meant the border lands between the Grand Duchy of Lithuania and the

Ottoman Empire (lands of the Zaporizhzhian Cossacks and Wild Fields). There were also terms such as "Ukrainian Russia Minor", "Lithuanian Ukraine", "Polish Ukraine", "Cossack Ukraine", but they did not stick. After the creation of the Novorossiya Territory, the term "Russia Minor" was used more often, referring to the Ukrainian lands stretching to the southeast.

Subsequently, the term "Sloboda Ukraine" became the most common name. This term is associated with "peripheral" territories, as Mykhailo Hrushevsky, Ukraine's greatest historian, wrote in the early twentieth century. This did not mean "backward", as Russian anti-Ukrainian propagandists insist, but "border" areas, because the lands of Ukraine were at the junction of three empires – Russian, Ottoman and Polish. From the end of the sixteenth to the eighteenth century "Ukraine" became a distinct geographical label, and from the eighteenth century it was commonly used, along with the church term "Russia Minor."

As an alternative to "peripheral", some Ukrainian historians and linguists have also put forward that the name "Ukraine" derives from the word "edge", "kraina" (Ukr. "kraïna"), that is "country", "land inhabited by its people", called Ukrainians. At the same time, it is argued that in the Ukrainian language the terms "ukra§na" and "okra§na" have always meant Ukraine as a separate and independent territory. As the national consciousness of the Ukrainians grew, "Ukraine" began to be perceived not only as a geographical term, but also as the name of an ethnic people at the turn of the nineteenth and twentieth centuries.

Ancient Ukraine

According to archeologists, the first *homo erectus* (upright man) appeared in the territory of Ukraine a million years ago, migrating from Western Asia through the Balkans and Central Europe – and were the first "Europeans". Then, more than 150 thousand years ago, other "Europeans" appeared – the Neanderthals, and 30 thousand years ago – the *cro-magnons*, our almost-contemporaries.

Another key moment in the history of Ukraine is occupied by the Trypillia culture in the fourth and third millennium BC between the Danube-Dnipro rivers, the heyday of which occurred in the period between 5500 and

2750 BC Trypillian ceramics were one of the most advanced in Europe of that time, excelling in sophistication and painting. Some Ukrainian scholars argue that the Trypillians are the "ancestors" of modern Ukrainians. Whether true or not, they managed to convince Viktor Yushchenko, President of Ukraine (2005-2010).

Archaeologists are still arguing about the presence of the Cimmerians in the southern part of Ukraine and in other regions, but many authors link the "Cimmerian era" (second half of the eight and seventh centuries BC) to Ukraine's Northern Black Sea coast. They were replaced in the seventh century BC by the Scythians, who displaced the Cimmerians from the Ukrainian steppes.

It is believed that the Scythians created their first state – the Scythian State, which fell to the Sarmatians in 200 BC. In the third century AD the Goths moved to Ukraine from the north-west and founded their own kingdom. In 375 BC the Goths were defeated by the Huns, who came from the depths of Asia, and migrated beyond the Danube to the borders of the Roman Empire, where over time they created their kingdom. The Hunnish empire, after suffering several defeats from the Romans and their allies, quickly lost power and disintegrated. After the Huns invasion, the hegemony over the present territory of Ukraine at the end of the fifth century passed to Slavic tribes. The left-bank part of the territory of Ukraine and Tauria became dependent on the Turkic Khazar Khaganate. At present, the northwest of Ukraine is considered the most probable origin of the Slavic tribes.

The Kyivan Rus and its disintegration (882-1240)

These Slavic tribes stood at the foundations of the origin of the ancient Russian state, first with its capital at Nizhny Novgorod, east of Moscow, and then at Kyiv, known to the world as Kyivan Rus – 'Rus' meaning men who row, a word with a Viking origin like the first rulers. Kyivan Rus occupied a territory enormous for its time – from the Crimea in the south; the Dnistro river and the upper reaches of the Vistula river in the west in Poland; and up to the upper reaches of the northern Dvina river in the north, beyond Nizhny Novgorod. Karl Marx compared it to Charlemagne's empire.

Kyivan Rus is also the cradle of Orthodox Christianity. In 988, Prince Vladimir baptized his subjects. Metropolitans appointed by Byzantium were at the head of its church. Vladimir's son Yaroslav, known as Yaroslav the Wise, succeeded in securing the borders of Kyivan Rus, developing trade relations with the Byzantines, the Khazars, the Scandinavians, and the peoples of Europe and Asia.

Dynastic marriages were the key to medieval diplomacy and power, and Yaroslav was jokingly called "father-in-law of Europe". He was married to Ingigerda – the daughter of Swedish King Olaf while his daughter Anastasia was married to the Hungarian King Andras, his daughter Elisabeth to the Norwegian King Gardardad, and his daughter Anna, known as Anna of Kyiv – to the French King Henry I (she was styled Queen of France). Arguably, Yaroslav was one of the first drivers of the integration of Ukraine into Europe and an invested supporter of a European union through peaceful means.

Yaroslav's successors continued his international diplomacy. During the existence of Kyivan Rus, until its collapse, there were more than 100 dynastic marriages, from Russian-Polish, Russo-Hungarian, Russo-Byzantine, German, Lithuanian, Bulgarian, Norwegian, English, to Austrian, and Croatian.

After the death of Yaroslav the Wise, internecine wars began between the separate principalities of Kyivan Rus and its disintegration. Although Vladimir Monomakh managed to briefly strengthen central power, the disintegration of Rus proved irreversible. In addition, the southern borders of Kyivan Rus were constantly being raided, and a significant part of the population had to seek refuge in the more secure lands of Rostov and Suzdal, where new cities were founded.

Russian history glosses over the fact that a coalition of eleven Russian princes took Kyiv by storm in 1169 and subjected it to plunder. As the sources recount, they plundered and burned "the mother of Russian cities" for two days. Many Kyivers were taken captive. In monasteries and churches, soldiers took away not only jewelry, but also raided all icons, crosses, bells and vestments. The Saint Sofia cathedral was plundered along with other temples and for all the people in Kyiv there was "inconsolable sorrow." It was the beginning of Kyiv's decline as a center of power and in 1362 the city was annexed to the Grand Duchy of Lithuania, then a rival to the Grand Duchy of Russia and one of the largest countries in Europe.

Galicia-Volhynia princedom (1199-1392) and the period of Polish-Lithuanian rule (1385-1795)

One of the largest principalities during the period of the political fragmentation of Kyivan Rus was the principality of Galicia-Volhynia, which stretched over 116 thousand square kilometers. Prince Daniel of Galicia was even raised to the title "King of Rus" by Pope Innocent IV. In spite of its vassal relations with the rule of the Mongolian Golden Horde, it pursued an independent foreign policy in Central and eastern Europe, competing with the kingdoms of Poland and Hungary as well as with the principality of Lithuania, and partnering with Rome, the Holy Roman Empire, and the Teutonic Order. However, in 1392 the principality of Galicia-Volhynia was divided between the Kingdom of Poland and the Grand Duchy of Lithuania and the lands of modern Ukraine in the thirteenth and fourteenth centuries were divided between its neighboring states.

Ukrainian identity, however, continued to persist as a result of the conflicts within Christianity. Poland and Lithuania were allied when the Lithuanian prince Yagaylo married the Polish queen Jadwiga and became the Polish king (under the name Wladyslaw). Their descendants ruled both states for the next three centuries, but Wladyslaw and Jadwiga were Catholics, which led to friction with the many Orthodox princes in their territory. Over a hundred years there were three civil wars, which resulted in a number of Ukrainian cities – Kyiv, Lviv, Vladimir-Volynsk, and much later (from 1760) Uman – becoming self-governing under, the "Magdeburg Law". The imposition of Catholicism also led to the separation of Chernihiv lands in northern Ukraine to the Orthodox Grand Duchy of Moscow. In the rest of Ukraine large estates (latifundia) worked by the Ukrainian population were developed by Polish nobles.

When the Polish-Lithuanian Commonwealth was divided in 1795 between Russia, Prussia, and Austria, Prussia got the capital and most of the Polish lands, Austria received Krakow and Lublin with their surrounding territory, including all of Galicia; whereas Russia received the West

Belarusian and West Ukrainian lands (without Lviv), and most of Lithuania.

The Cossacks *from khmelnytsky to Mazepa*

In the history of Ukraine's nation forming, the history of the Cossacks is very revealing. In the fifteenth century, much of the land in the southern part of Ukraine was sparsely populated and called "Wild Fields". Here, at the lower reaches of the Dnipro river, beyond the Dnipro rapids, lived peasants who had run away from the Polish-Lithuanian Commonwealth and the Russian lands, and who called themselves the Cossacks. They were based on islands along the river, where it was easy to hide and they could easily defend themselves, and from where they could raid the Crimean Khanate to the south and the lands of the Polish-Lithuanian Commonwealth.

Among the numerous rebellions against Polish-Lithuanian rule, the most successful was the rebellion led by Hetman Bohdan Khmelnytsky (1648-1654), which led to the formation of an autonomous region, Hetmanshchyna (1649-1782). Initially Khmelnytsky tried to find support from the Ottoman Empire and signed a treaty with it in 1649. But, having received no firm guarantees (the Turkish sultan merely asked his Crimean Khan to assist Khmelnytsky), he also sought other potential allies. Not finding support, the Cossack leader began rapprochement with the Russian government, which provided military and material support to his army, recognized Khmelnytsky as Hetman (ruler), and invited him to accept Russian citizenship.

In 1653, Khmelnytsky sent the embassy to Moscow to Tsar Alexis with the request to accept "all his Malorossiya and all the Zaporizhzhian Hosts [armies] as his eternal possession, citizenship and patronage". And after intensive exchange of diplomatic missions between him and Moscow in January of 1654 in Pereiaslav, not far from Kyiv, a secret council of representatives was held, who swore allegiance to Russia.

This event was widely referred to as "reunifaction" in historical literature written in Soviet times, although there was nothing to "re"-unify. Some modern scholars argue that only about 300 representatives of the Cossack nobility decided the fate of Ukraine for many centuries ahead and that the treaty to Moscow was not widely supported by other Ukrainian Cossacks.

The treaty itself does not mention "annexation" but uses the word "protec-torate", indicating self-governing status of Ukraine. Certainly, the privileges and liberties for the Cossack aristocracy were preserved, as well as for the broad masses of Cossacks, whose lands and estates were not taken away, and for their children who had the same "liberties as their ancestors and their fathers".

Khmelnytsky was unable to maintain the status quo and, as a result of the armistice in 1667 of the Russian-Polish war, the lands to the east of the river Dnipro (left-bank Ukraine) passed to the Moscow principality, and the right-bank Ukraine to the west remained under the authority of Poland-Lithuania. After his death, parts of Ukraine also came under Turkish rule, but Cossack self-governance continued in the parts of Hetmanshchyna that fell under Russian control. It had administrative and territorial borders with Russia, and customs duties were levied on imports. Private property rights were preserved and Russian laws did not apply to this territory (the courts applied Lithuanian law).

Khmelnytsky's dream of a united Cossack Ukraine on the left and right bank of the Dnipro remained alive, however, under Hetman Ivan Mazepa (1687-1708), who maintained trade relations with European countries though diplomatic representation was limited to Moscow. Unrest ceased and agriculture developed thanks to free Ukrainian farmers who were not serfs like Russian peasantry. The system of taxes introduced by Mazepa led to a flourishing economy, the construction of new buildings, monasteries and city churches in the Ukrainian Baroque style, while book printing developed and the Kyiv-Mohyla Academy became a university.

Despite initially having good personal relations with Peter the Great, Mazepa complained more and more that "Moscow wants to take the whole Ukraine into hard bondage". Mazepa was forced to maintain Russian troops at the expense of Ukrainians, which caused discontent among Ukrainian farmers who bore the financial brunt. Ukrainian Cossacks were drafted into the Russian army, but their commanders were Russian or foreign treating Cossacks with contempt. Peter also increasingly demanded money from Mazepa to build his own new Russia, including melting Ukraine's bells for weapons, which displeased Mazepa, who refused to destroy the churches, in which he himself had invested enormous funds. When the tsar refused to help him fight Poland (saying that even "ten men I cannot give you"), Mazepa dropped his alliance with Peter and turned to the Swedish King Charles XII. He was swiftly declared a traitor and, on orders from Moscow, Prince Menshikov massacred almost all the inhabitants of Mazepa's official residence Baturin.

When the raids of the Tatars and Turks from the south stopped, the need for Cossacks in the Russian army disappeared, and the Hetman gradually began to lose his military importance. In 1781, Hetmanshchyna, their administrative domain, was subsumed under direct Russian rule. On the right-bank part of Ukraine the Polish order of old continued (mainly in terms of its cultural and educational life), while on the left bank most of the Ukrainian farmers now fell under Russian law and became serfs of their landlords.

Novorossiya and Donbas

The last Hetman in the history of Ukraine within the Russian Empire was Cyril Razumovsky. After the demise of the Cossacks, their elite was integrated into the Russian nobility. Many became influential politicians, generals or even rose to the Chancellorship of Russia, such as Alexander Bezborodko. The Ukrainian nobility was allocated vast lands in the south of the Russian Empire, referred to as "Novorossiya."

The development of Novorossiya accelerated at the end of the eighteenth century under the leadership of Prince Potemkin, who had almost unlimited power to fulfill this task from Empress Catherine II. Under him, a new city, named after the empress – Ekaterinoslav (1776) now Dnipro, was built and, in 1783, Crimea was added to Novorossiya. Other subdivisions and reorganization within the Russian empire followed.

Despite Russian rule, few Russians moved to Novorossiya, then still a sparsely populated area. Instead, Tsarist authorities called for settlers and "Danube" Slavs who felt oppressed under the Ottoman Empire to move there, as well as Poles, Germans, French, Swedes and Swiss from Europe. It was a mass resettlement which occurred in the early nineteenth century. Settlers were guaranteed the status of free colonists and exemption for a time from taxes and military service. Instead, the "Trans Danube settlers" mixed with the local population, while Moldovans and Vlachs, Gypsies and

Jews were also moved here. In the Kherson region alone, the Ukrainians made up 71 percent, and the Russian population only 5 percent.

After 1917 the term "Novorossiya" fell out of use as a large part of its territory was incorporated by the Bolsheviks into the Ukrainian Soviet Socialist Republic (UkrSSR). In the part of Ukraine that remained independent, the term also disappeared. But the label in its Ukrainian spelling became relevant again in 2014, when a self-proclaimed confederative union of the Donetsk and Luhansk People's Republics was created in eastern Ukraine as "Novorosiya," although these territories had historically never been part of (Russian) Novorossiya before. Who introduced the idea will be discussed below. The term was also claimed by Ukrainian separatists in the Odessa and Nikolaev regions near the Black Sea.

Another region that is in the crosshairs not only of Russian and Ukrainian politics, but also of the international media, is Donbas. It is part of the Donetsk coal basin discovered in the eighteenth century: an area of about 60,000 km², with total coal reserves of 140.8 billion tons to a depth of 1800 meters. Its industrial development began in the late nineteenth century. Laborers moved there to work at the iron foundries. They were mainly Ukrainians from the right bank. The main investors in this region were Belgians, who founded its mining coal and building metallurgical plants, which is why the region was called "the tenth Belgian province". Russia, held hostage by its backward technological skills, opened the door to foreign investors from Europe and America, who brought with them the latest technologies in the production of metal that the Russian military required.

The third important historical region in the north-east of Ukraine is Slobozhanshchina. The name itself comes from the type of settlement – "sloboda" (freedom), which had significantly more privileges than the inland provinces of Russia. During the sixteenth through eighteenth centuries, this border region with Russia was actively settled by Tsarist authorities with right-bank Ukrainians from the Polish-Lithuanian Commonwealth, and by serfs who had escaped from Russia. Settlers were expected to do guard duty and military service near the fortresses of the Belgorod frontier, which defended entry to Russia proper.

All these regions together – Slobozhanshchina, Novorossiya, Donbas, and Crimea – constituted a vast territory inf southeastern Ukraine, were densely populated and industrially developed.

The Ukrainian Question in the nineteenth century

By the end of the eighteenth into the beginning of the nineteenth century, the regions of Slobozhanshchina, Novorossiya, the right bank with the whole Dnipropetrovsk region, Donbas, and Tauria (together with Crimea) constituted the so-called "Great Ukraine" within the Russian Empire. After numerous resettlements, both domestic and foreign, the population in this territory represented by now a colorful palette of different ethnicities – Ukrainians, Russians, Jews, Poles, Serbs, Bulgarians, and Germans. The most numerous were the Jews, who settled throughout the right-bank.

The nineteenth century saw the emergence of national identities throughout Europe, and in the Russian Empire in particular. Initially, it was limited to culture and education and the nascent intelligentsia was mainly interested in the study of ethnography, folklore, language, and literature. This posed no direct threat to the Russian autocracy, whose highest circles were favorably disposed to the emergence of interest in cultural and national issues of the Ukrainian people. Moreover, after the Polish revolt of 1830-1831, it even supported the birth of Ukrainophilism in order to weaken Polish influence over its right-bank Ukraine.

On the eve of the abolition of serfdom, the Tsarist government promoted the study of the native language in schools among the local population (the first two years of study), the Ministry of Education allocated the necessary funds to publish textbooks and literature in the Ukrainian language, and charity balls were held to raise funds for the publication of Ukrainian literature. True, a debate arose in Russian society: should the language spoken by the inhabitants of Ukraine be considered a Little Russian dialect or an independent Ukrainian language? A progressive part of Russian society perceived Ukrainian as an independent language, while others considered it "an adverb of the Russian language, corrupted by the Polish influence."

Societies and fraternities sprang up – the Cyril and Methodius brotherhood, Hromada (Unity), *Osnova* (Basis) magazine, etc. – which supported the national idea of Ukraine in an abstract fashion without ever touching on the question of self-determination. This would not have been permitted as the idea of a "Great Russian Nation," included all the Empire's Slavic people. Even so, in the southwestern region of the Russian Empire (including the Kyiv region) a number of secret societies were formed with the active participation of Polish national liberation movement activists and they did set political goals and spread the idea of autonomy.

However, after the second Polish revolt of 1863, when the Polish intelligentsia proselytized the unity of Poland, Lithuania and "Western Rus" (Ukraine) and created the idea of an independent Ukrainian state "from the Caucasus to the Carpathians," Russian authorities began to see the Ukrainian national movement as a threat. Repression of prominent figures of the Ukrainian national liberation movement followed. The "Valuyev Project" (named after Pyotr Valuyev, the Russian Interior Minister) was introduced, which prohibited the publication of scholarly literature in the "Little Russian language," except for "fine" writing, i.e. novels. As Valuyev himself wrote, the reason for creating this policy were "purely political circumstances – the emergence of separatist designs... under the pretext of promoting literacy and education". It was the beginning of the Tsarist drive to assimilate Ukraine wholesale into Russian culture and life.

The next step in solving the "Ukrainian question" was the signing by Tsar Alexander II in May of 1876 of the "Emskogo Decree" in the German town of Bad Ems, which sought to limit the teaching of the Ukrainian language in the Russian Empire and the publication of any writings in the Ukrainian language. The decree was the brainchild of the assistant director of the Kyiv school district, M.V. Yusefovich, who accused Ukrainian teachers of wanting a "free Ukraine in the form of a republic, with a Hetman at the head" and was a bitter enemy of Ukrainophilism. The law became known as the "Yusefovich Law."

The tsar's decree forbade import of books written in Ukrainian into the Russian Empire from abroad without special permission, to publish original works and make translations from foreign languages. The only exceptions were "historical documents and monuments" and "works of fine literature," with some restrictions and subject to prior censorship. Ukrainian spelling – "kulishovka" – was prohibited and only Russian orthography – "yaryzhka" – allowed. It was also forbidden to stage the Ukrainian theatrical performances (removed in 1881), any books in Ukrainian, or concerts with Ukrainian songs. In elementary schools teaching in Ukrainian language was prohibited, and Ukrainian books were removed from school libraries. The newspaper *Kyiv Telegraph* was also closed, and Ukrainian professors were fired from the Kyiv University.

In right-bank Ukraine, the Austro-Hungarian authorities, under whose rule the Galician lands fell, however, allowed Ukrainians to have their own publications, to study their language in schools and establish their own theaters, to develop Ukrainian culture. The Tsarist Emsk decrees ceased to have effect after the first Russian revolution in 1905, but in practice the ban on "anything Ukrainian" continued until the First World War.

The great upheavals that accompanied the late nineteenth and early twentieth centuries, caused by revolutions and two world wars, led to mass migrations of the Ukrainian population, mostly smallholders, to Russia, the Caucasus and the Far East, as well as to the United States, Canada, Brazil, and Argentina. But a historic new opportunity lay in wait after all its trials and tribulations.

The Russian Revolution and civil war in Ukraine

By the beginning of the twentieth century, Ukraine had settled into two parts much like the DDR and West Germany but for centuries instead of decades: the right bank, which gravitated towards its closest neighbors Poland, Austria and Hungary, and the left bank, which was drawn towards its closest neighbor Russia. In both cases, Russian was treated as the official language in Ukraine.

After the Revolution of 1917 in Tsarist Russia, left-bank Ukraine again regained the independence that it had lost under Catherine the Great. In the spring of 1917, Ukrainian political parties in Kyiv established the Verkhovna Rada (parliament). The Bolsheviks, for their part, as in Petrograd and Moscow, also tried to take power in Kyiv. This attempt, however, failed. Then in December 1917 the Bolsheviks left Kyiv, moved to Kharkiv, and there proclaimed themselves the seat of soviet power in Ukraine. At the same time, troops were sent from Moscow by Lenin to assist the Ukrainian Bolsheviks in seizing power in Ukraine. As the Red Army was successfully advancing and about to take Kyiv, the Verkhovna Rada decided to declare independence and establish the Ukrainian People's Republic on January 22, 1918.

The Ukrainian People's Republic first President was the famous scholar-historian Mykhailo Hrushevsky, who had previously been dismissed from his university post under the imperial "Yusefovich Law." He restored the Ukrainian language as a state language and created the Ukrainian Academy of Sciences, chairs of Ukrainian studies in universities, etc. It was a popular decision and the famous Ukrainian writer V. K. Vinnichenko, for example, wrote: "The Ukrainian people are Ukrainian, therefore all institutions should be for them as Ukrainian people: government, administration, school, court, and also the army".

At the same time, the Ukrainian government unsuccessfully negotiated with the Soviet Moscow government for the recognition of their new republic. For the first time in modern Russian-Ukrainian history, the question of the Crimea and its border territories reared its head. Initially, the republic included nine provinces – though not Crimea. Soon, however, two further Ukrainian provinces, and Crimea withdrew from Soviet Russia to join independent Ukraine. Even in the Bolshevik-Russian Donbas area, a splinter republic declared its separation from the Ukrainian Soviet Republic. This displeased Lenin, nor did the idea find support among the local population either and it disappeared.

Germany assumed the role of protector of Ukrainian People's Republic. However, the arrangement with the Verkhovna Rada was purely financial, and the fact that the Germans and the Austrians were taking money out of the country made Germany and Austria-Hungary responsible for economic troubles in the eyes of the population. Ukrainian proponents of independence were now anti-German, as they saw the Germans as "occupiers". Ukraine's soviet supporters were also anti-German, because they believed that it was only under German pressure Ukraine had declared independence and separated from Russia. Over time, the Verkhovna Rada adopted this anti-German stance and on April 28, 1918, Germany carried out a *coup d'etat*. They arrested the government and installed the puppet regime of Hetman Pavlo Skoropadsky who cleaved to a pro-German course.

After World War I, the Germans and Austro-Hungarians fled from their parts of Ukraine, and the Bolsheviks solved the "Ukrainian question" militarily by invading. The Red Army gradually occupied Ukraine and proclaimed a soviet Ukrainian state. It was called "war communism" in Ukraine, and included red terror as well as "prodrazverstka", taking all produce from farmers at a low fixed price. It also led to acute discontent by the summer of 1919. Requisitions made by Bolshevik "food squads" in favor of the Red Army and the Soviet government led to riots. Power in the country was slipping from the hands of the Bolsheviks. But Ukraine was also mired in civil war and internecine strife. Leaders such as the Ukrainian nationalist Simon Petliura, on the one hand, and the anarchist Nestor Makhno, on the other, emerged.

The Bolsheviks skillfully played off the Ukrainian leaders against one another defeating Petliura with the help of Makhno's armies and then wiping out Makhno. By 1921, soviet authority had been established in most of Ukraine and the UkrSSR was formed. Potentially significantly a century later, some western Ukrainian lands were not part of Soviet Ukraine and went to Romania, Czechoslovakia, and Poland. In December 1922, the UkrSSR, together with Belarus and Transcaucasia, under the auspices of Soviet Russia, created the USSR, which lasted until 1991.

The Bolsheviks who won in Ukraine promptly began a policy of Russification: the introduction of the Russian language in schools and universities, to the resentment of the Ukrainian population. Christian Rakovsky, comrade chairman of the first Soviet Ukrainian government, managed to convince the Bolshevik leadership at the Kremlin of the need to change tactics. In 1923, the equality of the Russian and Ukrainian languages was declared as part of the new Soviet policy of "cultural and national autonomy" for the peoples living in the USSR.

At the same time, the "korenizatsiya" ("Ukrainianization") of the party and state apparatus began. From this time, the Soviet leadership began to assist in the development of the Ukrainian language and even Ukrainian radio broadcasting aimed at Ukrainians who lived in Ukraine and beyond – in other Soviet republics, such as Russia, and in other countries: Poland, Czechoslovakia and Romania. Instead of Russians, Ukrainians were appointed to government positions in the UkrSSR.

In fact, Communist units were formed in Ukraine that worked with national minorities. Their work was coordinated by the subdivision of national minorities of the Central Committee of the Communist Party of Ukraine. Four sections were created: Jewish, German, Polish, and Bulgarian; the formation of thirteen national districts (seven German, four Bulgarian, one Polish, and one Jewish) began.

The policy of "korenizatsiya" as a method of Bolshevik nation-state building, provided for the training, upbringing and promotion of native nationality cadres, consideration of national factors in the formation of the party and state apparatus, organization of a network of educational institutions of various levels, opening of newspapers and magazines in native languages, book published in the languages of indigenous nationalities; profound study of national history, revival and development of national traditions and culture, and equality of regional languages. The essence of the policy was the Bolshevik leadership's attempt to control the processes of national-cultural revival in the UkrSSR and other satellite republics of the USSR.

Researchers distinguish three periods in the cultural policy of the Bolsheviks: the period of Russification in 1917-1922; the period of Ukrainianization in 1923-1932; and the period of Sovietization, which began in 1933 under the slogan of Stalin's fight against the Ukrainian "nationalist deviation." By this time in Ukraine, as in Russia, Stalin had carried out ruthless collectivization, leading to the end of freeholdings and the creation of poorly functioning collective farms. Many rich Ukrainians were resettled to Siberia, the Altai Territory, Transbaikalia, and the Far East.

As a consequence of Stalin's interference, a famine began in Ukraine that took the lives of millions of people. In addition, mass repressions began in Ukraine in 1933, and the most prominent figures of Ukrainian culture, intelligentsia and the Ukrainian elite were sent to camps and prisons. In 1938, the Soviet government announced the formal end of Ukrainianization and set a course for "accelerated assimilation" of Ukrainians with Russians. Russian laborers were sent to the eastern regions of Ukraine (including the Kharkiv and Donetsk regions). They settled permanently in Ukraine and were employed to build the giant factories planned under Stalinist industrialization of the USSR. At the end of the construction phase, the newcomers stayed to work in the factories, which is why Ukraine's industrial cities are largely populated by people who are ethnically Russian.

Ukraine between Stalin and Hitler

On the eve of World War II, under the Ribbentrop-Molotov Pact signed by the Soviet and German governments in August 1939, virtually the entire western Ukraine was ceded to the USSR and "joined the friendly family of nations". This meant that a part of Ukraine which had never been part of the Russian Empire now came under Russian dominion through the UkrSSR.

A year earlier, in 1938, as a result of the Munich Treaty, the autonomous Carpathian Ukraine, which was part of Czechoslovakia, was transferred to Hungary. Most of the western Ukrainian population were then deported by the Soviet government to Siberia, Kazakhstan, and Central Asia. A significant portion of the Ukrainian population of these areas was later forced to emigrate to the United States and Canada. One of the authors of this book, Michael Stanchev, was born during the deportations in Kazakhstan, where his parents were exiled. It was an horrific tragedy for the residents of western Ukraine. Many towns and villages were deserted, and those who remained experienced the friendly "new Soviet order."

Of the deported population, those who survived returned to their native lands only after Stalin's death and the de-Stalinization of the Soviet Union, which began after 1956. At the same time, the inhabitants of western Ukrainian towns and villages deported from Ukraine were labeled by Stalin as "Banderites" after Stepan Bandera, the Ukrainian national leader who headed the Organization of Ukrainian Nationalists (OUN) and fought for national Ukrainian interests first in Poland and then in Soviet Ukraine at the end and after World War II. Today the term "Banderite" has made a comeback and is once again used by Russian and pro-Russian propaganda to inflame tensions and provoke hostility between the western and eastern regions of Ukraine.

As a result of the Hitler's attack on the USSR and the war that began in 1941-1945, Ukraine was occupied by the Germans and divided into the Reichskommissariat "Ukraine" and the District "Galicia". In the latter police detachments and even the SS Division "Galicia" were formed from the locals, and the Ukrainian nationalist organizations were left relatively free. Not so in the Reichskommissariat "Ukraine". An attempt by the Ukrainian Insurgent Army (UIA) to create an independent state as protectorate of the Third Reich found no German support. As a result, the leaders of the insurgent movement, in particular Stepan Bandera, were arrested and sent to the concentration camps at Sachsenhausen and Auschwitz, where they remained for the rest of the war.

Through Bandera's followers, the idea of a united Ukraine lived on. In Nazi-occupied western Ukraine, its military branch UIA deployed guerrilla warfare. On Soviet territory, Ukrainian partisans fought under the command of the Soviet army. Soviet propaganda did not say a word about the involvement of the UIA, which fought behind the lines of the German army (apart from using the derogatory word "Banderites").

Meanwhile, the front line of World War II swept over Ukraine twice, first from west to east, then from east to west. More than five million Ukrainians died in the war, and about two million were deported to Germany as forced labor. Approximately 700 cities and towns and 28,000 villages were destroyed. Over ten million people were left homeless. In view of this, Vladimir Putin's comment that the USSR did not need the Ukrainians during World War II falls nothing short of being untrue.

In 1945, Stalin, paying lip service to international law, included Ukraine and Belarus as "independent" states in the newly formed United Nations, although they didn't play any independent role. Both the army and foreign policy of Ukraine and Belarus were an integral part of the armed forces and foreign policy of the USSR. Throughout the period from 1944 to 1991, the UkrSSR was completely subservient to the policies of Moscow, and any manifestation of independence was punished without mercy and labeled as "nationalist" or "Banderite."

When Petro Shelest, First Secretary of the Central Committee of the Communist Party of Ukraine and member of the Politburo of the CPSU Central Committee, published a harmless book called *Ukraina Sovetskaya Radianska* (Our Soviet Ukraine) in Ukrainian rather than Russian, he was accused of nationalism and removed from all government posts.

Ukraine played a hugely important role in the Soviet economy, and its eastern regions were the mainstay of the Soviet military-industrial complex, coal mining and metallurgical industries, high-tech industries, and student populations. During years of Gorbachev's perestroika and glasnost, the Ukrainian part of the soviet intelligentsia increasingly acquired a national flavor, as demonstrated by the first truly democratic elections to the Supreme Soviet of the UkrSSR, whose deputies proclaimed the Declaration of State Sovereignty of Ukraine. Finally, Ukraine was once again a unified state as it was under Yaroslav the Wise in 1054. It had taken almost a millennium to get there.

2

Dawdling in Europe

1991, the end of Soviet history: Michael Stanchev (co-author of this book), as deputy of Kharkiv's city council, assessed the city's international stature. In spite of its enormous economic and scientific arsenal of 240 industrial enterprises, 143 scientific-research institutes, and 23 higher educational institutions, he concluded that Kharkiv had no more than a provincial footprint.

Collapse of the Soviet Empire

The capital Kyiv has always been jealous of Kharkiv. Kharkiv was the "third" city, the "production line" of the Soviet Union. The city was home to such industrial giants as the Kharkiv Tractor and Aviation Plants, the Turboatom, which produced nuclear turbines, and the Kharkiv Tank Factory, home of the famous T-34 tank. In Kharkiv in 1938 a group of scientists led by Lev Landau was the first in the world to split an atomic nucleus. The Imperial University of Kharkiv was one of the four oldest universities of the Russian Empire. It gave the world three Nobel laureates – Ilya Mechnikov, Lev Landau and Simon Kuznets. Among its famous pupils were composers, writers, poets, and scientists – Mikola Lysenko, Isaak Dunaevsky, Nikolay Kostomarov, Dmitry Yavornitsky, Oles Gonchar. Novelist Leo Tolstoy, scientist Dmitri Mendeleev, the German naturalist

Alexander von Humboldt, the writer Johann Wolfgang Goethe, the Scottish geologist Roderick Impey Murchison, the British preacher and Marxist philosopher John Lewis, and the French storyteller Eduard Labule all accepted honorary doctorates from the university.

When the August putsch organized by the KGB and top-level Communist Party nomenklatura began in Moscow on August 19, 1991, many Soviet Ukrainian officials in Kharkiv suggested that Ukraine immediately "surrender to Moscow". Direct communication with Moscow was restricted, however. Only the City Council had one telex machine, donated by its twin city of Nuremberg,[3] to communicate with Moscow. Through the "Nuremberg telex," the Kharkiv leadership kept in touch with Yeltsin's headquarters. Kharkiv's newly elected mayor Yevhen Kushnaryov showed courage, speaking on the central square of the city in front of a rally of many thousands, and urged not to give in to provocations and support "Yeltsin's democracy." Three days later, the putsch was suppressed in Moscow and on August 24, the Verkhovna Rada (Supreme Council) of the UkrSSR proclaimed Ukraine's independence.

To legalize this decision, a referendum on independence was held in Ukraine on December 1, 1991.[4] At the referendum of December 1, 1991, a simple question was put on the ballot: "Do you want Ukraine to declare independence?" The turnout for the referendum for the independence of the Ukraine republic was 84.18 percent. A resounding 90.32 percent of those who voted answered "yes"; a mere 7.58 percent answered "no". The message couldn't have been clearer.

At the same time as the referendum, Presidential Elections were held.

President Leonid Kravchuk

Every President elected by the former Soviet Republics after the collapse of the USSR was a senior Communist Party (CPSU) official – with the exception of Belarus, which in 1994 elected Alexander Lukashenko who used to run a kolkhoz farm; he was an early example of someone who decade after decade proved unbeatable at the ballot box like neighbor Vladimir Putin after him. The other Presidents were most often the First Secretary of that Soviet republic, sometimes a member (as in Ukraine) of candidate for membership (as in Russia) of the Politburo of the Central Committee of the CPSU. In other words, all the Presidents of the newly independent states (except Lukashenko and Putin) were part of the *nomenklatura*. Leonid Kravchuk, who was elected President of Ukraine on December 1, 1991, was no exception.[5]

After the failed August putsch in Moscow, Kravchuk had resigned from the Ukrainian Communist Party, as did the rest of those who decided to stay on in Ukrainian post-Soviet politics. By the time the Presidential campaign began in Ukraine, he therefore already had the veneer of a non-partisan politician, and this is how Kravchuk presented himself to the voters. Since he was a former leader of the Ukrainian Communist Party, his candidacy was supported at the elections by his former Communist allies, though the party itself was banned at the time. The Communist Party representative at the elections, Oleksandr Tkachenko, for example, withdrew his candidacy in favor of Kravchuk. At the same time, Kravchuk was also supported by part of the National Democrats, who promoted him as the "Father of Independence" as he had retained his position as Chairman of the Verkhovna Rada, Ukraine's unicameral parliament. As a result, Kravchuk received 61.6 percent of the vote and became the first democratically elected President of Ukraine.

A week later, on December 8, 1991, Kravchuk signed with Russian President Boris Yeltsin and President of the Supreme Soviet of Belarus Stanislav Shushkevich an agreement to dissolve the Soviet Union and create the Union of Independent States (CIS). The agreement was signed in Belovezh Forest, near Brest, Belarus, and went down in history as the "Belovezh Accords." Two days later, the Supreme Soviets of Ukraine and Belarus ratified the agreement, and on December 12, Russia did the same.

The speed at which the former Soviet republics began to join the Belovezh Accords was staggering. On December 21, Armenia, Azerbaijan, Kazakhstan, Kyrgyzstan, Moldova, Tajikistan, Turkmenistan, and Uzbekistan joined the agreement. These countries together with Belarus, Russia and Ukraine signed in Alma-Ata the Declaration on the Aims and Principles of the CIS and the Protocol to the agreement on the establishment of the CIS. On December 25, Mikhail Gorbachev, President of what was left of the USSR and its fifteen founding republics, tendered his resignation.

Now that the republics had gained political independence, they needed to work toward creating a market economy. What was Ukraine like after declaring independence at the end of 1991?

Even before the official signing of the Belovezh Accords, on September 2, 1991, the President of the Supreme Soviet of Ukraine (and future President) Leonid Kravchuk declared Ukraine's intention to "become a direct participant in the European process and European institutions." At that time, Ukraine ranked seventh in the world in terms of its industrial and military potential and was one of the most developed republics of the USSR. Even Ukrainian agriculture was advanced by Soviet standards. Ukraine had a good number of scientific, engineering and managerial personnel. The country had a wide network of scientific institutes and industrial enterprises and a powerful military-industrial complex (mainly concentrated in the south-eastern part of Ukraine). By early 1992, Ukraine also had 1,240 nuclear warheads, 133 RS-18 strategic missiles, 46 RS-22 strategic missiles, 564 bomber cruise missiles, and about 3,000 tactical nuclear weapons.

The full-blown crisis of the 1990s, which engulfed all former Soviet republics, particularly affected Ukraine, as the largest and most closely associated republic with Russia. The severing of economic ties, which began very deliberately and was initiated by the former Communist-party nomen-klatura and the KGB, looked more like sabotage, although it was presented to the public as a "natural" result of the collapse of the USSR, the creation of a market economy, and the privatization of industrial assets. The strategy of those who failed to prevent the collapse of the Soviet empire in August 1991 was to bring former Soviet enterprises to complete bankruptcy and then, through the financial-industrial groups already under the Communist Party and KGB control, take them for next to nothing, and either keep them for themselves, or re-sell them at a profit. At the same time, no one was engaged in the real economy, reforming production and investing money. The companies that flooded Ukraine with foreign-sounding names, chief among which was the English word "invest", usually had little relation to abroad and were used exclusively for resale.[6] Former party functionaries and secret service officers became millionaires almost overnight. Party or youth

Komsomol apparatchiks, secret-service officers and their agents headed the banks and firms. Independent businessmen were usually suppressed or had to "accept" someone's powerful "protection", usually special services or gangsters, and the latter were eventually forced to hand over their clientele to the same special services.

The administrations which came and went, from Presidential to regional, did the same thing: they shook down the state or simply plundered it, "chipping away" at its budget. Their slogans may have been different: for European integration, or for union or reunification with Russia. But these slogans were just tactical weapons for the appropriation of state property or of funds. There appeared longstanding delays in the payment of wages to industry workers, teachers, and other state employees – and state employees made up the majority of Ukraine's work force. Inflation from 1992 to 1994 reached a thousand percent. The privatization of the Soviet state economy, especially industry, was accompanied by corruption on an industrial scale. The economic condition of the country as a whole was catastrophic.

On June 7, 1993, a strike of miners began in Donbas. On June 17, the Verkhovna Rada, at the request of the miners, scheduled a referendum of "confidence" (no confidence) for September 26. However, after consulting with the President, the Rada canceled the referendum at the last minute and scheduled early elections instead: the parliamentary elections on March 27 and the Presidential Elections on June 26, 1994.[7]

Kravchuk, who came to power on a wave of independence, failed to galvanize his political credo during his short months in power. Sometimes he was in favor of cooperation with European institutions, sometimes in favor cooperation with of the Commonwealth of Independent States. People used to call him the only President who managed to "run between the raindrops." As a result, the Ukrainian people neither became part of the new Europe nor returned to the old Russia. In the 1994 election, Kravchuk, despite his close ties to Russia, presented himself as a "national" politician, had broad support in western Ukraine, and contrasted himself with Leonid Kuchma, the former Prime Minister who advocated closer ties with Russia. It was Kuchma who in July 1994 defeated Kravchuk in the second round and became President.

Budapest Agreement, 1994

Since the collapse of the USSR, Washington had been very concerned about the nuclear arsenal which Ukraine, Belarus and Kazakhstan received as a result of the liquidation of the Soviet Union. The destruction of these weapons in the young republics, which had broken away from Russia and were no longer covered by the old Soviet international agreements, became a foreign policy priority for the newly independent states. Moscow was also keen to strip its new neighbors of their "nuclear power" status. Thus, Bill Clinton, who became US President in 1993, and Boris Yeltsin in Russia made promising statements about "economic incentives" and a favorable political climate in the world for Ukraine to agree to return its missiles and warheads to Yeltsin's Russian Federation.

Washington also resorted to political pressure. In particular, Clinton's official visit to Kyiv to meet with President Kravchuk was canceled. But, while under pressure from the two superpowers, Belarus and Kazakhstan managed to remove nuclear weapons in 1992, Ukraine still resisted, primarily under pressure from the leaders of the Ukrainian People's Movement represented by Vyacheslav Chornovil, who urged President Kravchuk not to relinquish them. It was Chornovil who voiced his fears about the threat posed by Russia, demanding security guarantees from the international community.

Those guarantees were given in 1994. On December 5, a Memorandum on Security Assurances in connection with Ukraine's accession to the Nuclear Non-Proliferation Treaty was signed during a summit in Budapest. Ukraine pledged to adhere to three non-nuclear principles: not to receive, not to produce or acquire nuclear weapons.[8]

Later, France, Canada, and China also signed the treaty, and Ukraine, in addition to offering to mediate security talks with Russia, received an invitation from European nations and the United States to participate in the Partnership for Peace program and to begin cooperation with NATO. Nothing else seemed to threaten Ukraine's security as its sovereignty and territorial integrity were securely assured by the international community.

In 2009, after the invasion of Georgia by Russian troops that followed in 2008, former Secretary of Ukraine's National Security and Defense Council

Volodymyr Horbulin called for a review of the Budapest Memorandum as not having met expectations and to convene an international conference to "start the process of demilitarization of the Black Sea."

Today it is obvious how right Horbulin was and how relevant his proposal was. He wanted the conference to include not only guarantor states, but also other leading world powers, such as Germany. Evidently, after the occupation of Crimea and the unilateral denunciation of the Russian-Ukrainian agreement on the Black Sea Fleet in March 2014, Russia, one of the guarantors of the Budapest agreement, is no longer likely to attend such a conference.

President Leonid Kuchma

During the 1994 election campaign, Kuchma's slogan "For an Alliance with Russia!" played an important role. Nostalgic for the old Soviet life, when everyone was poor but happy, Ukraine's Slavic soul perceived Kuchma as the best candidate, with the right path for the future – "Forward to the past!" But the reality turned out to be quite different: Kuchma had no plans to return Ukraine to the old Soviet Union. It was under Kuchma that financial and industrial clans began to form and gain strength, new political parties were created such as the Party of Democratic Renaissance of Ukraine, which gradually became the People's Democratic Party of Ukraine, supported by Kuchma.

Having gained strength from the mass privatization of state property, the new financial-industrial Ukrainian elite began "buying" their deputies. Seeing that these deputies were protecting not so much the interests of the elite as advance their own, the elite themselves began to look at the political seats that promised even greater profits than having a business. Why hope for anyone else to do your business, if you can run the state yourself and pass laws profitable to your business?

In 1995 the President signed a decree about the formation of financial and industrial groups (FIGs) "to promote structural reorganization of Ukrainian economy, speed up scientific and technological progress, increase competitiveness of Ukrainian goods." This act provided unlimited opportunities for those FIGs, which were not only close to political power, but in fact were created by them. They were allowed to independently approve the procedure of indexation of fixed assets. The Antimonopoly Committee, with the consent of the Cabinet of Ministers, could give FIGs a legal monopoly, if the latter carried out state programs for the development of priority sectors of the Ukrainian economy. Most importantly, FIGs enjoyed financial benefits and low taxation, which allowed them to launder money on a huge scale with impunity. An important element in the creation of FIGs was the presence of a leading enterprise in the group, its own commercial bank, through which all financial transactions were carried out, united by a single technological chain.

One of the main motives behind the creation of these FIGs was to streamline lobbying activities and distribution of state funds. That is why the supervisory boards of such groups included high-ranking officials directly or through front men. In fact, all the largest FIGs in Ukraine were members of the Union of Industrialists and Entrepreneurs. As a public organization, this union had the right to make proposals during the preparation of economic laws, as well as to lobby for them in Parliament. Many of Ukraine's leaders, such as Kuchma himself and former Prime Minister A. Kinakh, became President of the Union after they resigned. The merging of power and business became seamless.

It should be emphasized that these groups, which controlled the enterprises that produced the lion's share of the Ukrainian GDP during the Soviet times, had no intention of investing seriously in the development of the economy of the new Ukraine. They were not interested in introducing new technologies or innovations in production, although there were plenty of such inventions available in the country. Instead, FIGs tried to reduce the costs of the enterprises they controlled, gradually forcing out the state's share and privatizing them for next to nothing.[9]

We will not dwell on the characteristics of even the key players of financial and industrial groups in Ukraine, as this would require writing a separate book. We will only note that the groups have divided their spheres of influence throughout the country. The main ones are the Donetsk and Dnipropetrovsk groups. Each of them has its own parties and leaders. Donetsk traditionally supported the Regions (Rhioniv) party, led by Viktor Yanukovych, and Dnipropetrovsk supported the Fatherland (Batkivshchyna) party, led by Yulia Tymoshenko. It was they who determined the political direction in the country, periodically carrying out "orange" and "white-blue" revolutions, the main purpose of which was the redistribution of financial resources and the seizure of top government positions.

Europe

Immediately after the collapse of the USSR and the declaration of Ukraine's independence, a large part of society, especially young people, hoped that the country would follow the path of integration into Europe. The promises of the then Ukrainian leadership provided some optimism in this regard. When President Kuchma ran for President in 1999, he made Euro-Atlanticism a platform for his candidacy, fired his Foreign Affairs Minister and offered this position to Borys Tarasyuk, Ukraine's NATO representative and an ardent supporter of Euro-Atlanticism. His main diplomatic efforts were aimed at getting Ukraine to sign an association agreement with the EU, and getting at least some kind of reassuring signals from the EU about Ukraine's European prospects. A committee on European integration was created in the Verkhovna Rada, and an entire cabinet-level Ministry of European Integration was formed.

As Ukraine continued its cooperation with NATO within the framework of the Partnership for Peace, the European Union was in no hurry to embrace Ukraine. Many Ukraine-EU summits were held, during which the concrete steps towards the implementation of the Maastricht and Copenhagen criteria were carefully analyzed. At all the summits, the European Commission repeated the same thing: we support the intention and desire of the Ukrainian authorities to integrate into European institutions. But in practice little happened.

At the same time, at all levels and at all meetings with EU representatives, the Ukrainian leadership separated the prospect of joining the EU from the prospect of joining NATO. In 1997, this was discussed, for example, during the talks between the Chairman of parliament, the leader of the Socialist Party, Oleksandr Moroz, and the Prime Minister of Bulgaria, Ivan Kostov. When Kostov said that Bulgaria was seeking both EU and NATO membership, Moroz replied that Ukraine was not ready to join NATO, but was ready to join the EU.

In theory, the Ukrainian leadership was ready for the EU. In reality, they were not. Ukraine would have to undertake the difficult job of adapting its legislation to European standards, to have a truly democratic country, guaranteeing freedom of speech, elected executive bodies, local self-government, independent courts, and a free press, not to mention meeting the economic criteria of the EU. Meanwhile, the country continued to experience a systemic economic crisis. As a result of the first stage of mass privatization, Ukraine's unique technical, scientific, and industrial potential was subverted and stopped functioning. The ruling elite was in no hurry either to reform the way the state operated. Europe watched in silence and, seeing inaction of the Ukrainians, made no further promises.

Due to mismanagement at the highest levels from the mid to late 1990s, Ukraine's GDP plummeted as hyperinflation reared its head. In August 1996, Ukraine's nominal currency was devaluated 100,000 times and replaced by the hryvnia. Inflation and the decline in production in Ukraine far exceeded that of neighbors Russia and Belorus.

All this made the development of Ukrainian statehood more problematic and the crisis more protracted. Polarization in society intensified. The rich grew richer and the poor grew poorer. The oligarchy seized all levels of power and the parliament. The authorities became extremely sensitive to criticism. The European Union was forgotten about, and Ukraine's European direction all the more so.

Putin's first attempt to capture Ukraine

The country which never forgot about Ukraine was Russia. Or rather, its special services hadn't. The most important Russian agent in Ukraine was KGB general Yevgeny Marchuk. Born in Ukraine in 1941, Marchuk graduated from the USSR Alexander Pushkin Pedagogical Institute in Kirovgrad, Russia, where he studied from 1958-1963 to teach Ukrainian and German language and literature, and where he was recruited by the KGB.[10] In 1988, he was appointed Head of the KGB Department in the Poltava region. In 1990, when he was already a general, he was appointed First Deputy Head of the KGB of the UkrSSR. From June to November

1991, he was the Defense, State Security and Emergencies Minister of the UkrSSR and, during the August 1991 *coup d'etat*, he wholly supported the gang of eight who had started the putsch.

After it failed, Marchuk was not dismissed from his post in Ukraine as you might expect. Instead, he started to defy gravity and his influence increased. He was appointed as the first Head of the Security Service of Ukraine (SBU), Ukraine's national successor to the USSR's KGB. At the same time, he promoted himself to the rank of lieutenant general and, in August 1992, to the rank of colonel general. Marchuk stayed on as Head of the SBU until 1994. Shortly before leaving this post, on March 23, 1994, he elevated himself to Ukraine's top rank, a general with four stars. In July 1994, Marchuk was appointed Deputy Prime Minister for State Security and Defense in the cabinet of Vitaliy Masol. This position had not previously existed and was specially created for the general.

His rise and rise continued. On October 31, 1994, Marchuk became First Deputy Prime Minister and chairman of the Presidential Committee on Combating Corruption and Organized Crime, and on March 6, 1995, he was appointed Acting Prime Minister of Ukraine. On June 8, 1995, he became Prime Minister and held this post until May 27, 1996, when he was dismissed "for burnishing his own political image."

An interesting sketch about Marchuk's appointment as Prime Minister was left for us in an interview with Roman Kupchinsky, director of the Ukrainian section of Radio Liberty, and Major Mykola Melnychenko, the security officer in President Kuchma's protection detail who made unauthorized recordings of his boss:

"When Kuchma appointed Marchuk as Prime Minister, I was surprised at the lavish banquet the newly appointed Prime Minister threw for the so-called political elite in the state dacha in Pushcha, Kyiv. The tables were truly laden. I wondered to myself: at whose expense was this banquet arranged? I was very much surprised! I realized then that, well, maybe there is something fishy going on. Maybe you have to really thank the President when you become Prime Minister? It made a lasting impression on me."[11] Professionally speaking, Marchuk had been a remarkably unworthy statesman. From 1991 to 1994, when he was Head of the SBU, the agency failed to trace or prosecute a single case of embezzlement of state property by high-ranking officials. President Kuchma, who appointed him Prime Minister, did not like him much either.

Kuchma recalled that, "After becoming a chairman [of the State Committee for Monetary Reform], Marchuk showed a complete lack of interest in daily work and a restless passion for verbosity... At first, I attributed it to Marchuk's desire to understand all the problems himself, as he likes to say, "with scientific precision", to gather exhaustive information about them. But I soon began to suspect that he simply does not want to make decisions, and this fear is based on his lack of understanding economic mechanisms and his attempts to distance himself from any unpopular steps. Obviously, his long work in the KGB taught Marchuk only to collect information (and to make decisions based on it for others!), but he did not know how to implement this information in the interests of the economy. It was the summer and then the fall of 1995. For the first time, considerable arrears in pensions and wages began to accumulate, growing month by month. Production was falling. He obviously did not keep up with the situation, and inadequately reacted to the problems in industry and agriculture. Perhaps this was due to elementary incompetence? As, for example, the decision of [...] Marchuk in the autumn of 1995 against the recommendations of experts of the Committee not to introduce the hryvnia."

Of course, one cannot but ask: why appoint such an unfit person as Prime Minister in the first place? What forces were pushing former KGB General Marchuk to ever-higher offices? There are many indications that his involvement with the Moscow *nomenklatura* of the KGB continued all these years and we can safely assume that these forces were Marchuk's former KGB colleagues paving the way.

In October 1996, the newspaper *Den* (Day) was founded in Kyiv by Yevhen Shcherban, a Ukrainian oligarch and politician of the mid-1990s, and, from 1995-1996, the richest oligarch in Donbas as the main shareholder of Ukraine's largest conglomerate, Industrial Union of Donbas, which united hundreds of large enterprises in the Donetsk and Luhansk regions. On November 3, 1996, Shcherban was killed, a year after the previous "master of Donbas" and richest oligarch, Akhat Bragin, was killed on October 15, 1995. Both of these murders were committed by the

Kushnir crime syndicate.[12]

Shcherban was murdered on the airfield at Donetsk airport while returning from Moscow in his own Yak-40 jet from the birthday party of Iosif Kobzon, a famous singer, businessman, and longtime KGB agent. At least ten people were involved in preparing the murder. The actual murder was carried out by two criminals,[13] Vadim Bolotskikh ("Muscovite") and Gennady Zangelidi ("Animal"). Bolotskikh and Zangelidi entered the airport by car with fake documents; they had a flight and a police uniform. When Shcherban got out of the plane, Bolotskih shot him in the back of the head, and in a panic Zangelidi started randomly shooting at other people, after which both jumped into the car and fled, then burned the car somewhere in the city's outskirts. Apart from Shcherban, his wife, an aircraft technician, and a flight engineer, who died of his wounds in hospital, were also killed. In the firefight, Zangelidi accidentally also hit Bolotskikh.

It was after this murder that another Donetsk group, and a significant part of Yevhen Shcherban's property, ended up in the ownership of Rinat Akhmetov, who thereafter graduated to becoming the richest oligarch not only of Donbas, but of all of Ukraine. At one point, according to Bloomberg's 2012 ranking, Akhmetov was richer than Russia's billionaires.

The operation was planned by gangster boss Yevhen Kushnir. At some point, he was arrested in Ukraine, placed in a pre-trial detention center in Donetsk and killed in his cell under mysterious circumstances. In 2000, Russian police managed to arrest Bolotskikh and extradited him to Ukraine (Zangelidi was already dead by that time).[14]

The murder of Yevhen Shcherban became one of the most high-profile criminal cases in the Ukraine. Journalist Sergei Kuzin (author of *Donetsk Mafia*) believes that both Shcherban and Bragin were assassinated on the order of Russian criminal groups who wanted to control privatization in Donbas. In favor of this Kuzin cites the fact that Vadim Bolotskikh was involved in both murders – of Bragin and Shcherban. Former Ukrainian Prime Minister Vitaliy Masol[15] said that in his opinion, it was a business associate of Akhmetov who killed Shcherban: "I, for example, believe that Shcherban was killed by Yanukovych. He got him out of his way. This is Donetsk".[16]

Curiously Rinat Akhmetov, who was Bragin and Shcherban's partner at the Industrial Union of Donbas and who benefited more than others from the murder of a competitor, gave no evidence in Shcherban's case.

But there was another person who unexpectedly benefited from Shcherban's murder: KGB General Marchuk. He ended up owning the *Den* newspaper. This was the only daily newspaper in Ukraine with its own audience. Having turned *Den* into an opposition newspaper, Marchuk was able to attract high quality, opinion-forming authors and replaced editor-in-chief Volodymyr Ruban with a new editor, Larisa Ivshina, Marchuk's former press secretary, who later became his wife.

Gradually, Marchuk became a well-known and influential parliamentary political figure. In the March 1998 parliamentary elections, he was number two on the list of the Social Democratic Party of Ukraine (SDPU) and was elected to the Verkhovna Rada for the second time. From May to December 1998, he headed the parliamentary faction of the SDPU. At the same time, he decided to take part in the next Presidential Elections and become the next President of Ukraine.

Marchuk was to compete against Kuchma, the incumbent President. Another serious rival was Pavlo Lazarenko, Prime Minister of Ukraine from May 1996 to July 1997. After his resignation, he became Kuchma's opponent and, in 1998 was elected to the Rada as leader of the Unity (Hromada) party which he had set up.

As it happened, Lazarenko never took part in the Presidential race. On February 9, 1999, the Attorney General requested that the Verkhovna Rada deprive Lazarenko of his parliamentary immunity. On February 15, Lazarenko left the country, and on February 17, 310 deputies out of 450 voted for his arrest.[17] In collusion, the Attorney General's Office and Kuchma had forced Lazarenko out of the Presidential race.

Now the only obstacle to Marchuk's Presidency was Kuchma. Should we be surprised that in the spring of 1999, secret recordings of conversations were made in the office of the President. A participant in this operation was Kuchma's bodyguard, Melnychenko.[18] What follows below is based on his tapes, all of which he gave to Yuri Felshtinsky (co-author of this book). Felshtinsky assembled a group of experts – including former SBU wiretapping specialists – to transcribe the tapes and the spoken testimony given by the major.

It is important to remember the timing in 1999. In Moscow, Marchuk's KGB handlers were simultaneously plotting to take over the Russian Presidency from Yeltsin by inserting their own man, Lieutenant Colonel Vladimir Putin, Marchuk's colleague. In the event of a simultaneous victory parachuting Marchuk into the Ukrainian Presidency, the KGB would gain power not only over Russia but also over Ukraine. Evidently, this was the idea behind recruiting a member of Kuchma's security detail in order to record conversations in the President's office and leverage this information against Kuchma during the 1999 Presidential Election.

Melnychenko recalled that Marchuk gave him a thousand German marks.[19] They met at least ten times in different secret locations, at different times, using codes and a secret cell phone, changing cars frequently or meeting at the last moment.[20]

It proved a good investment. The wiretap helpfully revealed that Kuchma was doing some plotting of his own. In May, the head of the Central Election Commission Mykhailo Ryabets, had a meeting with Kuchma. At this meeting, "he told Kuchma how he would not allow Marchuk to participate in the Presidential campaign".[21] Marchuk immediately called Ryabets and told him that he knew about his plan to prevent him from running.

In less than a day Kuchma found out about the leak, said Melnychenko. "Near lunchtime, Aleksandr Volkov, a well-known oligarch, came in to see Kuchma and said: 'Leonid, I have two bits of news, one of which is very unpleasant'. He said: 'Marchuk knows everything about what you agreed with Ryabets yesterday, how to remove him from the electoral register – he knows all about it'." Kuchma immediately called Leonid Derkach, his Head of the SBU, and instructed him to sweep the Presidential offices for microphones. Melnychenko was only just able to escape detection when he was tipped off by chance that the SBU was about to descend on Kuchma's office with 15 agents, and removed the recorder just in time.[22]

The first round of the Presidential Elections was scheduled for October 31, 1999, two months before Yeltsin resigned in Moscow and made Vladimir Putin Acting-President of the Russian Federation.

Unlike Yeltsin, however, Kuchma had no intention of resigning before the first round in Marchuk's favor. This was despite the fact that "Marchuk had some pretty serious information that would have allowed Kuchma to be removed as President", Melnychenko said.

Having failed to persuade Kuchma to resign before the elections, Marchuk's Plan B was to remove Kuchma during or after the second round of 14 November, 1999. "Among other things, they planned to install a video surveillance system in Kuchma's office and film everything that was going on "on the second day after the first round of the Presidential Election" to record conversations that would prove that Kuchma had violated the election campaign during the first round", Melnychenko said.

But Kuchma had his own KGB connections and horse-trading ensued between the two rivals. At this time, Marchuk met with Aleksandr Volkov, a Russian member of parliament for United Russia (now led by Dmitri Medvedev). Volkov was KGB and held *kompromat* on Marchuk which Derkach handed on to Kuchma. This led Marchuk and Kuchma to negotiate together during the first round of the Presidential Elections about which role Marchuk would take in the government.

In the end, Marchuk cancelled the second wiretapping of Kuchma. Melnychenko stated, "He said: no, we won't do anything, we don't need anything anymore." Why soon became clear. In the first round of the Presidential Elections Marchuk came fifth, gaining just over 8 percent, in a crowded field of nineteen candidates. Marchuk was not destined to become Ukraine's first KGB President. And since that was the case, it made more sense not to throw Kuchma out, but to negotiate with him for Marchuk's position of secretary of the National Security and Defense Council, which is what Marchuk did.

When Yeltsin resigned, Russia was delivered to the KGB through its expert manipulation of him and the national elections, whereas Ukraine escaped that fate because the democratic process had – however imperfectly – leap-frogged sinister back-room corruption.

Marchuk lacked Putin's cunning and was increasingly marginalized. With the kompromat Marchuk had over Kuchma, he stayed in high office until he was forced to resign in 2004 as defense minister. Ostensibly this was because of explosions of old ammunition at artillery depots, but in reality, it was because President Kuchma was approaching the end of his final term in office. Marchuk tried to return to national politics at the 2006 parliamentary elections, but the moment had gone. Putin's Ukrainian equivalent had let absolute power over Ukraine slip through the hands of the KGB. Marchuk's party received only 0.06 percent of the vote and he left politics.

3

The Georgiy Gongadze Assassination

President Richard Nixon lived a long and interesting life. But he has gone down in American history primarily as the evil genius behind the Watergate affair, which precipitated his resignation. President Leonid Kuchma did not resign, though his entire second term was overshadowed by the Georgiy Gongadze murder case.

Journalist and media owner Georgiy Gongadze disappeared late in the evening of September 16, 2000. After preparing the latest issue of internet newspaper Ukrayinska Pravda (Ukrainian Truth). Gongadze disappeared on his way home. Nobody saw him again. Much later it transpired that the journalist had been killed on September 17. His decapitated body was found on November 2 in the Taraschansky woods about 100 kilometers from Kyiv.

Gongadze was born on May 1, 1969, in Tbilisi to the family of Georgian dissident and filmmaker Ruslan Gongadze and Ukrainian Lesya Gongadze (Korchak). Even before the fall of the Soviet Union, he was drafted into the army and served in Afghanistan. Following his father's example, Gongadze joined the opposition movement, heading the information center of the Georgian Popular Front. In 1989, he moved to Ukraine to his mother's hometown of Lviv (near Poland). After his father's death, Georgi joined the rebel army in Abkhazia, made several documentaries about the Georgian-Abkhazian conflict, was seriously wounded, and soon returned to Ukraine.

After graduating from the Faculty of Foreign Languages of the Lviv

National University, Gongadze became an anchor of TV programs on Lviv television.[23] In 2000, he founded Ukrayinska Pravda in which he and editor-in-chief Alyona Pritula sharply criticized the regime of Leonid Kuchma and published sensational materials about the President and his inner circle. The police constantly watched and harassed him and, before his disappearance on July 14, 2000, Gongadze had sent an open letter to Kuchma's Attorney General Mykhailo Potebenko complaining of being haunded by state officials.

While this was going on, Major Melnychenko was wiretapping the conversations of President Kuchma and his visitors for General Marchuk. Part of the more than 600 hours of recordings was Kuchma's discussion of the Gongadze case. We know this because Melnychenko left Ukraine and revealed his involvement and that the tapes were in his possession.

On November 28, 2000, Oleksandr Moroz, the Speaker of the Verkhovna Rada read out excerpts from the "Kuchma tapes" from the rostrum of Ukraine's parliament. Moroz was the leader of the Socialist party founded by members of Ukraine's Communist Party after it was banned in 1991 (this "Socialist" party would itself be banned in 2022, after Russia's invasion).

Moroz accused the President of involvement in the disappearance of the journalist, "We must stop society sliding further into a dark morass of criminality and gangsterism. Therefore, having sufficient grounds to do so, I am forced to make public that the President of Ukraine Leonid Kuchma ordered journalist Georgiy Gongadze's disappearance, someone who systematically criticized him. Kuchma's Chief of Staff Volodymyr Lytvyn was aware of the preparations from the very beginning. The one who executed the order and organized it was Yuriy Kravchenko, the Interior Minister".

At the press conference that followed, Yuriy Lutsenko, a member of Moroz's Socialist Party, read out a transcript in which the President asked Minister Kravchenko to "deal with" the journalist.

Yuri Felshtinsky (co-author of this book) was able to obtain the full transcriptions of the Kuchma tapes recorded by Melnychenko, including those that relate to the murder of Gongadze.

Leonid Kuchma and Oleksandr Zinchenko, Head of the Parliamentary Committee on the Freedom of Speech and Press, May 13, 2000
Kuchma: [On the phone] Oh, listen, I've been f**king fighting with

Zayts for an hour and a half instead of 30 minutes, for f**k's sake!

Zinchenko: [Enters] May I?

Kuchma: Yes, you f**king saved me, I didn't know how [to end that call with Zavts], I said: "Let Zinchenko enter." [Both laugh loudly.]

Zinchenko: Leonid, thank you. Well, if I may, I'll be very brief. There are a few problems that have cropped up, and a couple of more serious ones which, if you have the time, we will discuss later. As to the run ups, there are two dates: June 6 is Journalists' Day, and I would make a suggestion to try to initiate, you know, the problem of freedom of speech, journalists and so on. [...]

Kuchma: How "freedom of " gathers together the most, the most opposition journalists – scum. F**k. I'm sorry, there are talented journalists there too. [...] And that Georgian is there.

Zinchenko: Gongadze.

Kuchma: Georgadze, for f**k's sake.

Recording of Kuchma's conversation with TV host Vyacheslav Pikhovshek, June 12, 2000

Pikhovshek: I wanted to ask – I don't know if you saw it – about that story on ORT that Kuchma was elected with the help of criminal elements. I don't know who is behind it, but if any further information comes out, the press will start reprinting it, bringing up these allegations and so on: there was a meeting of criminal bosses in Kharkiv, and they agreed to support Kuchma in the elections.

Kuchma: Well, you know, it's absolutely, so to speak...

Pikhovshek: No, I understand, but you have to respond.

Kuchma: Now they will sort it out, so to say. Gongadze is behind those articles in *Nezavisimaya Gazeta* [A Moscow newspaper].

Pikhovshek: He's nuts.

Kuchma: But he is being financed. I don't want to deal with [it] now, they're double-checking it.

Recording of Kuchma's conversation with Leonid Derkach, Head of the SBU, June 12, 2000

Derkach: So, Leonid, I'll leave it to you, right?

Kuchma: Leave it to me.

Derkach: And one more thing. Why don't you read this for a few minutes. Read it. This is the man who is behind the article that the next Ukrainian Putin is Derkach. The whole thing, it's Gongadze.

Kuchma: Gongadze?

Derkach: Yes, yes.

Kuchma: So you can trace him,… to this very piece?

Derkach: He'll be f**ked. I'm going to f**k him up till the end. [Rada deputy Mykhailo] Brodsky gave him the f**king money.

Kuchma: Huh?

Derkach: Brodsky gave him the money [...] So, the fact is that he wrote this article. F**k it, it's all bullshit, we don't need this. But here's the thing [Derkach quickly flips through documents, speaks a few words inaudibly] here he wrote such libel against you, that it's like you and I are on each other [one word unintelligible]. Well, don't read it, it's stupid shit. His internet newspaper is behind it. We're going to make him pay for it this time. [...]

Kuchma: Gongadze! All right, I'll read it. Well, properly deal with him, he's total scum.

Derkach: Let's put Gongadze in his place.

Recording of Kuchma's conversation with the Head of the SBU Derkach, June 22, 2000.

Kuchma: Okay. So you are definitely sure that Georgadze, this Georgian, Georgadze is f**king financed by Brodsky, right?

Derkach: Well, that is our information. I say, we nailed him, but something, completely…

Kuchma: Should I tell Medvedchuk [First Deputy Speaker of the Verkhovna Rada and chairman of the Social Democratic Party (SDPU), and a close friend of Vladimir Putin]: "Why the f**k are you allowing Brodsky to help Georgadze."

Recording of a conference call between Kuchma and his Chief of Staff Volodymyr Lytvyn and an unknown person, July 3, 2000

Kuchma: Good day.

Lytvyn: Good afternoon.

Kuchma: Give me that one, from Ukrayinska Pravda. When you decide what to do with him let me know. He has completely lost it.

Lytvyn: I need a case.

Kuchma: Huh?

Lytvyn: I need a case.

Kuchma: Okay. [...]

[Two people enter the office, ostensibly, Lytvyn and the unknown.]

Unidentified man [with a Georgian/Chechen accent]: May I, please?

[Kuchma goes through papers.]

Kuchma: Ukrayinska Pravda – they are a f**king nightmare, of course, I looked him up. F**king bastard. He is Georgian, this Georgian.

Lytvyn: Gongadze or what's his name?

Kuchma: Gongadze. Well, who is financing him?

Lytvyn: Well, he actively cooperates with Moroz [...]

Kuchma: Let's haul him before a judge, let the lawyers deal with him... Yes, sue? That's what our Attorney General's office should do, right?

Lytvyn: I think we should order [Interior Minister] Kravchenko to use alternative methods.

Unknown: No, tell Kravchenko to talk to me. [...]

Kuchma: Well, are there any f**king measures taken against him, this f**king c***t.

Lytvyn: He should now...

Kuchma: Deport him, deport him to f**king Georgia and throw him the f**k out. Take him to Georgia and get rid of him there.

Lytvyn: I have already discussed this with someone.

Kuchma: Chechens have to kidnap him and demand a ransom...

Unknown: Precisely, that's what we should do.

A recording of Kuchma's conversation with Interior Minister Kravchenko, July 3, 2000

Kuchma: Before I forget. There is Gongadze.

Kravchenko: I remember that name.

Kuchma: Well, he's a f**king scumbag of the highest order.

Kravchenko: Gongadze? He's already on our radar.

Kuchma: So, he writes all the time for Ukrayinska Pravda – and he fills the internet. Do you understand?

Kravchenko: Yes.

Kuchma: Well, who exactly finances him?

Kravchenko: Danilovych [Kuchma], well, I know what to do…

Kuchma: And the main thing is that he, I say, well not me, but Volodya [Lytvyn] says, we need the Chechens to kidnap him and smuggle him to Chechnya. What the f**k. And have them ask for a ransom.

Kravchenko: Well, we have him somewhere… I'll tell you: we have great people who will sort it out, still no – does he not go anywhere…

Kuchma: Well, should he be deported to Georgia and left there?

Kravchenko: Yes I will figure it out, I will figure it out.

Kuchma: […] And Gongadze, apart from the fact that he cooperates with Moroz, he writes for Moroz in his *Hrania* newspaper… They all… finance him… Brodsky…

Kravchenko: Well, he's such a sh*t media whore that could well be the case. I wouldn't be surprised if he has connections with socialists as well, that's what… Danilovych, well we'll deal with him here, I think it's…

Kuchma: And Brodsky is Medvedchuk's and Surkis' [nicknamed 'Kyiv's Surkis and Co' after two oligarch brothers], more Surkis' really.

Kravchenko: Well, it is 100 percent certain that they are connected.

Kuchma: No, so now they… I remember the fight for ownership of the Kyiv newspaper. Surkis – I was on to that f**king Jew… I just read some of their conversations.

Recorded conversation between Leonid Kuchma and Head of the SBU Derkach, July 3, 2000

Derkach: Leonid!

Kuchma: Hello to you! How did you find out? I just read it, so Ukrayinska Pravda...

Derkach: Ah! It's that son of a bitch... We are listening to him on all channels, we identified all his connections and he went to Moroz just now.

Kuchma: I also heard that he was with Moroz.

Recording of Kuchma's conversation with Interior Minister Kravchenko, July 10, 2000

Kuchma: Let's not forget about this Georgian...

Kravchenko: Yes, we are working on it. I mean...

Kuchma: I say: get rid of him, kidnap him, give him to the Chechens, let them demand ransom.

Kravchenko: We will think it over. We will deal with it in the best way possible.

Kuchma: Or take him there, take his clothes off, leave him without his f**king pants, and let him sit there, asshole.

Kravchenko: We will do...

Kuchma: He's just a f**king asshole...

Kravchenko: My team reported to me today, we're setting up surveillance of him. We shadow where he goes, how he travels. We have to study him a little bit, a little bit, and then we'll do it. I've got a special ops team ready, they will do anything you want, Danylovych, so there. [...]

Recording of Leonid Kuchma's conversation with Interior Minister Kravchenko, August 30, 2000

Kravchenko: For three days I have been feeling like death. My elbow also hurts. I must have something with my joints. Leonid, what's new. So...

Kuchma: Is Gongadze f**king dealt with?

Kravchenko: The day after tomorrow, the day after tomorrow. We got [one word unintelligible] there today.

Kuchma: Are they watching [Rada deputy Sergey] Golovaty?

Kravchenko: Yes, they are! They found out about two or three of his associates. I want to punch him on the… So they found two dachas, where they… Two guys are watching him. I just want to confront him, head-on, that's the best way, and then… All the things they've been instructed to do, it's getting results. Well, I think that Gongadze's… Well, we'll see how it pans out. I looked at his materials on the internet. That's him.

Recording of the conversation between Kuchma and Interior Minister Kravchenko, September 11, 2000

Kuchma: How are you? Please. So that I don't forget. Gongadze just keeps carrying on.

Kravchenko: Yes, I am aware of it. We made a mistake there.

Kuchma: There's a team, headed by – he told me his name…

Kravchenko: So [Gongadze] complained to the Attorney General. But I think…

Kuchma: Who?

Kravchenko: He did. I messed up a little here. But I am just seeing how it spun out of control. I blame it on the Deputy Chief of the Kyiv police, Opanasenko. Well, that Opanasenko… Well I have a group there – in prison, right? Opanasenko started trying to find out through his own people what kind of cars they use, and he wrote to [Attorney General] Potebenko.

Kuchma: Who? Opanasenko?

Kravchenko: No, no – Gongadze. Well he published number plates that were already withdrawn a year ago. I am changing my tactics a little, because I just want, that's why I want to remove this Opanasenko. I had my doubts when I was told over there, in Kyrgyzstan, that Opanasenko was interested in these number plates. So I said: "Don't do anything." When I got there, they said there was a complaint. I will fix it, Leonid. I'll fix it! I just don't want it to go wrong… But it will be done. He writes that it "may be retaliation for his writing". He's such a…

Kuchma: But he writes such shit in the Russian media…

Kravchenko: On the internet?

Kuchma: Not to the internet, but yesterday in Russia… […]

Kravchenko: I'm not letting Gongadze off the hook, because for me this issue is already too… There are contacts in his team. I've also set up outside surveillance on him now. I want to look into his contacts, what it is…

Kuchma: And Gongadze has a team, thirty or so, penning this shit.

Kravchenko: No, three people. I know who they are. I have all of their names. But I want to start with him. Well, I'll still see how the Attorney General responds. They're getting jittery, so I don't know.

Kuchma: Well, does the Attorney General have to do that for every c***t?

Kravchenko: Well, it's a legal complaint.

Kuchma: So what – it is just a complaint.

Kravchenko: Well, I'll see how they will react.

Kuchma: Why does every shithead write to the Attorney General?

For all the accusations against President Kuchma made in the Verkhovna Rada by Moroz, it should be pointed out that the tapes themselves do not unambiguously prove that President Kuchma gave the order to kill Georgiy Gongadze. It is impossible to conclude with certainty from the recordings that Kuchma was involved in the actual murder. Almost all the recordings in the office of the Ukrainian President were of extremely poor quality and had to be deciphered by specialists, and despite the efforts made, many texts could not be transcribed. The incompleteness of phrases and not always clear meaning is not due to mistranslation from Ukrainian or "surzhyk" (a mixture of Russian and Ukrainian), the language used in Kuchma's office, but is, unfortunately, evidence of the poor level of the original recording.

Undoubtedly, however, Kuchma hated Gongadze and he did order his Interior Minister to harass the journalist. His inflammatory remarks might also have been perceived by subordinates as an unspoken instruction to punish or even kill the dissident.[24]

But, with hindsight of the KGB's attempt to capture the Ukraine Presidency at the same time as the Russian Presidency, another point needs to be considered. General Marchuk told Melnychenko to wiretap Kuchma, but also told him to stop shortly after the body was found. In other words,

Kuchma was being recorded exactly until enough compromising material had been gathered. After Gongadze's murder, the people who controlled the recordings considered their work complete: Kuchma was tainted. One high-profile murder was sufficient for their ends and so in October 2000, wiretapping of the Ukrainian President's office was no longer needed.

The last recorded conversations concerning Gongadze belonged to the period when the journalist had already been kidnapped and murdered. The people who discussed Gongadze in Kuchma's office, including Kuchma himself, Derkach, Kravchenko and others, did not appear to know that Gongadze was dead already. There is no suggestion of this in the recordings made after September 16, 2000.[25]

Having been fed Gongadze's articles, Kuchma obliged, however, by raging on tape about the journalist. The simultaneous disappearance (and murder) of Gongadze and publication of the tapes before the elections, created the perfect plank for ousting him through blackmail.

As we know, it didn't work. Kuchma had no intention of yielding power to the KGB and Marchuk. But when Gongadze's body was found in November 2000, the country was ready to explode. Public opinion firmly believed that the order to kidnap and brutally murder Gongadze came from Kuchma.

Gongadze's name was constantly in newspapers or on television programs. Tens of thousands of articles were written. In December mass protests began, initiated by public figures in Ukraine who were outraged by the lawlessness of its government, demanding the resignation of the President, the Interior Minister, the Attorney General, and the Head of the SBU, as well as an independent expert examination of the Gongadze case. The protesters advocated "changing the system of social, economic and political relations in Ukraine," including the elimination of the system of "Presidential authoritarianism" and the transition to a parliamentary republic. The protest was supported by some 24 political parties, public organizations and movements across the political divides.[26] "Kuchmagate" managed to unite into one bloc those who would otherwise be sworn enemies.

Gaining further momentum, on January 30, 2001, the opposition began a second wave of anti-Kuchma demonstrations. A tent city sprang up in Kyiv on Khreshchatyk Avenue – city authorities had started repair works on Maidan Nezalezhnosti (Independence Square) for the anniversary of

Ukraine's independence and where the original tent city had been set up. On February 6, the opening day of the new parliamentary session, the opposition organized a demonstration in the center of Kyiv under the slogan "Ukraine without Kuchma".

In response, Kuchma's government went on the offensive. The tent city was attacked by the police; Yulia Tymoshenko was arrested on February 13; and on the same day a "three-way letter" was published – signed President Kuchma, Verkhovna Rada Chairman Ivan Plyusch and Ukrainian Prime Minister Yushchenko – in which they condemned the protesters' actions and branded them fascists. Yushchenko, of course, had no idea that sometime later he himself, along with some of these "fascists," would have to lead the opposition movement and overthrow the Kuchma regime. At the end of February, under public pressure, the Attorney General's Office was forced to recognise Gongadze's death and open a criminal case investigating "premeditated murder".

Kuchma said on February 19 that he was ready to swear on the Bible and the Constitution of Ukraine that he did not give an order to kill Gongadze. At the beginning of March, the tent camp on Khreshchatyk Avenue was demolished by the police. On March 6, 2001, the Trudova Ukraina (Labor Ukraine) party, led by Serhiy Tihipko, a close associate of the Kuchma family and Kuchma's son-in-law Viktor Pinchuk, hired US firm Kroll Advisory to conduct an "objective" investigation into the murder and the allegations that Gongadze was killed by order of the Ukrainian President and that he was in some way involved in the murder. Kroll's experts (as expected) concluded that there were no grounds for the allegations.[27]

On March 9, there were renewed clashes with the police near the Presidential palace, more than 200 people were arrested, and about fifty[28] were convicted of organizing mass disturbances. In spite of this, however, new tent cities were set up in at least 15 regions, which became the focus of protests against the existing regime. In many cities, governors and mayors organized retaliatory rallies in support of Kuchma, but this did not deflate the general anti-Kuchma spirit of the protest movement.

In parallel, the official investigation into Gongadze's murder continued. Kuchma announced that he was placing the Gongadze case under his personal supervision. At the same time, the Attorney General's Office tried to mislead the public by claiming that the murder had been committed "out of hooliganism" by two criminals who had died in December 2000. No one believed this, however. Information emerged about the involvement of Interior Ministry officers that, interchangeably, either confirmed or disproved by the investigation.

Finally, on October 22, 2003, Attorney General Svyatoslav Piskun signed an arrest warrant for General Olexiy Pukach, the Head of Surveillance of the Interior Ministry, whose officers had been tracking Gongadze. However, Kuchma did not like this show of "independence" by the Attorney General. On October 28, he decided to dismiss Piskun, and on November 18, the Attorney General was fired together with his deputy. The investigative team in charge of the Gongadze case was re-organized, and the arrested General Pukach was released on November 5 (he would be re-arrested on March 1, 2005).

In June 2004, the British newspaper *The Independent* published the materials of the investigation, which contained the testimony of Lieutenant Colonel Igor Goncharov, deputy head of the Department for Combating Organized Crime of the Kyiv region, arrested in May 2003 on charges of murdering eleven people. He died either from poisoning or from a blow to the head in custody on August 1, 2003. Goncharov claimed that Gongadze's abduction and murder were carried out by gang members on the orders of the Ukrainian Interior Ministry, that is, on the orders of Interior Minister Yuri Kravchenko, acting on behalf of President Kuchma. Goncharov called his colleague, police officer Yuri Nesterov, a direct participant in the murder. For his part, Nesterov suggested that Gongadze's murder was a conspiracy by the Russian secret services and that Lieutenant Colonel Goncharov himself took part in this Russian conspiracy aimed at "killing Gongadze and laying the blame for it on Ukrainian President Kuchma".

On May 22, 2005, Nesterov gave an interview in the program "Closed Zone" with host Vladimir Aryev where he claimed without providing evidence that Goncharov was in fact an FSB agent and that he cooperated with General Marchuk. He also claimed without evidence that Goncharov had Melnychenko's tapes in his possession even before they were made public by Moroz on November 28, 2000.

On March 1, 2005, the new President, Viktor Yushchenko, who came to power thanks to the Orange Revolution that broke out in part because of the Gongadze murder, announced that the journalist's killers had been identified. The next day, Svyatoslav Piskun, who had been reinstated as Attorney General, presented the public with all the available information about Gongadze's murder. He said that four police officers took part in the murder, two of whom had already been arrested, one was in hiding and one was a witness. Piskun said that he knew the names of those who ordered the killing but could not name them yet.

It also became public knowledge that one of the suspects summoned to the Attorney General's Office was former Interior Minister Yuriy Kravchenko. His interrogation was scheduled for 10 a.m. on March 4. It never took place. Three hours earlier Kravchenko was found dead with two bullet shots to the head. According to Deputy Attorney General Viktor Shokin it was suicide, despite the fact that there were two shots. He left, however, a suicide note: "My dearly beloved. I am not guilty of anything. Forgive me. I became a victim of the political intrigues of President Kuchma and his entourage. I leave with a clear conscience. Farewell." Interior Minister Yuriy Lutsenko, nevertheless believed that his successor had been assassinated.

4

The Poisoning of Viktor Yushchenko

Viktor Yushchenko and Yulia Tymoshenko

Viktor Yushchenko was a renowned beekeeper, and he loved bees more than he loved power. Born in a small Ukrainian village with the unpromising name of Horuzhivka, in eastern Sumy, a region on the Russian border, he received his secondary education. His teachers remembered him as a diligent student, but without leadership ambitions. After graduating from the USSR Ternopil Financial and Economics Institute, he served in the Soviet Army and after his discharge worked on rank-and-file positions in the kholkoz collective farm system. Yushchenko then worked in various divisions of Ukrainian banks in Sumy and Kyiv and became a staff member of the then Governor of the National Bank of Ukraine (the central bank), Vadym Hetman. The latter promoted Yushchenko to director, first at Agroprombank of the USSR, later at Ukraine Bank. In 1993, on Hetman's recommendation, Yushchenko became the National Bank of Ukraine's third Governor since 1991.

In this position, Yushchenko managed to push through several important reforms. He was responsible for monetary reform and the introduction of the new national currency – the hryvnia. He also created the State Treasury and State Mint. Being under the close guardianship of Vadim Hetman, he rarely made his own decisions, but he took responsibility for the currency reform and promised the people that they would not suffer from the reform. The successful implementation of the monetary reform and the introduction and strengthening of the national currency put Yushchenko among the best bankers in the world, and the European Bank for Reconstruction and Development nominated him as the best banker of the year. Yushchenko's popularity skyrocketed. It was in this context that he decided to participate in President Kuchma's re-election campaign (for a second term) and was eventually proposed by Kuchma for the post of Prime Minister of the country. The post of Deputy Prime Minister in Yushchenko's government was taken by Yulia Tymoshenko.

Tymoshenko was in charge of fuel and energy. In this position she pursued a policy that displeased the President's inner circle.[29] The Donetsk politicians Mykola Azarov and Viktor Yanukovych, and Dnipropetrovsk oligarchs Medvedchuk and Surkis & Co did not like Tymoshenko either. It was she who insisted on the real privatization of three regional energy distribution companies.[30] She also publicly accused Naftogaz Ukrainy of stealing Russian gas and concealing its real debts to Russia, which led to the resignation of the management of the company. Tymoshenko then insisted that Fuel and Energy Minister Serhiy Tulub (a representative of the Donetsk clan) be fired. Due to disagreements with her, Economy Minister Serhiy Tihipko, who was close to the President's family clan in Dnipro, was forced to resign as well. Tihipko was the inventor of a short-term loan scheme under which the government borrowed money from private banks at high interest rates (up to 70 percent per annum) to pay salaries to state employees and pensions to pensioners. Tihipko was the head of Privatbank and lobbied for its interests before taking up a government post. The ruinous (for the state) but profitable (for banks) practice of short-term loans was stopped by Yushchenko, who balanced the state budget.

In addition, Yushchenko and Tymoshenko forced big businesses to make their empires transparent, pay taxes to the state, and give up hidden barter deals that deprived the Treasury of revenue. Yushchenko and Tymoshenko also ensured that the Tax Service, headed by Mykola Azarov, no longer reported to Kuchma but was subordinated to the Prime Minister, Yushchenko. In June 2000, they presented a law modernizing operations in the Ukrainian energy sector, which helped increase state revenues sixfold.

This bold step by Yushchenko's government allowed the state to repay its debts to pensioners, students and state employees. At the same time, the Fatherland faction in the Rada, controlled by Yulia Tymoshenko, took an anti-Kuchma stance on the Gongadze case, blaming the President for the journalist's death.

Given their losses, the Donetsk and Kyiv oligarchs close to the President, whose interests were under attack from Tymoshenko, easily convinced Kuchma to get rid of her. The first move came from the Attorney General Potebenko, who opened a criminal case against her. It compromised her both as a state official and as an entrepreneur. Tymoshenko's husband Oleksandr and her childhood friend Valeriy Falkovich, who was a board member of United Energy Systems of Ukraine (UESU), a company controlled by Tymoshenko, were arrested in August 2000. On January 5, 2001, the Attorney General followed this up with two criminal cases against Tymoshenko herself, and on January 19, at the recommendation of Potebenko, Kuchma removed her from the government.

Tymoshenko was accused of illegally withdrawing from Ukraine more than $1.1 billion through her company. On February 13, she was arrested in connection with the charges, as well as the accusation of transferring about $80 million to the Swiss accounts of former Prime Minister Pavlo Lazarenko. The transfer was carried out when Lazarenko was the Prime Minister. Tymoshenko was also accused of bribery and of involvement in a Russian financial scandal at the Ministry of Defense.[31]

After serving for over a month and a half in Kyiv's Lukyanivska prison, Tymoshenko was released on her own recognizance and transferred from the detention center to a hospital. In March 2001, from the hospital, she demanded President Kuchma's resignation and declared that she would fight for the Presidency. Seeing Tymoshenko re-emerge, Kuchma again tried to put her behind bars. The Attorney General appealed against Tymoshenko's transfer to a hospital, and a Kyiv court ruled that Tymoshenko should be returned to prison. Yushchenko, who had intended to meet his former deputy in hospital, called the decision a "display of muscle" and urged the President to establish a dialogue with the opposition instead. Tymoshenko's lawyers managed to appeal the Kyiv court's decision to the Supreme Court of Ukraine, which overturned the lower court's decision. Upon her release,

Tymoshenko reiterated her intention to run for President: "If I knew of a real leader in Ukraine who is ready to give his life for the country... then I am ready to do my laundry at his campaign headquarters. But I do not see this team yet. I want to form it myself."

After the publication in November 2000 of audio recordings of President Kuchma's possible involvement in the disappearance and death of journalist Georgiy Gongadze and the beginning of mass protests called "Ukraine without Kuchma," Kuchma's rule became so unpopular that the movement took on a pan-Ukrainian scale. The organizers of the protests were the leader of the student unrest of the 1980s and 1990s, Volodymyr Chemerys, and the socialist Yuriy Lutsenko. The protesters demanded the resignation of the President and his inner circle – the Interior Minister, the Head of the SBU and the Attorney General, as well as an independent examination of the Gongadze case. Under public pressure, Kuchma eventually had to dismiss his associates.

At the same time, another high-profile murder of a Ukrainian journalist occurred in Donbas: Ihor Aleksandrov, director of the TOR television company in Sloviansk, who was brutally beaten to death with baseball bats on the premises of his own television company. From 2000-2001, Aleksandrov hosted a television program called Unvarnished that revealed the links between Donbas organized crime and the police and prosecutors in the region. His follow-up program was planned to show a videotape in which members of the Kramatorsk organized crime group "17th Precinct" discussed how much they had paid or should pay their patrons in police and prosecutor's offices. The broadcast was never aired due to his assassination in July 2001.[32]

Of course, international pressure on Kuchma intensified. The President's actions were sharply criticized. Western countries now publicly declared their support for Yushchenko as an alternative to Kuchma. To crown it all, on October 4, 2001, during air defense exercises in the Crimea, a TU-154M passenger plane of the Russian "Siberia" airlines flying from Tel-Aviv to Novosibirsk with 144 Russian and Israeli passengers and 12 crewmen on board was shot down by a Ukrainian missile over the Black Sea. Initially Ukraine categorically denied its involvement in the crash, but international experts proved the responsibility of the Ukrainian Defense Ministry. As a result, Ukraine was forced to admit its connection to the tragedy and a trilateral agreement was reached between Russia, Israel and Ukraine to pay financial compensation to the families of the dead.

At the height of the 2001 political crisis, in which many government levels, including the Presidential administration and virtually the entire cabinet, were embroiled, Kuchma searched frantically for ways to survive. US philanthropist and billionaire George Soros suggested that the Ukrainian President should step down and appoint Viktor Yushchenko, who was supported by the West, as his successor. But the only conclusion Kuchma drew from Soros' recommendation was that, in order to retain power, he had to double down on eliminating all his rivals, above all Yushchenko.

The forced departure of Yulia Tymoshenko meant that the Yushchenko government did not have much time left. The confrontation between the Kuchma entourage and the Prime Minister moved to the Ukrainian parliament. Viktor Medvedchuk, Deputy Speaker of the Verkhovna Rada and Putin's friend, insisted that a coalition government be formed by April 5, 2001, during a government Q&A. Yushchenko called this threat by Medvedchuk "a good way of destabilizing the situation in the country" and called for a meeting with the President and the Deputy Speaker of parliament to discuss the ultimatum delivered to him. Kuchma made it clear that he supported Medvedchuk and was in favor of a coalition government. In turn, Yushchenko decided to fight his corner in parliament.

Speaking in Parliament on April 26, during a vote of no confidence in his government, the Prime Minister said that Parliament was following the lead of the oligarchic clans and acting as their mouthpiece. He suggested that any political actions be temporarily suspended in order to gradually hand over power in the country to the people, but stressed that "I will not quit politics" even if "democracy in Ukraine has suffered a serious setback". Yushchenko then famously said: "I will leave to come back!" The next day, April 27, Kuchma resigned, instructing the government to perform its duties until a new government was formed. Yushchenko refused to stay on, telling the President that the position of "acting President was not for him."

Many Ukrainian and foreign analysts agreed that Yushchenko's government made the first attempt in a decade of independence to reform the country's political and economic system.[33] Prior to this, Ukraine's elite had caused the stagnation of not only economic but also democratic developments. Any reformist government became a threat to the wealth of these people.

Against the gray mass of the faceless politicians, Yushchenko and Tymoshenko became the most charismatic and colorful politicians in Ukraine. That is why Ukrainians believed in them. Yushchenko did not give the impression of being anything other than a mild-mannered man. Tymoshenko, on the other hand, looked determined and courageous. She was called "the only man in Ukrainian politics", paraphrasing Ukrainian writer Ivan Franko's (1856-1916) words about Lesya Ukrainka (1871-1913), "the only man in Ukrainian literature".

The Ukrainian people, tired of political squabbles and clashes between the President, the government and parliament, always imagined that after a change of this or that President, government or even Rada, the country would experience long-hoped-for prosperity. But each time the change merely resulted in a redistribution of power, property and money between the new names and the emergence of new political alliances between the well-known players. While the Rada voted to dismiss Yushchenko's government, a crowd of 7,000 supporters of the Prime Minister gathered outside the parliament, shouting that his government was a reformist one that fought for the country and its people. Yulia Tymoshenko said that she would support Yushchenko's candidacy at the next Presidential Elections in 2004 and created an initiative of 50 parties and organizations in order to force a referendum (which failed).

This referendum was to ask just one question: "Do you think that Leonid Kuchma should resign, further to articles 108 and 109 of the Constitution of Ukraine, for destroying the rights and freedoms of the Ukrainian people contrary to the rule of law". Naturally, the government did not allow the referendum to take place. Then in July 2001, the undaunted Tymoshenko created the cross-party political alliance "National Salvation Forum" (NSF).[34]

In an attempt to thwart Tymoshenko's political activity, in late January 2002 the Attorney General's Office issued a new warrant for her arrest and put her under house arrest. On January 29, 2002, while driving her Mercedes to a hearing at the Court of Appeals, Tymoshenko had a car accident and was hospitalized.

Parliamentary Elections of 2002

The March 31, 2002, parliamentary elections were fast approaching. Both Yushchenko and Tymoshenko, now ousted from power, began preparing by rallying a large number of supporters who really thought that the Yushchenko-Tymoshenko tandem would radically change things for the better. The country was readying itself for an election that would radically change the political landscape and life in Ukraine.

The pre-election months were marked by a regrouping of political forces and blocs, some of which tried feverishly to retain power while others tried to seize it. According to the new law, Ukraine created an election system in which 50 percent of deputies were elected from party lists and 50 percent from first-past-the-post constituencies. To enter parliament, a party or political bloc had to pass the four percent threshold. While Tymoshenko created an opposition bloc under her own name, former Prime Minister Yushchenko announced his intention to create an opposition bloc of political parties called "Our Ukraine".[35]

At the Verkhovna Rada elections of March 2002 no fewer than 62 political parties (united in no fewer than 30 electoral blocks) took part. Our Ukraine headed by Yushchenko was the winner with 23.55 percent of the votes.[36] He received support in central and western Ukraine; the Communists – in southeastern Ukraine and Crimea;[37] Tymoshenko's bloc was supported mainly in Kyiv and Dnipropetrovsk.[38] The newly elected deputies and parties now formed new factions. Twelve deputies, however, remained independent, which turned out to be advantageous in the finely balanced Rada. They could vote without a party whip for this or that bill (proposed by different factions) and earn handsome fees.

As is always the case in politics, some win and others lose. In 2002, it just took a long time for the dust to settle: the struggle for a parliamentary majority, and consequently for the position of Prime Minister, lasted from May to December. The pro-Presidential forces took advantage of the heterogeneity of the opposition, which was unable to develop clear principles of cooperation, to draw the Socialists and Communists to their side and form a parliamentary majority. Having gained a majority in parliament, supporters of

President Kuchma cleared the way to government power, increased economic and political influence in the country, revival of the old corrupt privatization schemes, used the opportunity to appoint people they liked to senior government positions and fired those who stood in their way.

The Presidential Elections of 2004

Yushchenko lost, but for the first time in the years of Ukraine's independence, a coalition government had been formed. Regrettably it turned out to be one headed by Viktor Yanukovych, who was in the pocket of oligarch Rinat Akhmetov and his Donetsk clan. The opposition could only continue its struggle for further democratization and work out a new strategy to fight for power in the forthcoming Presidential Elections. They began preparing long before the officially announcement. The majority of Ukrainian voters hoped that these elections would be a watershed in the country's history. The ruling elite realized that they could not win fair and democratic elections. Yet, they had no intention of giving up their lucrative position.

Thus, the Constitutional Court, which was controlled by President Kuchma and his supporters, decided that under to the new Constitution of 1996, President Kuchma had really only been in power for one term, as he had been elected for the first term before the new Constitution of Ukraine had been adopted. This meant, the court ruled, that Kuchma could run for a "second" term if he wanted to even though he had "technically" already served two full terms. The government-controlled Ukraine's mass media began to explain to viewers and listeners the "correctness" of the Constitutional Court's conclusions, and Kuchma himself was carefully monitoring public opinion. Not knowing yet whether he should run for the Presidency or not, he initially supported Yushchenko's candidacy in the media.

At the same time Kuchma understood that if they came to power Yushchenko, and even more so Tymoshenko, would come after him, and that he would most likely be prosecuted for corruption, or worse, for killing Gongadze. But there was one more option left for him: to support the Donetsk clan who offered their protégé for the Presidency – Viktor Yanukovych. For all the disadvantages of handing power to the Donetsk oligarchs, had one great plus side: he would definitely not want to start a corruption witchhunt and see Kuchma behind bars.

Another candidate, Viktor Medvedchuk (of the Kyiv oligarchs "Surkis and Co"), then Kuchma's Chief of Staff, also promised Kuchma that if he won, he would not prosecute him, and guaranteed (like Putin to Yeltsin) an untroubled existence when no longer in power. Both candidates did not have deep popular support, but they did have powerful oligarchs behind them, ready to fight for their survival to the bitter end. Meanwhile, the opposition went on the offensive, denouncing to the people the constitutional "sleight of hand" played by the Supreme Court. In the end, Kuchma declined to run in the Presidential race, bet on Yanukovych, the incumbent Prime Minister, and lost everything.

While waiting for the situation with the incumbent President to become clearer, a whole army of candidates (26) rushed into the election race, each one trying to convince voters that it was they who could change the lives of ordinary people for the better. Ukraine had never seen such a number of candidates wishing to relieve the suffering of its people. The most popular ploy of the candidates was to cover their opponents in muck, and the Presidential Elections campaign of 2004 turned out to be the dirtiest ever.

No one paid attention to the programs of the candidates because there was not much difference. Among the general monotony nevertheless two stood out: Viktor Yanukovych and Viktor Yushchenko. Completely different and dissimilar, these two candidates very soon emerged as the main ones in the race. Prime Minister Yanukovych was publicly supported by Putin, for whom Yanukovych, after the frustation of the 1999 Marchuk plot, was the new vehicle to take the reigns in Ukraine. As Russian President, Putin had been consolidating his power for four years by inserting former intelligence officers in key government and business positions. He was keen, finally, to start doing the same in Ukraine, courtesy of Yanukovych's election. The former Donetsk governor was also the preferred candidate of the Ukrainian oligarchy, especially of course the one in Donetsk. Not least, Yanukovych could also count on the support of his own ministers.

Unusually for a Prime Minister, Yanukovych had a serious criminal record involving both theft and the use of force. Born near the town of Yenakyivo into the family of a locomotive engineer, Fedor Yanukovych, and a nurse,

Olga Leonova, Viktor Yanukovych was motherless at an early age and was raised by his grandmother, Kastusya Yanukovych. After graduating with good grades from high school, he worked at the local metallurgical plant while he also studied at its mining college, and later graduated from the Donetsk Polytechnic Institute. At the age of 17, he was first sentenced to three years in jail for participating in a robbery, and as soon as he got out was sentenced to serve two more years in another prison for inflicting grievous bodily harm. These physical-violence charges were later dropped "for lack of corpus delicti," as Yanukovych and his supporters pointed out many times.

For more than twenty years, Yanukovych worked as a manager of a number of Donetsk enterprises, which allowed him to break through to politics in the end and from 1996 to 2001 he was the Governor of the Donetsk Region. He received a degree from the Faculty of International Law of the Ukrainian Academy of Foreign Trade and, while a governor, defended his doctoral dissertation on the management of infrastructure development. Following his dissertation, Yanukovych not only received his doctorate but also the title of "Professor". But when he wrote down this title in the electoral questionnaire, he spelled it with two letters "ff" and one "s" – "proffesor", which was how he was known in Ukraine ever since – "Proffesor Yanukovych".

"Big Ya" (another nickname for Yanukovych, in the narrow circle of his supporters) successfully coped with his task – up to a point. The government tried to create a positive image for their candidate through all possible means at their disposal – some not entirely legal – deploying administrative resources, demagogy, and compromising evidence against political opponents. On the eve of the election, the Prime Minister also made populist decisions, such as increasing wages and pensions, which depleted the budget and almost imploded the entire economy.

The opposition focused its forces around Viktor Yushchenko, who at the time had the highest popularity rating in the country. Tymoshenko wanted to become President, but realized that her hour had not yet come. She joined his "Our Ukraine" party, remaining in the shadows of her former boss. The European Union also made no secret of its sympathy for the opposition candidate, hoping that he would gradually free Ukraine, the center of Europe, from Russian influence. Yushchenko himself said he did not really want to become President but would submit to the will of the voters.

All the polls showed that Yushchenko and Yanukovych led the election race and the official election results announced on October 31, 2004, showed a tie: Yushchenko received 39.87 percent of the vote; Yanukovych, 39.32 percent.[39] Voter turnout was a record high 75 percent. Observers noted that there were numerous violations during the election campaign. No one could say how much these irregularities might have influenced the election results. But since none of the candidates gained more than the 50 percent required to win in the first round, a second round was scheduled for November 21.

Geographically, voter sympathies were clearly split. The central and western regions of Ukraine voted for Yushchenko with the exception of the Transcarpathian region, where Ruthenians and Hungarians live. The population of these regions spoke mostly Ukrainian and belonged to the Greek Catholic Church and the Kyiv Orthodox Church. The southeastern regions and the Republic of Crimea, where residents preferred to speak Russian and were members of the Moscow Orthodox Church, voted mostly for Yanukovych.

The election campaign for the second round of voting proved to be unprecedented. The entire propaganda and administrative machine of the ruling party, which Yanukovych represented, worked at full capacity. The state-controlled TV channels and media were also working for his candidate. Every city in Ukraine was plastered with Yanukovych's portrait. In his election program, he promised to make Russian the second state language.

Vladimir Putin himself came to Kyiv twice to support the pro-Russian candidate. All the CIS leaders (except for Georgian President Mikheil Saakashvili, who supported Yushchenko) also took part in Putin's propaganda campaign to get Yanukovych elected, assuring the Ukrainian people of their eternal friendship and the importance of preserving the economic ties and cooperation built in Soviet times. The leitmotif of these statements was that, if Yanukovych came to power, Ukraine would take its rightful place in the CIS, becoming once again a driving force in the economic and customs union of former Soviet states, and that its economy could only survive and thrive in close cooperation with Russia and the others.

Of particular "concern" to Ukraine's neighbors, primarily Putin's Russia, was the "oppressed" position of the Russian-speaking population and the situation with the infringement of the Russian language in Ukraine. Pro-Russian and Russian analysts warned Ukrainians that if Yushchenko came to power, Ukraine would join NATO and become financially dependent on the International Monetary Fund and the US

At the same time, on Kuchma's orders, the press was told that Yushchenko's wife Kateryna Chumachenko was an employee of the Central Intelligence Agency and had been sent to Ukraine by the US as a sleeper agent. In the press it was claimed that she was "attached" on purpose to Yushchenko, then Governor of the National Bank of Ukraine, and that that their first meeting on the plane, where their seats were next to each other, and their subsequent marriage were also organized by the CIA. There had never been a more dramatic and crooked Presidential Elections in the history of Ukraine.

The poisoning of Viktor Yushchenko

As the unauthorized recordings in President Kuchma's office in 2000 were made on the orders of General Marchuk (further to the instructions received from the Russian secret service in Moscow) in order to force Kuchma to resign and hand over power to a pro-Russian candidate, the operation was a failure: Kuchma did not resign, despite a whole chain of scandals and revolutions. He remained President until the end of his constitutional term. In 2004, however, Putin was not taking any chances during his second attempt to seize control of Ukraine. In September Viktor Yushchenko was poisoned.

The poisoning took place in the evening of September 5, 2004, during a dinner at the dacha of secret-service General Volodymyr Satsyuk,[40] where the former Prime Minister candidate Yushchenko was meeting with the SBU leadership. We can ignore the explanation that was given to misinform the press both by the poisoners themselves and by Yushchenko's political opponents[41] that there was no poisoning, merely a reaction of Yushchenko's body to the sushi he had eaten. Yushchenko was poisoned with dioxin, a diagnosis made by doctors at the clinic Rudolfinerhaus in Vienna, where Yushchenko was taken on September 10.[42]

The Austrian doctors said that the poison must have entered

Yushchenko's body five days before hospitalization, that is September 5. Yushchenko's appearance had changed beyond recognition and his face was disfigured. He hovered between life and death. For about a month after the poisoning he was unable to speak. Meanwhile, the elections were scheduled for October 31. And Yushchenko had to spend a substantial part of precious campaign time in intensive medical treatment. Given the confusion, Yushchenko's ratings were plummeting. Moreover, if Yushchenko had died as a result of poisoning, or had withdrawn his candidacy for health reasons, his pro-Russian rival Yanukovych would have remained the sole leader of the Presidential race.

The Attorney General duly opened a criminal investigation into Yushchenko's poisoning. SBU General Satsyuk was considered the main suspect. He was interrogated several times but was not charged or arrested. Despite the interrogations and examinations, the Attorney General concluded there was no case that Yushchenko was poisoned at dinner at Satsyuk's place and that Satsyuk was involved. The general subsequently fled abroad and it was not immediately known that "abroad" was Putin's Russia. Later, when under President Yushchenko Ukraine requested the extradition of Satsyuk, the Russian government replied that Satsyuk had received "political asylum" in Russia and could not be deported.

As Yushchenko did not resign or die, the campaign against him didn't stop. On November 21, 2004, the day of the second round, another attempt was made to assassinate him and, at the same time, Tymoshenko. On that day, city police detained two Russian citizens, Muscovites, with three kilos of explosives in their car in the center of Kyiv. The detainees were 35-year-old Mikhail Shugai and 33-year-old Marat Moskvitin. A second car with explosives was parked near the election headquarters of Yushchenko on Borychiv Tik Street, in front of the residence of the US Ambassador. The car contained an explosive device with a radio-electronic control. Shugai and Moskvitin confessed that they were paid to murder Yushchenko and Tymoshenko. Who exactly was behind the organization of this assassination attempt remained unknown, though circumstantial evidence pointed to the top of the Interior Ministry under Prime Minister Yanukovych.

Under Yushchenko as the new President, the Ukrainian media published a recording of a telephone conversation between the Head of the

Surveillance Department, Oleksiy Prilipko,[43] a position formerly held by
General Pukach, and Serhiy Klyuyev, the brother of Yanukovych's campaign
manager and former Deputy Prime Minister Andriy Klyuyev. Prilipko had
been Pukach's deputy, and it was he who had organized the surveillance that
preceded Gongadze's abduction and murder in 2000 (which at the time of
the second round of Presidential Elections in 2004 had not yet been
solved).[44]

The two officials spoke in detail about the exact location where the
second assassination attack took place. The revealing nature of this conversation is also crucial to our understanding who was behind the deadly events
in Kyiv on February 20, 2014. In 2004, Andriy Klyuyev was one of
Yanukovych's energy ministers. But his official title clearly belied his real role
in Prime Minister Yanukovych's entourage as there would have been no
reason for Ukraine's Head of Surveillance to discuss a covert operation of
any nature – and certainly not regarding political opponents – with someone
tasked with gas policy. By February 2014, Klyuyev's real importance to
Yanukovych became public. He was then President Yanukovych's Chief of
Staff and the most powerful man in Ukraine after the President, appointed
only a few weeks before the events that would change Ukraine's history.

Klyuyev: That's where Yulia is, etc.

Prilipko: No, Yulia has her own…

Klyuyev: And where all the leadership, is there, where they gather?
Well, still, there's where they gather for the most part.

Prilipko: That's it – on Borychiv Tik, all the services in Yaroslavskaya,
all in one square, as it were…

Klyuyev: And that place where the leadership gathers, where is that?

Prilipko: They go to Yaroslavskaya 1/3d, he has 8a… He also meets
there in a smaller circle, and I think there's a 22 there as well.

Klyuyev: There's no such main place as ours.

Prilipko: His office is on 8a.

Klyuyev: How much security is there?

Prilipko: There are a lot of guards there, there's an American embassy
nearby.

Klyuyev: In all three, yes.

Prilipko: Yes, yes.

Klyuyev: Okay. But we have a number of agents there. And the entrance is free, how's the entrance? There are a whole lot at the entrance, right?!

Prilipko: Yes, yes there's cover there.

Klyuyev: Okay, good, thank you.

Prilipko: Thank you, goodbye.

There was no third assassination attempt that day. However, another crime did take place. The Central Electoral Commission announced preliminary results of the second round of the Presidential Election, according to which Viktor Yanukovych, the incumbent Prime Minister, had won by a 3 percent margin.[45] The published results of the second round shocked everyone. People were reminded of Joseph Stalin's saying that it is not how one votes, but how votes are counted. In Russia Vladimir Putin had followed this sage advice and made sure that electoral counts always ended up in their favor.[46]

The problem with the preliminary voting results was that, according to exit polls, the election results were the exact opposite: Yushchenko had won. In addition, numerous irregularities were revealed. It turned out that voters dependent on the state – students, prisoners, and military personnel – had been "strongly encouraged" to vote for Yanukovych. Voters were allowed to vote by so-called absentee ballots, and many active Yanukovych supporters traveled around the country and had voted several times. In the eastern part of Ukraine (especially in Donbas), which voted mostly for Yanukovych, there was also a significant increase in the number of voters between the first and the second round – almost 20 percent. At some polling stations, the number of voters even miraculously exceeded the number of officially registered voters. (These were all methods from the rule book Putin had developed to lock his own people in elected positions in the years after 2000, up to and including assassination.)

It was apparent that the government was deceiving the voters and were stealing the victory from Yushchenko. This opinion was shared by the majority of voters, the opposition, and the international community. All official observers from international organizations (the European Parliament, NATO Parliamentary Assembly, Council of Europe, OSCE,

PACE) were vocal about the large-scale fraud committed during the Presidential Elections in Ukraine, and their undemocratic nature and incompatibility with European standards.

Information on how exactly President Kuchma and Prime Minister Yanukovych's people falsified the results began to transpire. The SBU had recorded the telephone conversations of the conspirators and it also turned out that voting figures in the regions were first sent to Yanukovych's headquarters, where the data was amended, and only from there was it sent to the computer of the Central Electoral Commission (CEC).[47] To create extra votes pushing up Yanukovych's percentage, hundreds of thousands of fraudulent ballots printed in Russia had been filed into ballot boxes across the country. In telephone conversations with Russian members of the conspiracy, these fake ballots were referred to as "cookies".

Nonetheless, on November 24, the CEC announced that, according to the official electoral count, Yanukovych had won and was President. Putin and the KGB had succeeded. Four years late, Ukraine was now at last theirs through Yanukovych. At any rate, so it was in the script that Putin had prepared.

5

The Orange Revolution

Once again Ukraine humiliated Putin's certainty. On November 25, the Supreme Court of Ukraine ruled against ratifying Yanukovych as President until ´Yushchenko's complaints about possible falsifications had been examined. At the same time, the finely balanced Verkhovna Rada refused to recognize the election results announced by the CEC.

On November 27, the parties sat down for talks with Polish President Aleksander Kwasniewski, EU representative Javier Solan, Russian State Duma Speaker Boris Gryzlov, and Verkhovna Rada Speaker Volodymyr Lytvyn. Kuchma insisted that the protesters stop blockading the buildings of the Government, the Presidential Palace, and the Rada.

Yushchenko, however, did not back down. Then Kuchma decided to resort to force. Late in the evening of November 28, Deputy Interior Minister Sergei Popkov ordered a 10,000-strong force to clear the center of Kyiv of protesters. Still, the transition of power to Yanukovych (and thus Putin) was thwarted. The Ukrainian army sided with the protesters and opposed the Interior Ministry. The "cleansing" of the center of Kyiv did not take place.

The government's election fraud had created a broad revolt among Ukrainians. Mass demonstrations began in the western and central regions demanding a review of the election results. Another political crisis loomed against the backdrop of civil disobedience. It went down in Ukrainian history as the "Orange Revolution", based on the color of the flag and scarf of the main Presidential contender Viktor Yushchenko.[48]

The mother lode of the Orange Revolution was the center of Kyiv – Maidan Nezalezhnosti, Independence Square, where many thousands of protesters held continuous rallies for two months. Over time, this phenomenon came to be called "Maidan" (an Ottoman word) to mean something that translates as "Open Air".

It started as early as November 21, 2004, when, after the CEC announcement of the preliminary results, Viktor Yushchenko and his team called on voters to gather in the evening for a rally to defend their choice without waiting for the official results. At the rally, Yushchenko, disfigured by the dioxin, rejected the election results as having been rigged and called for a general political strike that would not disperse until there had been a recount.

As in 2002, a tent city was erected on Kyiv's central square. Roman Bessmertniy, a supporter of Yushchenko, was appointed as the "mayor" of the Maidan (later, when Yushchenko was President, he would become Deputy Prime Minister). In the beginning, Maidan was chaotic but over time ordinary citizens of Kyiv, and then small and especially medium-sized business, tired of the corruption at the top, began to sponsor the protesters. Food, medicine, and firewood were brought in to keep the protesters warm around the fires. A huge stage was erected on which opposition leaders and numerous artists performed for free.

The opposition factions called an extraordinary parliamentary session the next day to debate the crisis. However, of course, the Communists and pro-government factions did not show up. It proved a tactical mistake of the Yanukovych-Putin faction. At this session of the Verkhovna Rada, Yushchenko took his oath as President, which caused a new massive wave of support. Between 500 thousand to 1.5 million protesters now gathered in the center of the capital.

The police and special forces acted in a relatively neutral and respectful way, and they did not respond to provocation. Despite the large concentration of Interior Ministry personnel in the capital, bloodshed was avoided. Both sides, the opposition and the authorities, behaved with restraint.

From the capital, the Maidan movement spread to the provinces. As in Kyiv, the viability of the Maidans in the regions was made possible by the active support of the middle-class businessmen, who allocated people and money for the construction of tent camps and the provision of food and medicines for the protesters.

Despite the mass protests, the Central Electoral Commission announced its official results on November 24 and declared Viktor Yanukovych the winner. In response, protesters besieged the Presidential Palace and Kyiv's central-government building. To counter these protesters, Yanukovych supporters from eastern Ukraine and especially from Donbas were bussed into the capital, camping out in the garden opposite the buildings. There were rumors about more than 300 thousand miners from Donbas to Kyiv who would "wipe out the Maidan activists" and prevent Yushchenko from coming to power. Ultimately, the number of Yanukovych supporters in Kyiv did not exceed 20 thousand people. These were mostly miners who were paid wages and a "traveling allowance" for the time they spent participating in the counter-protests. They slept in train carriages located on the spare tracks of the Kyiv railway station. A violent confrontation between the two camps and the use of force by the authorities to disperse the demonstrations hung heavy in the air.

On November 27, the Rada adopted a resolution about the political crisis, passing a resolution that stated that the Presidential Elections had been falsified and that annulled their results. While expressing mistrust of the Central Electoral Commission, it called for peaceful resolution of the conflict. In the western regions of the country, local governments decided to recognize Viktor Yushchenko as the legitimate President. In the eastern regions, leaders of the Donetsk, Luhansk, and Kharkiv regions closest to Russia initiated the convening of a congress of local councilors to create an autonomous state and recognize the legitimacy of Yanukovych's election as President.

The Southeastern Ukrainian Autonomous Republic

In contrast to the events taking place in the western regions of Ukraine and in Kyiv, November 28, 2004, saw a meeting of all elected officials from the south-east of Ukraine in Severodonetsk (in the Luhansk border region with Russia). It would be referred to as the "Severodonetsk Congress".[49] The key organizer behind the congress was the governor of Kharkiv, the well-known Ukrainian politician Yevhen Kushnaryov. It was attended by about 3,500 delegates from 17 regions of eastern and central Ukraine and Crimea, including 159 deputies or a third of the Verkhovna Rada. The aim of the congress was to develop a common strategy in the event of an escalation of the conflict.

At the congress it was argued that if Yushchenko and his "orange team" came to power, deputies of the southeastern regions and Crimea reserved the right to create southeastern autonomy from the government in Kyiv. At the same time, Viktor Tikhonov, head of the Luhansk regional council, stressed that the goal of the congress was to create a council of regions without yet declaring autonomy, as that question should be resolved by a referendum. Delegates at the congress were unanimous in condemning the "Orange Revolution" in Kyiv as a *coup d'état*, and called on residents of southeastern Ukraine to fight the "Orange Plague."

Even before the start of the congress, a number of region councils adopted resolutions to expand their powers over the national government. Thus, on November 24, 2004, the Luhansk Regional Council decided to create an Autonomous Southeastern Ukrainian Republic and appealed to Putin for his support. On November 27, neighboring Kharkiv Regional Council on the border with Russia invested local executive committees of its own creation in its territory.[50]

The Kharkiv Region, prompted by Yevhen Kushnaryov, stopped transferring funds to the Treasury until the political situation in Kyiv had resolved itself. At the same time, representatives of the Odessa Regional Council and its city councils announced their intention to call a meeting of all elected officials of southern and eastern Ukraine to decide on the proclamation of "Novorosiya" along the Black Sea.

Yanukovych, still only a Presidential candidate and not a President, arrived late at the Severodonetsk Congress. Borys Kolesnikov, chairman of the Donetsk regional council, was the first to speak and suggested that if "illegitimate" President Yushchenko was installed as President of Ukraine, there should be a referendum in southeastern Ukraine on a vote of confidence in the central government and on an independent republic that is part of a federation of Ukrainian states. He said, "The situation is out of control. Until the very last moment, we were hoping for a peaceful resolution. But now it is clear that this has become fundamentally impossible. We have an obligation to protect the interests of our constituents. And if we are not allowed to defend our voters, we are ready to opt for extreme measures. We have no confidence in the national bodies of state, as they have violated the law. We want to create a new southeastern Ukrainian state as part of a federal republic. The capital of our new state would be Kharkiv."

It was understood that the "main address" would be given by the governor of the Kharkiv region, Kushnaryov. His speech was emotional and seductive:

"There is no doubt that within a week a carefully planned and prepared, amply financed anti-state coup was carried out in Ukraine. Using the latest techniques in brainwashing the people, they tried to coronate a self-proclaimed President using any method, including force... But do not test our patience... We have our own answer to any outrage, including the most extreme measures you can think of. And I want to remind the fanatics with their orange banners: from Kharkiv to Kyiv it is 480 kilometers, but to the border with Russia it is – 40! [applause] We want to live in a state where everyone is protected. Where our rights, our culture, our [Russian] language, our history, our traditions and our customs are protected. We know that our eastern Ukraine is very different from Galicia, we don't impose our way of life on Galicia, but we will never allow Galicia to teach us how to live! We must protect and preserve the main spiritual pivot that unites us, our faith. We will not accept a way of life imposed on us, we will not accept someone else's symbols, our symbol is [Moscow] Christian Orthodoxy! Dear friends, we want to live, work, create in peace, but there is a terrible orange threat hanging over our country, over our future. So once again I call on everyone to be unwavering, to stand tall and defend our choice."

Moscow Mayor Yuri Luzhkov, known for his anti-Ukrainian statements back in 1998 in Sevastopol, was present at the invitation of the congress organizers, also sparkled with rhetoric. Known for being bald and wearing a cap, he said:

Two polar forces are now at work in Ukraine. On the one hand, there is crude interference in Ukraine's affairs, and on the other hand, there is Russia, which fully respects the sovereignty of your country. As mayor of Moscow, I am ready to take off my favorite cap in order to look like Viktor Yanukovych.

Everyone was now waiting for the Presidential candidate to speak, confident that Yanukovych would galvanize the fight against the supporters of the Orange Revolution and call for decisive action. But his speech disappointed those in attendance who expected their leader to be intransigent:

> I will never betray you, I will always march with you. And whatever you decide will be the law for me…. One more step and everything will collapse. Let us try to find a solution, without resorting to drastic measures. If even one drop of blood is spilled, there will be no stopping the tide. Protecting laws and rights is our goal. Please chose the solution that will ensure the integrity of the country and the rule of law….

In the end, it was decided to create an Interregional Council of Local Self-Government Bodies of Ukrainian Regions centered in Kharkiv.[51] The Luhansk and Donetsk regions decided to hold a referendum in the first half of December 2004 to found independent republics. In addition, the Luhansk and Donetsk regional councils, following the Kharkiv one, announced that the police and other state agencies were to fall under their direct orders and that they would also stop contributing to the state Treasury.

On December 11, a second congress was scheduled to take further steps to autonomy, but the congress never happened. Neither Yanukovych nor the oligarchs around him had a clear understanding of what they really wanted: to surrender or fight, to secede from Ukraine or remain as an autonomous part of it, or even to join Russia. Ten years later, in 2014, after the annexation of Crimea, a second congress of the same regional officials took place in Kharkiv. It faced the same dilemma, but this time Yanukovych shone by his absence.

When Yushchenko came to power, criminal cases were filed against Kharkiv Governor Kushnaryov and Donetsk Regional Council Chairman Borys Kolesnikov, as the organizers of the Severodonetsk Congress, accusing them of separatism and "attempting to change Ukraine's borders by aggression". Both were imprisoned, but the criminal cases were soon dropped "for lack of corpus delicti" and the prisoners were released. But calls for federalization and autonomy of eastern Ukraine and Crimea as well as demands for strengthening traditional ties with Russia became a permanent fixture in Ukrainian politics. From being one country since the Bolshevik conquest of 1917, Ukrainians once again divided themselves in west (right bank) and east (left bank). The political and business elite of these two parts of Ukraine held opposing views: the desire to follow the European path of development was towed in the western regions of Ukraine. The desire to strengthen ties with neighboring Russia and create a federative state with autonomous regions was claiming the east.

Viktor Yushchenko's Victory

The European Union weighed in on the conflict in Ukraine by sending an EU mediation mission to Kyiv, as well as one from the Organization for Security and Co-operation in Europe (OSCE), to meet with Kuchma, Yanukovych and Yushchenko and representatives of Russia, Poland and Lithuania. As a result, a compromise was reached to "redo" the second round, that is, to schedule a new, third round, subject to ratification by the Verkhovna Rada.[52]

The session in parliament was televised so that the whole country could follow the process. More abuses and falsifications during the elections were revealed: appearance of "dead souls" on the voter lists, i.e. people who died but were recorded as voters (an evergreen in Russian elections) etc.

Before the Verkhovna Rada's vote was taken, President Kuchma flew to Moscow for consultations with Putin, whom he met at the airport. Putin had already been wrong-footed when he hurried to congratulate his candidate Yanukovych on his victory. After the mass protests, Putin was no longer able to manipulate Ukraine's election results as if they were genuine, and nor did he publicly get involved in Ukraine's civil conflict. Perhaps Kuchma convinced Putin of the need for neutrality. On December 3, 2004, having previously blocked the investiture of Yanukovych, the Supreme Court ruled that it was impossible to determine a winner on the results of the second round, and on December 26 it scheduled a third round.

On December 7, President Kuchma agreed to comply with the court ruling, as well as to Yushchenko's demand that Prime Minister Yanukovych be placed on leave[53] and that a new Central Election Commission be formed to oversee the results. At the session of the Verkhovna Rada of December 8, amendments to the laws on Presidential and local elections and the Constitution were introduced, which set in motion the political reform about which the opposition had been talking about for so long. Parliament also approved the new CEC. Kuchma, present at the parliamentary session, signed the laws so that they came into effect immediately. The political crisis seemed to have been averted and protests stopped, though Kyiv's tent city remained.

Twelve thousand international observers came to the third round of the Presidential Elections in Ukraine. Each of the political parties also had observers at almost every polling station in the country. The political bloc that supported Yushchenko's candidacy was the coalition "People's Power" (uniting Yushchenko's Our Ukraine and Yulia Tymoshenko's Fatherland). The Socialist Party of Ukraine also agreed to support Yushchenko. In all Our Ukraine included about a dozen national-democratic parties.[54]

Despite a few attempts by the Ukrainian government to favor its candidate Yanukovych, something that should have happened in the second round took place: the re-vote held on December 26 led to the victory of Yushchenko with a landslide margin of about 8 percent. Yushchenko received nearly 52 percent of the vote; Yanukovych, just over 44 percent. As expected, the central and western regions of Ukraine gave their votes to Yushchenko, while the southeast and Crimea gave theirs to Yanukovych. The elections were deemed to have been held fairly, with no significant violations.

Nonetheless, Yanukovych filed a complaint, similar to the one previously filed by Yushchenko, with the Supreme Court. On January 20, it was rejected, however, and the CEC published the election results. There was general jubilation in Ukraine, people congratulated each other on the victory of Maidan, considering it their personal victory over authoritarianism, bureaucracy, and oligarchy. For the first time ever, the majority had truly won the Presidential Elections and, for the first time, Ukrainians believed that a new democratic and fair Ukraine had been born. It would follow the path of European history and the party-economic stranglehold that had dominated the country since 1991 would finally end.

The change in the political top of the Ukraine, and its radical reorientation of foreign policy, prompted many analysts to talk about a series of "color revolutions" in the world after 2004. The Orange Revolution in Ukraine followed the model of the 2000 overthrow in Serbia, when citizens fought against the regime of Slobodan Milosevic, the "Rose Revolution" in Georgia (2003), the "Cedar Revolution" in Lebanon (2005), and the "Tulip Revolution" in Kyrgyzstan (2005). A characteristic feature of these revolutions was, apart from the use of color, spontaneity, and the main driving force of all revolutions was the youth, especially students. They all began with discontent about the results of elections in which the candidates in power won, and ended with mass riots and protests in the country, until the resistance won and real elections were held.

On January 20, Yushchenko resigned his parliamentary seat. The Verkhovna Rada scheduled the inauguration of the new President for January 23, 2005. His inauguration was attended by heads of state and government from many countries. The official ceremony was held at the Verkhovna Rada, where the chairman of the CEC announced the election results. The President of the Constitutional Court confirmed the legality of the results and Yushchenko stepped on to the podium and took the oath of office for the Ukrainian people, placing his hand on the Constitution of Ukraine and on the Peresopnitsky Gospels, on which all previous Presidents had been sworn in. Having received the symbols of state, Yushchenko delivered his inaugural address and the Speaker announced the resignation of the government.

Having become President, Yushchenko and his family went to Kyiv's Maidan where about half a million people awaited him, who greeted him with standing ovations shouting "Yushchenko, Yushchenko!" Addressing his supporters, Yushchenko said, "After the Orange Revolution we live in a different state – a country where there will be honest journalists, judges and officials. Today Ukraine is famous throughout the world. Now everyone knows that we are not only in Europe but that we are in the heart of Europe.

Addressing his son, Yushchenko said: "You have the country that I didn't have. And we have created Ukraine where none of us will be ashamed." Yushchenko ended his speech by saying to those gathered in the square, "I believe that you will not give away our victory!"

He visited many places in the capital that day, where ordinary people were waiting for him and warmly congratulated him and themselves on their victory. In the evening, a ball was held for at the Ukrainian House to celebrate Yushchenko's inauguration. It seemed that Ukraine was breathing in freedom.

The phenomenon of Yulia Tymoshenko.

Was it an illusion? Hardly anyone would dispute that Yushchenko owed much of his success to his closest supporter Yulia Tymoshenko. She was a politician on whom many epithets were lavished: initially they were "Lady Yu" and "Orange Princess" or "Princess of the Orange Revolution"; but, after repeated attempts by the authorities to put her behind bars: "Joan of Arc" and even "Countess of Monte Cristo" due to being imprisoned in the Kachanovskaya prison in Kharkiv.

During the Orange Revolution, Tymoshenko was especially popular. Ukrainians associated her and Yushchenko with the European future of the country. Tymoshenko's charismatic personality, her assertiveness, fearlessness, for which she was nicknamed "the samurai in a skirt", made her the mascot of the Maidan. She knew how to make an impression. When the public inauguration of President Yushchenko took place on the Maidan, people were waiting for him to arrive and greeted Yushchenko affectionately. A little later, breaking protocol, which no one paid attention to at the time, the Queen of the Maidan, Tymoshenko, appeared and was greeted with even more cheers. Yulia really looked like a queen. She knew how to stand out, unlike her faceless "fellow fighters".

Tymoshenko's biographers note her "uniqueness" as a politician. Perhaps it stemmed from a very difficult childhood, after her father left her and her mother. Her mother was a taxi-dispatcher in Dnipro, raising her daughter as best she could, trying her utmost to not make her daughter feel poor. From an early age, "Lady Yu" learned to make her own decisions, to protect herself from overbearing boys and she preferred dolls over soccer, volleyball, table tennis. In high school, however, Yulia began training in gymnastics and excelled as a junior champion. "The sports competitiveness of my childhood came in handy when I joined the 'men's club' of politics."

After graduating from high school Tymoshenko entered the Dnipro Mining Institute, but realizing that it was not for her changed to studying economics at the Dnipropetrovsk State University of Internal Affairs, graduating with honors. At 18 she married Oleksandr Tymoshenko, whose father was a well-known party functionary in the city, and at 19 she gave birth to her only daughter Eugenia.

In the mid-1980s, at the height of perestroika, Tymoshenko realized that she would not make much money as an economist and joined as "cooperator" a Soviet cooperative called "Terminal," which dealt in video rentals. Not without the help of the Dnipro Komsomol committee, the youth division of the Communist Party (where the head of the propaganda department was later Kuchma supporter Serhiy Tihipko, who gave her invaluable help), the young and enterprising Tymoshenko managed to open video shops in many areas of the city.

In order not to pay taxes to the state, many cooperators registered their firms offshore or created joint ventures. Cyprus became an offshore paradise for such Soviet cooperators. Thus, Tymoshenko became director of Ukraine Gas, a monopolist in supplying petroleum products and lubricants to the agro-industrial sector. At the same time, she created an international company called Sial, which quarried natural stone. In addition, she got a 25 percent stake in the Took company, the only red granite quarry in the world, and in the mid-1990s, she created the Sodruzhestvo gas company together with Viktor Pinchuk, Kuchma's son-in-law.

But Tymoshenko's main business asset was her meeting in 1995 with Pavlo Lazarenko, "Lord" of the Dnipropetrovska region, who became Prime Minister in 1997. Her close acquaintance with Lazarenko enabled Tymoshenko to become a major oligarch in Ukraine's gas market, ousting her former partners. Her company Ukraine Gas, reborn as UESU (Ukrainian-British United Energy Systems of Ukraine Ltd), controlled 25 percent of the Ukrainian economy. Having ousted Ihor Bakai, another oligarch close to Kuchma, Tymoshenko became virtually the sole supplier of Russian gas to Ukraine, earning her the nickname "gas princess".

Tymoshenko joined the Unity party founded by Lazarenko, and was elected to the Verkhovna Rada. By then her fortune (according to the British newspaper *The Times*) was $6 billion, making her the most powerful woman in the country. An Investment Institute in Poland nominated her even for the title of "Man of the Year" in central and south-eastern Europe.

The interest in Tymoshenko by men and politicians was understandable. But she kept people at a distance. Some were afraid of her influence, others of her character. But public interest in her as a high society woman never faded. Women wanted to know what cosmetics she used (apparently French cosmetics by A-Studio, and Angel perfume), what clothes she liked (Chanel and Dolce & Gabbana). Men liked how she always looked elegant. It cast a spell on many. Her fashion consultants and makeup artists thus created an immediately recognizable image of Tymoshenko today with golden hair and a permanent braid. Ordinary citizens wrote her letters confessing their love for her. But this was already a different kind of love, and here, perhaps, was the key to another of aspect of her uniqueness: a love of people.

When she became an oligarch, the public was interested in her as a businesswoman. When she became a public figure, she drew attention to herself as a politician, able to overcome her opponents effectively and ruthlessly. Her speeches, vivid and entertaining, were the envy of any speaker. Unlike her dense-speaking male counterparts, Tymoshenko was articulate, fluent and intelligible in both Russian and Ukrainian; she said what the people wanted to hear.

Tymoshenko's uniqueness also lay in the fact that she was exceptionally ambitious and arrogant. To achieve her goals she had no mercy, throwing allies under the bus along the way. The meaning of her life was determined by the struggle for power, for the highest level of power, for the Presidency. To achieve this goal, she was ready to make temporary compromises even with her enemies. But ultimately, she worked only for herself, was implacable and driven, regardless of the office she held, never forgetting for a moment that the ultimate goal was the Presidency. After losing another Presidential Election, she hid in the shadows for a while, but never gave up her fight for Ukraine's highest public office.

6

The Sfinx

In 2005 Yushchenko's Presidency promised a bright future. At that time, everybody was unanimous in condemning "the Kuchma regime" and praising the new President and his team, calling him "the hope of the nation". His favorite Ukrainian phrase "Love My Friends" was widely used in the population, not without some irony. Upon taking office as President on a wave of euphoria, Yushchenko had to tackle a whole set of problems for the country. In his January 23 inauguration speech, the new President announced that his goals would be to fight corruption with determination, keep politics and business separate, and commit to freedom of speech and open government.

He began by reforming the civil service. The Presidential administration was renamed the Secretariat. Oleksandr Zinchenko, head of Yushchenko's election headquarters, was appointed its Chief of Staff. The new President also announced a reduction of the civil service, replacing all the regional governors and dismissing over 18 thousand employees. Yulia Tymoshenko became his Prime Minister. As happened under previous administrations, it was open season against political opponents, against whom the Attorney General started criminal proceedings, accusing them, among other things, of separatism in favor of Russia.

Yushchenko immediately made it clear that the main strategic foreign policy objective of his Presidency would be the European Union, while maintaining positive Russian relations. This is why President Yushchenko paid his first official visit to Russia, where he arrived on January 25, 2005. On the plane, just before its departure, he made public the appointment of Yulia Tymoshenko as Prime Minister, dispelling rumors circulating in Kyiv that her candidacy would be subject to Russian approval. "A terse message to the Kremlin: Kyiv plans to build relations with Moscow on an entirely different basis," the Russian newspaper *Kommersant* wrote, "As the new Ukrainian authorities see it, it will be a relationship of equal partners, not of the younger and elder brother. It is even possible that Ukraine will play the role of the elder brother."

Another delicacy of the situation was that, at the time Tymoshenko was appointed Prime Minister, a criminal case was opened against her in Russia, and she was put on the Interpol's most-wanted list. But Tymoshenko's criminal case was dropped after Yushchenko's visit to Moscow, and Yushchenko assured Putin that the Ukrainian people were keen on friendly terms with Russia. Yushchenko reiterated that Russia was and remains Ukraine's strategic partner, and he wanted to build up Ukrainian-Russian relations on a basis of trust and mutual benefit.

A few days later, Yushchenko was supposed to arrive in Brussels, but his January 27 trip was unexpectedly canceled due to "weather conditions". Yushchenko arrived in the capital of the European Union only in February. There he tried to convince EU officials that Ukraine wanted to become, if not a full EU member, then at least an associate member with a prospect of joining the European community. The EU leadership assured Ukrainians of its support, yet also stressed that Ukraine was not yet ready to join the EU. Ukraine was left with little choice but to throw itself back into the "brotherly embrace" of the Russian bear.

"My government has clean hands and will never steal."

On January 23, 2005, at the inauguration ceremony, the newly elected President said with a famous catchphrase: "My government has clean hands and will never steal". Most people believed him, though not everyone did, because Yushchenko did not quite fulfill his promise. An indication of this was the appointment to high government positions of quite a few cousins and others without relevant experience apart from a close personal relationship to himself.[55]

The first stumbling block for Yushchenko was the constitutional reform that changed the Presidential-parliamentary system to a parliamentary-Presidential one. Kuchma had prepared this reform under Rada pressure, but Yushchenko was in no hurry to implement it, justifying himself by the fact that he had received a broad vote of confidence from the people and did not have to transfer some of his powers to parliament. Nevertheless, before the parliamentary elections of 2006 Yushchenko had to agree to implement this reform and limit his powers, which he had to share with the Prime Minister.

The result was a constant tug-of-war between Tymoshenko and the President. Business was suffering. The population was waiting for real change, not the perennial reshuffling of government offices. No transformation of the economy or politics were happening. Instead, a scandal broke involving Prime Minister Tymoshenko and the head of the National Security and Defense Council (NSDC), Petro Poroshenko, resulting not only in the resignation of Tymoshenko's government but also in the disappointment of the masses in the ideals of the Orange Revolution and its leaders.

While struggling to reduce the civil service, Yushchenko simultaneously increased the size of his Presidential Secretariat to 600 people. Yushchenko's office now cost 1.5 billion hryvnia, while the cost of maintaining the Verkhovna Rada was "only" 1 billion hryvnia and the cost of maintaining the central government was 500 million hryvnia. All state decisions were controlled and ultimately approved by the Secretariat and its Chief of Staff who, in effect, became the second most powerful person in Ukraine.

Intentionally or not, Yushchenko carbon-copied the system Putin created in March 2000 in Russia after he became President. When Putin came to power in Russia, his Chief of Staff Alexander Voloshin issued a decree (signed by Putin) under which he became the second most powerful man in Russia. And because the Chief of Staff was appointed by the President himself, he was responsible only to him and could be removed from office by no one but him. Unelected by the people, Putin's Chief of Staff was more powerful than the Prime Minister who was accountable to parliament. Yushchenko followed suit.

It was the Secretariat that Yushchenko had created that ultimately led to dissatisfaction and a drop in his approval rating. Under the circumstances, he had to slightly reduce the size of the state apparatus.[56] Under Yushchenko there were three top centers of power: the Presidential Secretariat, the Prime Minister, and the National Security and Defense Council (NSDC). The Secretariat duplicated the functions of the Prime Minister's government and interfered with its policies as not a single government decree could be issued without the final approval of the Secretariat. This in itself led to clashes. The expansion of the NSDC staff to 220 people, and giving it the right to adjust and prepare government decisions (i.e. duplicating the role of the government), created even more tension and were a constant cause for personal accusations against each other by ambitious politicians Tymoshenko and Poroshenko.

In Russia, Putin controlled the entire civil service and government through his Chief of Staff. In Ukraine, Yushchenko may have thought that he would always be able to "divide and rule" as the neutral arbiter between politicians who fought with each other under him. But this is what ruined his own prospects. People saw Orange Revolution leaders Yushchenko and Tymoshenko as one, as a team of like-minded people who complemented each other. Instead, they turned out to be "A Swan, the Crab and a Pike" who could never agree, as in a popular fable by the Russian writer Ivan Krylov. The discord between the former allies disappointed their supporters, and the rating of the Orange Revolution began to plummet.

Nevertheless, despite his reduced Presidential power over economic and social policy, especially after the constitutional amendments, Yushchenko was able to partially implement the "Ten Steps Toward the People" program. The standard of living in the country went up a little, and child support for mothers increased to, in some cases, ten times basic subsistence.[57] During 2007-2008, Yushchenko also introduced the internet campaign "Ask the President", believing it would help him get feedback from the people and raise his own rating. Here, too, Yushchenko copied Putin, who would communicate with the "people" on air at that time. But after Yushchenko received the question: "Dear Mr President, please tell us how much we ordinary people should pay you, so that you, together with all the deputies of the Verkhovna Rada, ministers, members of the government, will emigrate forever and stop interfering with Ukraine's development?", he took offense, and stopped the program.

An import social policy of Yushchenko's Presidency was to build affordable housing, needed by more than 17 million citizens of Ukraine. But this promise was never fulfilled, neither by him nor by his successors. In 2007, at a meeting with Ukrainian businessmen, Yushchenko also initiated a family program to support low-income children, large families, orphans, and troubled children without parental care, and he brought up the issue of adoption support in parliament, arguing that every child without parental care should find a family. In this he was supported by oligarchs, and other businessmen, thanks to whom the program was partially realized.[58]

Yushchenko considered reform of the legal system, the Interior Ministry, the Attorney General's office and the SBU to be the main plank of his Presidency. But the widely proclaimed reorganization of law enforcement did not happen, as the public expected it would. The changes he made further confused the relationships between the legislative, executive, intelligence, and judicial branches of power. All Yushchenko succeeded in doing was to change the heads, appoint supporters instead, and then limit their influence by breaking all these services into smaller independent units.[59] Yushchenko's reform of the State Automobile Inspectorate, however, was extremely popular with motorists he unexpectedly announced the elimination of this agency.

Yushchenko planned, but did not carry through, a reform of the health service. In fact, all he managed to do was hold a meeting on the need for reforms in order to preserve a free medical service. The result was an increase in government funding of medical institutions, where doctors (who swore allegiance to the Oath of Hippocrates, and not "Pythagoras" as Yanukovych had once claimed) could perform their professional duty. But it did not change the health system and the efficiency of medical services did not improve. Patients were forced to come to doctors with their own bandages and medication in some cases, and with money and gifts.

Yushchenko most wanted to bring the "Gongadze case" to a conclusion, to arrest and convict not only the perpetrators of this murder – officers of the Interior Ministry, who carried out the order to dispose of the unwanted journalist – but also the unidentified masterminds of the crime. Numerous trials of the case, however, led only to the escape, or death, of key witnesses, suspects, and defendants. As we saw, the main witness, Interior Minister Yuriy Kravchenko, was found dead in his country house the day before the summons to the Attorney General's office. The masterminds remained unknown and, thus, remained at large.

Yushchenko – Tymoshenko conflict

Already in the first months of his Presidency Yushchenko and his entourage began to lose the credibility of the 2004 Maidan. The Yushchenko-Tymoshenko duo, which had seemed an ideal match during the election race, began to crack. Part of the reason was that the government headed by Tymoshenko had virtually no supporters (though she could count on Oleksandr Turchynov, Head of the SBU), and not a single member of her party was appointed as regional governor. So the Prime Minister's position was not strong and was dependent only on the support of Yushchenko himself. At the same time, as the confrontation between Yushchenko and Tymoshenko intensified, ministers and governors supported the "princess" of the Orange Revolution, not the President.

Since there was a prior agreement between Yushchenko and Tymoshenko to appoint Tymoshenko as Prime Minister, Yushchenko should have let her form a government of her own choice and thereby make Tymoshenko politically responsible for her policies. But this did not happen. Tymoshenko's government was anything but a team of like-minded people. As it was a cabinet based on political compromises between different political forces, she could hardly be held responsible for all their decisions. Moreover, Yushchenko's avowed principle of the separation of business and politics was never executed. Ministers were appointed on the basis of their business interests, including Tymoshenko herself.

Despite disagreements with the Presidential staff and Poroshenko's NSDC, the government still attempted to fulfill the pre-election promises of the Orange Revolution. Ukraine's thirteenth independent government was the youngest and most European-oriented, and even the key enforcement ministries were headed by civilians for the first time. The government had a Deputy Prime Minister in charge of European integration, and each ministry had a department in charge of European integration.[60] Wages, pensions, and tipends were increased 1.5 to 2 times.

Many analysts believed that the main reason for the disagreements between the "perfect duo" was not so much personal animosity, but rather fundamentally different vision of the reformers' perspectives, their methods, as well as the protection of interests of different financial and industrial groups. In order to stop land grabbing by oligarchs, foreigners, and foreign companies, Tymoshenko's faction in parliament prevented the adoption of laws on land sales and secured a moratorium on sales of farmland. This populist move by Tymoshenko led to a conflict with Yushchenko, who believed it was necessary to introduce private ownership of land in order to increase agricultural productivity and boost Ukraine's second largest export item after iron and steel.

Tymoshenko accused Yushchenko of lobbying the interests of the Swiss company RosUkrEnergo (RUE), half of which belonged to the Russian company Gazprom, and the other half to Yushchenko's oligarch friends Dmitry Firtash and Rinat Akhmetov.[61] Yushchenko and Tymoshenko also disagreed on the issue of transferring the shelf of the Black and Azov Seas under a long lease to the Venko company, which was also backed by Firtash and Akhmetov.[62] Tymoshenko considered it a betrayal of Ukraine's economic interests and said that Yushchenko was in the pocket of local oligarchs who owned RUE and Venko.

Vladimir Putin unexpectedly turned out to be her ally. He supported Tymoshenko in her attempt to remove all intermediaries from Russian natural gas supplies to Ukraine. The net result of this removal would be that Gazprom – part-owned by the Russian state and, it was rumored, 4.5 percent by Putin himself – would supply gas directly to the Ukrainian state company Naftogaz Ukrainy without having to pay these middlemen.

Tymoshenko decided to go all the way in her "Stop Fraud" campaign to bring oligarch businesses that did not pay taxes into the open. It affected not only large but also medium-sized companies.[63] The most high-profile and perhaps the only major review undertaken at Tymoshenko's own insistence was the re-privatization of one of the largest metallurgical conglomerate, Kryvorizhstal. The business was purchased at a relatively modest price of $800 million by the Interpipe company of Viktor Pinchuk while his father-in-law Kuchma was President. Claiming that the privatization had broken the law, the Yushchenko-Tymoshenko government announced a new tender and resold it for $4.8 billion to British metallurgical magnate Lakshmi Mitall. The proceeds from this deal did end up in the Treasury.[64]

Ukraine's leading businesses began to sabotage Tymoshenko's policies. Gasoline and sugar crises were artificially created and prices rose by 50 percent. Tymoshenko did not give in and her government forced an end to the crisis. The standoff continued, however, and in June 2005, Yushchenko, Tymoshenko and parliament were forced to guarantee existing property rights. In addition, at a meeting of the NSDC chaired by its head Poroshenko, himself a major Ukrainian businessman like Tymoshenko, Yushchenko criticized Tymoshenko for her "large-scale re-privatization" and "pressure" on gas companies. It was the beginning of a conflict between Tymoshenko and Poroshenko, who was plotting to take her place.

"Lady Y" did not back down, however. She declared another war: first of all, against Russian oil companies Lukoil, TNK-BP, and Tatneft, which controlled domestic oil in Ukraine. Re-export of Russian oil from Ukraine was banned.[65] Tymoshenko's government also began to pressure Russian oil companies who owned the refineries that supplied oil products to Ukraine. In order to avoid dependence on these Russian refineries, Tymoshenko proposed creating new state-owned gas stations, and building her own refinery in Odessa port for oil purchased from the Middle East and other countries, in order to significantly increase Ukraine's supplies of non-Russian oil. Yushchenko personally intervened to block her plans and issued a decree that vetoed Tymoshenko's government's measures against Russian oil refiners.

The manipulative hand of Vladimir Putin was never far away. During Ukraine's Independence Day celebration on August 24, 2005, Yushchenko claimed that Tymoshenko's government was the most successful of all the years of independence, but the simmering conflict between the three centers of power – Yushchenko, Tymoshenko, and Poroshenko – was becoming ever more and more apparent. Yushchenko had surreptitiously instructed Poroshenko to head a bilateral Russian-Ukrainian commission set up by Yushchenko and Putin. The President stated that the NSDC and not the government should be "the only place where strategic decisions are made". Thus, Yushchenko derogated a set of state powers that had previously belonged to the Prime Minister from her to Poroshenko.

Publicly, Yushchenko categorically denied that this conflict might trigger the dismissal of Tymoshenko's government. Nevertheless, that is what happened, though it was on the face of it triggered by an entirely different event: Yushchenko's Chief of Staff Oleksandr Zinchenko unexpectedly tendered his resignation. At a press conference he accused Poroshenko of gangsterism. "Most Ukrainians do not understand what is happening in the country," Zinchenko said, "There are enough decent people in the President's entourage, but a small group of adventurist politicians is trying to use the achievements of the Orange Revolution... Poroshenko illegally influences judges, systematically uses the telephone taps, is involved in 'protection' bribery at customs, and forces business representatives to share profits and assets with him... In his actions, Poroshenko says he acts on behalf of the President. But he is making it up because the President gave him no such instructions".[66]

Poroshenko flatly rejected all accusations and added "I would very much like to sue" (he did not).[67] He also said, "The President has never told me about any claims against me", and nor had Zinchenko. "Zinchenko is deceitful, claiming that he has been briefing this to the President for two or three months. The only disagreement with Zinchenko during this time was the fact that the Presidential Secretariat is still in charge of law enforcement in Ukraine. I proposed to the Chief of Staff that we change this, but he didn't agree with me."[68]

Nevertheless, on September 8, 2005, Poroshenko tendered his resignation as Head of the NSDC as a result of the corruption charges.[69] On the same day, the Verkhovna Rada deprived him of his immunity as a government executive by 269 votes in favor (of 450), and the SBU launched an investigation into corruption allegations against Poroshenko.[70]

On September 8, 2005, Yushchenko dismissed Tymoshenko's government as a result of the Poroshenko scandal. The next day every major newspaper in the world devoted front pages to this event. The *New York Times* neatly summarized what had happened:

The Orange Revolution is coming to an end at least its first act.... If Mr Yushchenko hopes to salvage any of their spirits, he needs to convince his country and a very wary West that not only does he believe in democracy, free markets and the rule of law, but that he is also able to lead Ukraine in that direction.[71]

On September 20, 2005, Attorney General Svyatoslav Piskun said that his office had found no evidence that Poroshenko was involved in corrupt practices.[72] However, on October 10, his office announced that it had opened a criminal case against Poroshenko on suspicion of interference with two firms that were constructing a building on 9-a Mykhailo Hrushevsky Street in Kyiv that could lead to imprisonment for a maximum of 10 years.[73]

The prosecution was never followed through but at the next political crisis that gripped Ukraine, public opinion was no longer on Yushchenko's side. In the March 2006 Rada elections, Tymoshenko's party outnumbered Yushchenko's for the first time. She won 129 seats, while the Presidential Our Ukraine party received only 81. In 2002, Tymoshenko had 22 seats and Yushchenko 112.

The gas conflict with Russia

After dismissing Tymoshenko's government, Yushchenko invited his close friend Yuriy Yekhanurov, then governor of the Dnipropetrovsk region (and a businessman like most Ukrainian politicians), to head the national government as Prime Minister. After graduating from the Kyiv Institute of National Economy in 1973, Yekhanurov worked as CEO in the construction industry and had held several ministerial positions in independent Ukraine and had been Yushchenko's Deputy Prime Minister under President Kuchma.[74]

Yekhanurov's candidacy for Prime Minister fell three votes short in parliament, however. Because of this, the President had to seek the opposition support from his former rival Yanukovych. He got it, but Yanukovych extracted concessions, confident that, at the next parliamentary election in 2006, his party would gain the upper hand. The Communists and Social Democrats also received a volley of promises in exchange for refusing to oppose Yekhanurov, and they abstained in the second vote on Yekhanurov. As a result, the new Prime Minister was in office but not in power, trapped as he was in a web of promises by both himself and Yushchenko.

During Yekhanurov's premiership (2005-2006), a major gas conflict broke out between Ukraine and Russia. Russian monopolist Gazprom wanted to bring prices for gas supplies to the former Soviet republics such as Ukraine in line with international market prices: for several years gas had been fetching record prices. After the collapse of the Soviet Union, relations over gas contracts had gradually morphed from a purely economic one to one dominated by Putin's foreign policy agenda. Russia began to use gas to put political pressure on the former Soviet republics, as they were totally dependent on Russian supplies.[75] The worse the relations with Russia, the higher the price.

In March 2005, under Tymoshenko, Naftogaz Ukrainy had suggested that Gazprom abandon its gas barter scheme and switch to direct cash payment while revising at the same time upwards the price Gazprom had to pay for gas transit (some 80 percent of Russia's gas exports) through Ukraine's pipelines to Western Europe. The background to this conflict was that Slovakia, the Czech Republic and Germany were charging from $3 to $13 per 1,000 cubic meters per 100km transit to Gazprom, whereas Ukraine received a mere $1.09 in barter value. Naftogaz proposed that Gazprom raise it to $1.75-2.00 from the $1.09. Until the summer the parties worked out different versions of a new cash-based agreement. In the end Gazprom drew the line at $1.60 per 100km, balancing this against charging Ukraine $160 per 1000 cubic meters for its domestic gas usage – some 60 percent more than it charged other CIS countries that had belonged to the USSR. Ukraine balked at this and rejected the deal. Here at least Yushchenko showed he ran Ukraine's foreign policy with a measure of independence from Putin.

Ukraine's refusal to sign the agreement resulted in cancellation of Russia's Prime Minister minister's visit to Kyiv. More to the point, Russia unilaterally raised the price it charged Ukraine for gas to $230 when the current agreement came to an end. It was a blatant shake-down of the country. The Ukrainian delegation interrupted its negotiations in Moscow and returned to Kyiv as winter set in. Putin's government meanwhile unleashed an anti-Ukrainian propaganda campaign blaming its neighbor for insufficient gas supplies passing through Ukrainian pipelines to Europe. Many European countries were concerned about the situation and called upon both parties to come to an agreement. Not minded to give in, Gazprom stopped supplying gas to Ukraine as of January 1.

The day before, Putin, speaking at the Security Council of the Russian Federation, said that "Ukraine is first and foremost our brother. And we have to consider relations between Russia and Ukraine: that is why I am instructing the Russian government and Gazprom to ensure gas supplies to Ukraine in the first quarter of 2006 on 2005 terms and prices, provided that our Ukrainian partners sign before the end of this day what Gazprom proposes and switch over to market prices in the second quarter of 2006. In case of no clear agreement, we will consider our proposal rejected."

On the night of January 3 to 4, 2006, Gazprom and Naftogaz reached an agreement on the terms and conditions of gas supply via Swiss middleman RUE (RosUkrEnergo) and on the condition of uninterrupted Russian gas transit to Europe for the next five years, ending in 2010. RUE earned about $1.5bn from reselling Russian gas to Ukraine. Under the agreement, Gazprom undertook to deliver gas to Ukraine at a price of $95 per thousand cubic meters in the first quarter of 2006, as Putin had set out days before, and then at the "European market price" of $230. At the same time, Gazprom and Naftogaz Ukrainy agreed to hand over to RUE their contracts for the purchase in 2006 of 56 billion cubic meter of gas from Central Asia.[76]

Putin and Yushchenko stated that the gas conflict between the two countries was now over. However, if the conflict was considered solved at a political level, problems remained at the level of relations between the two companies, leading occasionally to the resumption of aggravation. After the signing of the gas contracts with Russia, the Verkhovna Rada heard a report on these energy negotiations from Yekhanurov's government, and, dissatisfied with it, passed a resolution for his government to resign. Yushchenko managed to persuade parliament with great difficulty to have the government continue as a minority government until the upcoming parliamentary election, in the hope that the new Rada would reverse its decision.

Parliamentary elections 2006-2007

Parliamentary elections were approaching. The election itself took place on March 26, 2006, but the election campaign had started much earlier, and all political crises between the Presidential and parliamentary branches of power were focused on the upcoming election. The disintegration in the "Orange" camp fueled the interests of Viktor Yanukovych's "Blue-White" regions. The electoral system itself had also changed.[77] While in the 2002 elections 33 political parties and blocks participated, in 2006 there were no less than 45 of them vying for the 450 seats.[78] The more than 3,500 international observers present agreed that the elections had been held without violations and passed international voting standards.

The 2006 parliamentary elections had a special significance for President Yushchenko because the political reform and constitutional amendments debated under Kuchma were finally signed into law as a result of the horse trading during Yushchenko's term. They curtailed his influence as important powers were transferred to the Verkhovna Rada. Henceforth parliament had to approve the country's Prime Minister, Defense and Foreign Affairs ministers, and the Prime Minister now had sole discretion to appoint their ministers.

Even though the pro-Presidential Our Ukraine came in third, Yushchenko tried to recreate an Orange Coalition in the Rada by negotiating with Tymoshenko and the Socialists. That coalition had 243 seats in parliament. A coalition of Yanukovych party (the largest in the Rada with 189 seats), Socialists and Communists would have received more – 240 votes. It made the Socialists the Rada's king makers in the 2006 parliament.

Socialist leader Oleksandr Moroz wanted to become Speaker and when the Orange Coalition advanced Poroshenko instead, Moroz went over to Yanukovych and joined his "Anti-Crisis" coalition.[79] It nominated Yanukovych as Prime Minister and Moroz as Speaker of the Rada. Yushchenko waved through Yanukovych as Prime Minister, but tried to sabotage Moroz's appointment, hoping to strengthen his position in parliament.

Talks between Yushchenko and Yanukovych about their power sharing lasted from August to September 2006 but led nowhere. Nevertheless, in September 2006 the parties signed a "Universal Principle of National Unity", declaring their intention to pursue greater European integration and eventual accession of Ukraine to NATO, stating the need to depoliticize the state, creating a legal basis for the opposition's role, and proclaiming the need to create the conditions for privatization of agricultural land. It was signed by all Rada parties, except Tymoshenko's.[80]

Tymoshenko argued that the declaration was the result of a bargain between Yushchenko and Yanukovych. In many ways she was right.[81] In December 2010 WikiLeaks published classified reports of the US Ambassador in Ukraine. They said that on 22 March 2006, i.e. four days before the elections in the 2006 parliamentary election, Defense Minister Anatoliy Hrytsenko, who was a member of Yushchenko's inner circle, met with the US ambassador for a meeting on NATO.[82] He leaked to the Ambassador that an alternative coalition between Yushchenko's and Yanukovych's parties was being explored.[83]

While Yushchenko failed to reach an agreement with the leaders of the "Anti-Crisis Coalition", he did manage to insert in Yanukovych's government eight of his own ministers, including his Defense Minister Hrytsenko and Foreign Minister Borys Tarasyuk.[84] Yuriy Lutsenko became Interior Minister. All three had a pro-western orientation.[85]

It made little difference. For example, during his visit to Brussels in September 2006, Yanukovych stuck closely to what Putin liked to hear and stated that "Ukraine is not ready to join the EU and NATO," arguing that there was no political and civil consensus in society. According to Yanukovych, only a popular referendum could decide whether or not Ukraine should move toward Euro-Atlantic integration. Although in theory there was nothing wrong with this, in the context of Ukrainian politics Yanukovych's statement meant a complete and abrupt change of all previous Ukrainian policies aimed at European integration.

Not surprisingly, Yushchenko and his supporters called Yanukovych's position a "betrayal of Ukraine's national interests," especially since the Prime Minister made an unscheduled visit from Brussels to Moscow, where he met with Putin and his Prime Minister Dmitri Medvedev to discuss expansion of Ukrainian-Russian economic cooperation and they agreed to dial down again the price of Russian gas for Ukraine to $95 per thousand cubic meters as a reward for Ukraine for changing its pro-European political course to a pro-Russian one.

In October 2006, Yushchenko's faction announced its withdrawal from the parliamentary coalition, switching to the opposition and recalling its ministers. A new political crisis had begun which continued throughout 2007. The defense and foreign ministers who remained in the government under the "President's prerogative" declared that they would continue to focus on Europe as part of the NATO-Ukraine program and prepare the ground for Ukraine's associate membership in the European Union. Yanukovych then demanded their resignation and, on December 1, 2006, secured a parliamentary decision to dismiss the ministers who opposed his policies – as per their right in the new Constitution. In response, however, Yushchenko refused to sign the decree required to release them. The fight between the President and his Prime Minister was now a full-blown constitutional crisis.

The political crisis of 2007

The power struggle between Yanukovych and Yushchenko had to be resolved. Although the President did not recognize the parliament's decision to dismiss his foreign and defense ministers, Yanukovych continued to insist on his right to appoint and dismiss ministers. In January 2007 parliament passed a "Law on the Cabinet of Ministers" which limited the President's authority, and which Yushchenko in turn vetoed. Yanukovych also tried to expand his coalition to 300 deputies in order to be able to overturn Yushchenko's Presidential veto and make changes to the current constitution.

The climax came on April 2, 2007, when Yushchenko ordered the dissolution of the Verkhovna Rada and called new elections for May 25. Yanukovych's government coalition, of course, did not accept this and refused to provide funds for early elections, and began organizing numerous protests in the capital. Since Donbas was Yanukovych's base, miners from Donbas were again paid and bused into the capital for rallies. They received the wry epithet, "bus rallies".

Yanukovych's coalition also challenged the legality of the Presidential order dissolving parliament in the Constitutional Court. The court tried to sidestep a conclusive decision, not wanting to be drawn into a political showdown between Yushchenko and Yanukovych. For their part, the opposition parties to Yanukovych also called upon their supporters to protest. Another period of civil unrest began, and with some frequency the rallies continued until the winter of 2007.

Again, the police as well as Interior Ministry special units called "Berkut" (Golden Eagle), were mobilized to patrol the political strife, barricading various government institutions from protesters. The Berkut, in particular, were unpopular, having been formed after independence from Ukrainian officers who had been part of the USSR's anti-riot units.

Defense Minister Hrytsenko declared that he would follow the orders of the country's Commander-in-Chief Yushchenko rather than civilian Prime Minister Yanukovych. There was an implied threat of involvement of the armed forces in the conflict, but attempts to concentrate troops in the capital were unsuccessful. The Railway Minister, who followed Yanukovych's orders, refused to transport the armed military units to the capital. A personnel reshuffle began in the security and law enforcement agencies – who were under Yushchenko's control. Having shown "insufficient zeal" to defend the President, Yushchenko fired the President of the Constitutional Court and a number of judges (under his "Presidential prerogative"), as well as the Attorney General.

As a result of lengthy negotiations, violent clashes between the factions were avoided. Yushchenko agreed to postpone the elections from May to June, and then to July 2007. Many observers believed that during this crisis Yushchenko (unlike Tymoshenko) did not follow a consistent course and tried to compromise with Yanukovych, which only prolonged the crisis. The boycott of the Rada by Tymoshenko and other parties supporting the President paralyzed its work.[86] Eventually, after a long confrontation all sides agreed to elections on September 30.[87] A total of 20 parties and blocs entered the race, almost half the number of the previous elections.[88]

The second government of Yulia Tymoshenko (2007-2010).

In August 2007, Yushchenko and Tymoshenko met and talked about forming a coalition of "democratic" forces in parliament if they won the election. They scored a victory, as their parties were returned with 228 seats, a majority of 3.[89] Tymoshenko once again became Prime Minister and Yushchenko once again had to "play a duet" with her.[90] But the salvation from political chaos that the voters expected did not come. The political crisis just entered a new phase.

Tymoshenko's election as Prime Minister did not go smoothly. Despite the new Orange Coalition and its majority of three seats, Tymoshenko was not confirmed at the first attempt on December 11, 2007. She gained 225 votes out of 226 needed. She was one vote short. Why? As it turned out later, the electronic voting system malfunctioned and did not take these two votes into account. On December 18, there was a second round without using the electronic system; by a simple show of hands she got in.[91]

In mid-January Tymoshenko submitted to the Verkhovna Rada her program "Ukrainian Breakthrough: for People, Not Politicians." While populist, it otherwise contained no practical measures.[92] The program was subjected to extensive criticism at the Rada's commission meetings. Before being adopted, it underwent more than 300 amendments.[93] Nevertheless, according to the program, the priority tasks for the government were, apart from developing industry and fighting corruption, increasing wages and pensions. This the government could deliver, as three quarters of the economy were still run by companies whose shareholder was the state. Years after Tymoshenko's departure, people still remembered their increase of salaries and pensions.[94]

NATO was again the cause of a crisis. In January 2008, Foreign Minister Volodymyr Ohryzko gave NATO Secretary General a letter signed by Yushchenko, Tymoshenko and Speaker Arseniy Yatsenyuk about Ukraine's ambition to join the "NATO Membership Action Plan" at the Bucharest Summit in April 2008.[95] The contents of this letter had not been discussed in Tymoshenko's cabinet or by the Rada before it was sent to Brussels.

As public opinion was split on Ukraine joining NATO, this gave Yanukovych and the Communist faction the opportunity to criticize Ukraine's top leaders harshly. In a statement written by them on January 21, 2008, they damningly accused them of secretly hijacking the issue, "Being afraid of its people, [the government] decides the fate of our state behind closed doors, behind the scenes, in threes".[96] The scandal around the "secret negotiations" with NATO paralyzed the Rada for two months as opposition deputies boycotted its agenda. Only on March 6, 2008, did parliament resume work, after Yanukovych accepted a resolution stating that the decision on Ukraine joining NATO "shall be taken on the basis of the referendum that may be held on the people's initiative".

Only six months later, on September 16, 2008, Ukraine lurched into a new crisis. It was caused by Putin's attack on Russia's former Soviet satellite Georgia. Despite Georgia being a member of CIS, the Russian equivalent of the EU formed after the USSR's collapse, Ukraine's political top was not united in its foreign policy response to Putin's aggression.[97] It caused the implosion of the ruling "Democratic Alliance" in the Rada as two government parties, one of them Tymoshenko's Fatherland party, split during a parliamentary debate on the Russian-Georgian armed conflict. Yushchenko and his supporters supported Georgia and condemned Russian aggression. Tymoshenko took a measured stance, however, calling on both sides to stop the bloodshed and resolve the conflict peacefully. For this she was sharply criticized by Yushchenko's Secretariat and his Our Ukraine party, which accused her of betraying national interests.

Yushchenko's Secretariat's sniping at Tymoshenko had begun as early as August 2008, at the height of the Russian invasion of Georgia. Deputy Chief of Staff Andriy Kislinsky accused the Prime Minister of "systematically working for Russia," saying that "she has no way back. They dictate her position on the war in Georgia." Tymoshenko's neutral view on the Georgian issue had a financial context. During these very months she was involved in difficult gas negotiations with the Russian government. Tymoshenko's "impartiality" towards the Russian-Georgian war was likely the quid pro quo Putin had extracted in return for a lower offer on Ukraine's domestic gas supply.

Yushchenko tried to glue together the splintering alliance, but he failed to achieve his goal. On October 8, he dissolved the Verkhovna Rada and called early parliamentary elections for December 7. Now it was Tymoshenko's turn to claim the Rada's dissolution was illegal. Tymoshenko and her lawyers spent two days preparing the legal grounds for her complaint, and on October 10, a court in Kyiv suspended Yushchenko's decree. Frantic discussions ensued with one of the opposition parties, promising its leader appointment as Speaker.[98] A deal was struck and on December 8, the newly elected Speaker announced the restoration of the coalition. Tymoshenko's government avoided resignation. Its plans were highly ambitious: to settle the perennial Ukrainian-Russian gas conflict once and for all.

Another gas conflict with Russia

The new gas conflict with Gazprom, which erupted at the beginning of 2008, was directly related to Tymoshenko's attempt to cut Swiss intermediary RUE from the Gazprom deal for Ukraine's gas. Having received support from Putin (who was nominally Russia's Prime Minister from 2008), her government announced it was cutting ties with the company, which by then owed Gazprom nearly $1.5 billion in gas payments. Tymoshenko said in February 2008, "Ukraine and Russia do not need intermediaries in their gas supply, and the government will stand firm on this". At that time, while on a visit to Moscow, she managed to put together an agreement that Russian gas supplies to Ukraine would be delivered directly under a contract between (Russia's state-owned) Gazprom and (Ukraine's state-owned) Naftogaz. Russia had offered Prime Minister Tymoshenko a joint Russian-Ukrainian venture to sell gas inside Ukraine. But this carrot she rejected, saying that Naftogaz was capable of selling Russian gas domestically without Russian help.

Having secured direct gas supplies, Tymoshenko then raised the issue of the $1.5 billion debt, arguing they were not Ukrainian state debts, but debts of RUE to Gazprom. The intermediary company, however, had no intention of paying the balance which by now had risen to $2.2 billion. Trying to off-load the debt on to the Ukrainian Treasury, RUE received unexpected support in this matter from President Yushchenko himself.

More horse-trading ensued. In October 2008 Ukraine and Russia officially agreed to exclude the middlemen as of January 1, 2009. Having realized that RUE's $2.2 billion debt had to be paid off, Tymoshenko suggested a barter by buying more than 11 billion cubic meters of Russian gas and pumping it into RUE Ukrainian storage facilities as payment for the debt.[99] At the same time, Tymoshenko assured European countries that the new agreement provided for uninterrupted Russian gas transit to Europe on a long-term basis. The new contract, with all its terms now agreed, was to be signed on December 31, 2008. Meanwhile, RUE did everything possible to derail the signing of this contract and even offered Gazprom to pay a price of $285 instead of $235 for the supply of Ukraine's gas (all to be paid for ultimately by the ill-starred Ukrainian population, of course).[100]

They failed. Except, on December 31, 2008, Yushchenko ordered the CEO of Naftogaz[101] to return from Moscow and not to sign the Tymoshenko agreement with Gazprom. He blamed his Prime Minister for derailing the talks, saying she was working on behalf of Russia, whose government had accommodated her in the gas negotiations and bought her silence on the Georgian issue.[102]

On January 1, 2009, Gazprom announced that it was once again cutting off Ukraine's domestic gas. Under the Tymoshenko agreement, Gazprom was supposed to set Ukraine's new price based on eastern European prices for Russian gas. Instead, Putin made it clear that Ukraine would now have to pay $470 per thousand cubic meters. At the same time, Russian gas supplies to Europe via the Ukrainian pipeline were sharply reduced. And, on January 6, European countries once again called on Russia and Ukraine to settle the dispute as soon as possible and resume regular gas deliveries.

This time parties returned to the negotiation table as late as January 18-19, but these were negotiations unlike any other.[103] Dmytro Firtash and Ivan Fursin, the Ukrainian co-owners of RUE, were accused by Gazprom of being a front for Semyon Mogilevich, the Ukrainian-born godfather of the Russian mafia who had deep ties to the KGB/FSB. Mogilevich himself may have been on the most-wanted list of many countries, but he lived undisturbed in his dacha outside Moscow where no one ever made any attempt to arrest him. In fact, he shone at local social events.

After much haggling, the price of Russian gas for Ukraine was brought down from the $450 Putin had threatened Tymoshenko with to $291.23 per thousand cubic meters, on which Naftogaz was given a "fraternal" 20 percent discount to $232.98. The transit price Russia paid for gas export to Europe through Ukraine was simultaneously raised by over 50 percent to $2.7 per 1000 cubic meters per 100 kilometers.[104] And the Russian Interpol warrants for the arrests of Firtash and Fursin were as quickly filed away as the Red Notice for Tymoshenko herself had once been issued and withdrawn.

An important result of the agreement was that it finally fixed the cost of the gas delivered to consumers in Ukraine. Immediately after signing the contract, the NSDC (to which Yushchenko had just appointed a new head), recommended to Ukraine's energy regulator that gas prices be increased by 35 percent for domestic users and by another 5-10 percent for businesses that used large amounts of gas. The latter charge mostly affected Ukraine's industry which was concentrated in the east. When Naftogaz raised consumer gas tariffs Tymoshenko intervened, however, and said: "I categorically object to raising the price of gas for people. I undertook a commitment that during this year price on gas for people will not change, and I will stick to my word... I do not understand the President."

Tymoshenko prevailed in this dog fight. In a desperate effort to reduce Ukraine's energy dependence on Russia, her government planned energy savings programs, diversification to other sources of energy, and again mooted alternative sources: Central Asia, Azerbaijan, the Middle East, Arab countries, and even Europe.

Having overcome Yushchenko, in the second half of 2009 she herself tried to negotiate with Yanukovych to form a coalition in parliament. She, too, was after an absolute majority to amend the Constitution and further limit Yushchenko's Presidential powers. However, Yanukovych considered an alliance with his eternal rival too risky and pulled out of discussions at the last moment.

7

A Burglar as President

The 2010 Presidential Election

The failure of the Orange Revolution will be analyzed by economists, historians, and political scientists for a long time to come. As some observers point out, the problem was not even the fractious nature of the Yushchenko-Tymoshenko tandem, or that they never became allies throughout their political cohabitation, seeing each other as rivals rather than comrades-in-arms. The problem is that these two could not change the political system in Ukraine, uproot authoritarianism and corruption (it strengthened under Yushchenko), change the hold of the oligarchy over political parties. Viktor Yanukovych, who replaced Yushchenko, made a sharp return toward the Kuchma period. As Volodymyr Chemerys, one of the leaders of the "Ukraine without Kuchma" movement, noted, "Ukraine has remained stuck with Kuchma, only he has a different surname – Yanukovych."

Yushchenko took part in the Presidential Elections, though he polled a dismal 3 percent in pre-election surveys. Everyone wanted to try their hand, and 15 men and 3 women were officially entered on the ballot, whereas 40 candidates were excluded. Ten candidates were independents, the others were party members. At 50, the average age of the candidates was relatively young.

It didn't matter. The real contest was between Prime Minister Tymoshenko and opposition leader Viktor Yanukovych. The latter's popularity was so formidable by now that he did not need a pre-election alliance with his rivals' parties. He was careful, however, to clarify that he was not against coalitions as such in parliamentary elections to ensure that he would be able to engineer a pro-Presidential majority in the Verkhovna Rada.[105]

What about NATO and the EU? Analysis of the candidates' programs, by civic thinktank "Women's Alternatives", showed that most of the candidates had no clear foreign policy for the country and ranged from a union with Russia to accession to NATO.[106] Tymoshenko and Yushchenko saw Ukraine as part of the European Union, while Yanukovych favored a neutral status, but at the same time believed that it was necessary to restore friendly relations with Russia and the CIS countries, while seeking membership in the G20 (somewhat of a stretch given Ukraine's GDP ranking below 50 in the world). Only one of the Presidential contenders, the head of the Ukrainian People's Party (UPP), Yuri Kostenko, advocated the need for Ukraine's accession to NATO. At the same time all candidates were united in saying that the main direction – whatever it was – of foreign policy should finally be decided.

Practically all candidates included in their programs fighting unemployment, increasing the country's birth rate, quality health services, a social safety net… But none detailed how they were going to achieve these noble goals. Of course, the programs of the candidates also paid a lot of attention to the issues of education and science, the only difference being that the candidates for the highest state office could not decide for themselves whether to join the European system of higher education in Ukraine or to defend the national one. They were united in the need to create modern facilities in educational institutions, knowing full well that there was no money for this.

Many of the candidates studiously avoided the elephant in the room: the status of Crimea and the Russian Black Sea Fleet which had been based in Sevastopol for the past two centuries, with a section based in Odessa. Only Yushchenko addressed it head on and thought that the Russian Fleet had to leave Sevastopol after 2017.

Incumbent President Yushchenko had promised that elections would be democratic and that he would not deploy state resources for his candidacy, which is why many billboards throughout the country carried pictures not so much of him as of Yanukovych and Tymoshenko. The first round of the Presidential Elections was exemplary, without the usual vitriol poured on the heads of candidates and without violating election rules: the candidates had equal opportunities not only on TV but also on the public squares of Ukrainian cities. Joao Soares, special coordinator of the Organization for Security and Co-operation in Europe (OSCE, an organization closely aligned with the EU) observation mission, said that "these elections were very good. They were high quality elections. According to him, the current electoral process was "a step forward compared to the previous elections. Along with that, Soares stated that the election campaign was calm and organized and the apprehensions of mass falsifications were not justified.[107]

The official count of the first round showed that Yanukovych had 35.32 percent (slightly more than 8.5 million votes) and Tymoshenko 25 percent (slightly more than 6 million voters). The incumbent President Yushchenko took a modest fifth place with 5.45 percent. His result, as compared to other Presidents, was the lowest on record.[108]

Unlike the first round, the run-off between Yanukovych and Tymoshenko was fierce and brutal. Both tried to enlist support from other parties,[109] but Yanukovych got 48.95 percent (12,481,268 voters) and Tymoshenko won 45.47 percent (11 593 340 voters).[110] He had won by a handsome margin.[111] Unusually, the ballot also had an "Against All of Them" choice, which polled more than 1 million voters. In the first round of voting, wishing to take votes away from Tymoshenko, one of the Presidential candidates – Vasyl Humenyuk had changed his last name to "Against All of Them". It made little difference in that round as he got only 0,16 percent (a little over 40,000 votes). In the second round he urged his supporters to vote for Yanukovych.[112]

Immediately after the announcement of the official results,[113] Russia, Belarus, Poland, the United States and Kazakhstan were the first to congratulate Yanukovych. Perhaps for the first time in history a convicted burglar was elected to be a nation's head of state.

The inauguration took place on February 25, 2010. Unlike previous ceremonies, only Kuchma was present. Neither Yushchenko, nor Tymoshenko, nor the first President of Ukraine Leonid Kravchuk attended the ceremony, demonstrating to the world their disappointment with the results. Yanukovych, on the other hand, zealously took control of the unfettered Presidential power Yushchenko had created in the image of Putin. His first task was not governing, but the destruction of the political power of his Prime Minister, Yulia Tymoshenko.

Yulia Tymoshenko's court case

Yanukovych skillfully removed the party of the Rada's Speaker from Tymoshenko and Yushchenko's coalition by promising to keep him in the post. The Speaker's party duly joined Yanukovych's new coalition called "Stability and Reforms" (dubbed by journalists "the coalition of carcasses"). Having lost her majority in parliament, Tymoshenko understood that her days as Prime Minister were numbered.[114] President Yanukovych repeatedly urged her to resign and join the opposition, but Lady Y was not going to go without a fight.

On March 3, 2010, the Verkhovna Rada passed a vote of no confidence in Tymoshenko's government by 243 votes (including seven deputies from her own party). Still, she did not resign and on March 11, 2010, parliament dismissed her government with 237 votes.

With control over the government as well, the real persecution of Tymoshenko, began. As early as April 28, the new Prime Minister Mykola Azarov stated in parliament that "the actions of Tymoshenko's government caused 100 billion hryvnia of damage to the state, and therefore Tymoshenko and her officials should be held criminally responsible."[115] Immediately after the May holidays, the Attorney General reinstated a criminal case from 2004 that Kuchma had suspended, in which she was accused of "attempting to bribe" (based on a video-recorded conversation between Tymoshenko and a judge) in order to influence the decision of the judge who handled the case of her father-in-law Gennady Tymoshenko and the CFO of gas company UESU.[116] At the same time, the government decided to audit the activities of Tymoshenko's 2007-2010 government.[117]

Using the case against Tymoshenko as a smokescreen, Yanukovych also executed a paper palace-revolution Under the cryptic cover of the "Tymoshenko case", the Constitutional Court of Ukraine reviewed Yushchenko's amendments in a closed session on September 30, 2010, and declared unconstitutional the "Law on Amendments to the Constitution" of 2004 because of the "violation of the procedure of its consideration and adoption". The court returned Ukraine to the sweeping Presidential powers with which Kuchma had controlled Ukraine.

After Ukraine's elections were over, the Control and Revision Office announced the completion of an audit of the government.[118] Tymoshenko was charged with embezzlement of 320 million euros received under the Kyoto Protocol, by which her government redirected carbon funds received to plug a gap in Ukraine's pension fund instead of reforesting as the Protocol stipulated. In 2009, the Tymoshenko government had signed several agreements with Japanese and Spanish government agencies and corporations to sell Ukraine-owned greenhouse gas emission quotas totaling 319.9 million euros, which became the source of funding for a special state budget fund to finance projects aimed at reducing emissions or increasing greenhouse gas absorption in the country. However, the amount received was paid into Ukraine's pension fund to pay pensions, as well as to cover the operating costs of a number of state institutions.

On December 2, 2010, Tymoshenko was summoned to the Attorney General for the first time and was charged. On December 30, the interrogation continued for 12 hours. She denied all accusations against her.[119]

In January 2011 she was facing a new accusation – of buying at the end of 2009 thousands of Opel Combos for the needs of rural medicine. The purchase was not covered by the state budget. At the same time, Attorney General Viktor Pshonka said that he did not accuse Tymoshenko of stealing money or causing damage, but only of misuse of budget funds, abuse of power, violation of budget legislation and abuse of office.

Tymoshenko countered that this Kyoto money had been paid in December 2010 when her government had already resigned. It appeared that the money had in fact been misappropriated by Azarov's government under Yanukovych.[120]

The European Parliament expressed concern about "the growing

selective prosecution of political opposition leaders in Ukraine...
especially in the case of Tymoshenko" and stressed "the importance of
guaranteeing maximum transparency in investigations, prosecutions and
courts" and warned "against any use of criminal law as a tool to achieve
political goals". The crisis around the Kyoto Protocol led to a United
Nations investigation, which sent its experts to Ukraine.

On May 24, 2011, on the day of the international holiday of Slavonic
literature and culture, Tymoshenko was "invited" to the Attorney General's
office to be indicted and arrested. Having been informed of this,
Tymoshenko in turn "invited" the ambassadors of leading European states
and the United States, as well as the ambassador of the European Union,
who expressed their protest over Tymoshenko's illegal detention. Many
foreign diplomats demanded personal meetings with Pshonka and
President Yanukovych. A number of European and US statesmen also
personally called Yanukovych in connection with Tymoshenko's planned
arrest, voicing their concern. Yanukovych decided to back down and
instead of charging Tymoshenko, the criminal cases were closed.

However, it was just a short reprieve. New criminal cases against
Tymoshenko followed. First of all, they remembered the gas agreement
with Russia, signed by her government in 2009. Prompted by Yanukovych's
party, the Verkhovna Rada set up an *ad hoc* investigative commission to
investigate "indications of treason of Ukraine's economic". A month later,
on April 11, the commission published a report accusing Tymoshenko of
falsifying directives on gas agreements during negotiations with Russia,
accusing her of "betraying Ukraine's national interests," signing "onerous
for Ukraine agreements" and colluding in favor of Russia when signing gas
contracts.

On the same day, the Attorney General launched a criminal case against
Tymoshenko "for abuse of power and official authority when signing the
gas contracts". Tymoshenko was charged with inflicting $195 million in
damages as a result of the consequences for state-owned Naftogaz.
Tymoshenko's charges were supported by Firtash (as expected), the co-
owner of RUE, and former President Yushchenko (not expected at all), as
well as Arseniy Yatsenyuk, leader of the "Front for Change" party, who
stated that "Tymoshenko worked for Russia," "betrayed Ukraine a year

before Yanukovych," and "is pulling us into bondage to Moscow."[121]

The ad hoc parliamentary commission investigating Tymoshenko's government also brought up a 300 million debt of UESU owed to the Russian Defense Ministry which was never paid off. From this the commission concluded that Tymoshenko had spent this money on her Presidential campaign in exchange for the gas contracts she had signed. At the same time, Azarov's government stated that Ukraine would not pay off the UESU debt to Russia.[122]

Tymoshenko's trial over the "gas affair" began in the Kyiv Pechersky Court on June 24, 2011. The judge for the case was appointed personally by Yanukovych without senior judicial scrutiny. It was a grievous violation of Ukrainian due process, if not unambiguous evidence of collusion between the President and the court in charge of Tymoshenko's case. The day before, a crowd of thousands of the former Prime Minister's supporters, Rada deputies and representatives of international organizations gathered in front of the court building.[123]

On July 22, prosecutors read Tymoshenko's indictment, which was clearly prepared in a rush and contained numerous mistakes. Tymoshenko denied all accusations against her. The interrogation of witnesses, including ministers, officials, deputies and even ex-President Yushchenko, began. The judge also allowed two representatives of Tymoshenko's defense to speak. However, the witnesses for the prosecution testified in Tymoshenko's favor. Because of this, the live broadcast of the trial was stopped – parliamentary deputies who remained there filmed the proceedings on their cell phones.

Many of the witnesses invited by the prosecution testified that the gas agreements signed by Tymoshenko did not harm the state because the price was fair, taking into account the gas discount that the former Prime Minister had achieved and against the cost of buying gas from gas held in Ukraine's storage facilities.[124] Oleh Dubyna, the former head of Naftogaz, who also acted as a witness, pointed out that Russia deliberately raised the price of gas so that the problem of the "gas agreements" would turn from economic to political.

Because of her frequent arguments with the judge and Tymoshenko's remarks during witness statements, the judge repeatedly ordered

Tymoshenko out of the courtroom, and on August 5 she was arrested "for systemic violations" and for "obstructing the questioning of witnesses". It happened on the same day that Prime Minister Azarov appeared in court as a witness.

According to Tymoshenko, she was arrested because of her uncomfortable questions regarding Azarov's corrupt relations with RUE and his son's business that benefited from Ukraine's state budget. Tymoshenko's arrest could also be explained by the fact that during this period many "prosecution witnesses", in particular former Deputy Attorney General Tatyana Kornyakova and former Energy Minister Yuriy Prodan, began to give testimony that exonerated Tymoshenko, which clearly did not please the "show masters" of the hearings.

Tymoshenko's arrest caused a wave of indignation among the protesters, who were gathered outside the court building and tried to break into the building through the backdoor. However, riot police managed to take Tymoshenko to the Lukyanivska detention center in Kyiv.

What was going on? Tymoshenko believed that Yanukovych was planning to kill her. Therefore, after her arrest, she issued a statement to that effect: "I want to state that I have no inclination of committing suicide. They should not try to repeat what they did with Kirpa and Kravchenko. I will never end my life by suicide."

Another international scandal erupted. The European Union, the US and leaders of a number of countries expressed their concern about what had happened and demanded the immediate release of Tymoshenko. Even the Putin's Foreign Minister issued a statement that all the agreements between the two countries were concluded in accordance with national legislation in both countries, international law and the orders of the Presidents of Russia and Ukraine.

The public awaited Yushchenko's speech spellbound. His testimony evoked opposite reactions: "joyful" among supporters of the regime, and negative – among supporters of Tymoshenko. Yushchenko claimed that Tymoshenko had concealed from him the real gas price and that he did not summon Naftogaz CEO Dubyna to leave Moscow without signing the new gas contract. Meanwhile, numerous eyewitness accounts testified to the contrary. The Russians also confirmed that they understood the negotiations were terminated on Yushchenko's instruction. Yushchenko's testimony in court underlined the position defended by Firtash's RUE, although Yushchenko himself denied any involvement in this company in court.

When Tymoshenko's supporters were leaving the courtroom, they threw eggs at Yushchenko's car chanting "Shame on you!" The "Committee against Dictatorship", which consisted of eleven opposition parties, demanded that his party cancel Yushchenko's honorary chairmanship, while Tymoshenko, in a show of indignation, refused to question him, noting only that she did not agree with his testimony.

A short break was announced in the trial in September 2011 "to get acquainted with the materials of the case". Political analysts believed it was linked to the negotiations between Ukraine and the EU over the preparation of an association agreement between Ukraine and the European Union, which was taking place at the time. The European Commission had set as one of the conditions for such a signing "an end to the persecution of the opposition" and, in particular, of Tymoshenko. This point was one of the important requirements of the EU for the political leadership of Ukraine during the entire negotiation process of the country's associate membership.

It made no difference. On October 11, 2011, a court found Tymoshenko guilty under Part 3 Article 365 of the Criminal Code of Ukraine (abuse of power and corruption) and sentenced her to seven years in prison with a ban on holding public office for three years after serving her sentence. This would neutralize her politically for at least ten years and deny her any chance of running as his opponent in 2015.

The court also allowed the civil claim of Naftogaz, which personally claimed from Tymoshenko compensation for $189.5 million in losses incurred as a result of signing the agreements in January 2009. Tymoshenko commented that she was not being sued for signing the agreements, but for eliminating RUE from its profitable role as intermediary. Yanukovych responded by calling Tymoshenko's arrest an "unfortunate incident" that hindered Ukraine's European integration, and failed to mention that the sentence was read out by the judge he had appointed.

The Kharkiv Agreements of 2010

With Tymoshenko behind bars, Yanukovych turned his attention to foreign policy. On April 21, 2010, without any discussion with the Ukrainian parliament or the public, Yanukovych signed the so-called Kharkiv agreements with (nominal) Russian President Dmitry Medvedev, which established a radical change in the legal status of the Russian Black Sea Fleet in Crimea. Kharkiv was not chosen as the place for signing the agreements by accident. The people of Kharkiv refer to their city as the "capital of Ukrainian-Russian relations" because of the regular summits between both states held there. Located in Yanukovych's eastern power base, it was an important symbolic choice.

Negotiations covered a wide range of issues, but the main ones were gas deliveries to Ukraine and Russia's Black Sea Fleet. In fact, the price Yanukovych agreed was identical to the one that was agreed upon in 2009 by Tymoshenko.[125] But Tymoshenko had insisted on linking the gas price to the price of Russian gas transit through Ukraine – an increase in the price of gas led to an automatic increase in its transit price. This clause was absent from Yanukovych's Kharkiv Agreements. Ukraine's Treasury was worse off.[126] There were no major changes to the general agreement signed by Tymoshenko in 2009.[127] But in exchange for minor commercial concessions in the gas contract, Yanukovych bowed to important strategic concessions to the Black Sea Fleet, despite Article 17 of the Ukrainian Constitution, which states that "foreign military bases may not be stationed on Ukrainian territory". Putin's long-standing investment in Yanukovich was paying off.

All previous Presidents of Ukraine, with the belated exception of Yushchenko, had turned a blind eye to this clause in exchange for advantageous Ukrainian-Russian gas agreements. When Yushchenko said in his Presidential re-election program that on May 28, 2017, when the Russian Black Sea Fleet's lease expired, all of its deployment facilities (and there were over 4,600) were to be relocated to Russian territory, he brought up a costly point for Putin. This relocation would have cost the Russian Treasury about $10 billion. Ukraine received from Russia $100 million annually in rent for basing of the Russian Black Sea Fleet. It could have stayed in Crimea for another 100 years for $10 billion.

Yanukovych agreed that the lease of the Russian Black Sea Fleet base in

Sevastopol was to be extended for another 25 years, until 2042, and that Russia was to be allowed to modernize its fleet from Soviet times. Strategically the Russian Black Sea Fleet was severely limited in tonnage due to Turkey's restrictions on the passage of military vessels through the Dardanelles. Russia was unable to secure its strategic advantage in the Black Sea region as NATO naval bases were located in Romania, Bulgaria and Turkey while the US Sixth Fleet controlled the Mediterranean Sea. The planned purchase by Russia of two of the latest Mistral helicopter carriers from France did not significantly change the overall balance of power.

Within a week of extending the lease of the Black Sea Fleet, both parliaments ratified it. In Russia no one paid any attention, but in Kyiv drama unfolded. Opposition deputies blocked the rostrum, egged the Speaker and prevented a debate of the ratification. Some deputies started throwing smoke bombs, turning the parliament's session hall into what looked like battlefield. It made no difference. Yanukovych's party controlled the Rada and the Kharkiv agreements were ratified by a majority vote on April 27. The opposition covered their seats with the blue-and-yellow banner of Ukraine and left the session hall in protest.

The criminal prosecution of political opponents affected not only Yulia Tymoshenko and Interior Minister Yuriy Lutsenko, but also Economy Minister Bohdan Danylyshyn, Defense Minister Valeriy Ivashchenko, deputy Ihor Markov, former deputy head of Naftogaz Ihor Didenko, former Chairman of the Customs Service Anatoliy Makarenko and many others. Yanukovych even took a swing at former President Leonid Kuchma, who was accused of being involved in the murder of journalist Georgiy Gongadze, which allowed Yanukovych to strike fear of reprisals in Kuchma and the entire entourage of the former President.

Yanukovych's duplication of Putin's "vertical of power"

Like many of his predecessors, Yanukovych began by reducing the civil service. He even intended to reduce his own Secretariat by 20 percent. Restyling it as the "Presidential Office", he appointed as his Chief of Staff the oligarch Serhiy Lyovochkin, who owned a portfolio of foreign companies and a number of valuable minority stakes in Ukrainian enterprises.[128] Lyovochkin had "supported" Yanukovych when he was governor of the Donetsk Region, assistant to President Kuchma, and Prime Minister under Yushchenko. Now he was Ukraine's second most powerful man.[129]

Interestingly, Yanukovych made it clear that Ukrainian would remain the only state language in contradiction to his pre-election promise to make Russian the second state language. But he underlined that that Ukraine would adhere strictly to the European Charter for Regional Languages and in 2012, the Verkhovna Rada passed a law on regional languages, which was essentially a cover for legalizing Russian as a local official language in Crimea and the south-east. An attempt by settled minorities (Romanians, Poles, Bulgarians, and others) to use this law to give their languages also the status of regional languages failed.

By the end of his first year, Yanukovych reduced the number of business areas subject to regulation, from 66 to 43. The procedure for obtaining permits was simplified for investment activity, although this did not lead to an "rush" of foreign investors into Ukraine. Yanukovych cancelled compulsory military service, inserting a professional army in its place, without setting it up, however, as combat ready reducing Ukraine's defensive power.

On the eve of the New Year 2011, despite vociferous protests of small and medium entrepreneurs, a new tax code was adopted. While on the face of it providing for a threefold reduction of local taxes, it did not change the tax burden for domestic producers. On the contrary, small and medium-size businesses became even more indebted to authorities, with whom they had to share their revenues. But Ukraine became a paradise for its billionaires connected with power. All the major companies with close ties to the President and his entourage flourished. After Yanukovych's first year in power, the number of Ukrainian oligarchs mushroomed from 8 to 21. Together they were worth $58 billion, or roughly $20 billion more than the entire Ukrainian national budget.

Determined to avoid Yushchenko's mistakes, Yanukovych began creating his own "vertical" power base cutting through Ukraine's state hierarchies, closely mirroring Vladimir Putin's path to absolute power after his election in 2000.[130] He replaced the country's regional governors and administrators.

All the government enforcement ministers and judges of the Constitutional Court, who were appointed under Presidential prerogative, were replaced. Having stealthily annulled Yushchenko's 2004 changes to the Constitution,[131] Yanukovych introduced censorship of the mass media, and oligarchs from his closest circle became the owners of the largest media outlets. The opposition could only chronicle the establishment of the President's autocratic system and helplessly protest against his usurpation of state power.

Under the guise of a crusade against corruption, Yanukovych and his entourage adopted a system of raiding businesses from both their political rivals and their own allies. European OSCE experts documented over 50 cases of business deals by Yanukovych's circle using corrupt law enforcement agencies, courts, prosecutors, tax inspectors, and ministers. Owners were forced to hand over half of their shares, or even saw their entire business taken away through the courts. According to the Anti-Raiders Union of Entrepreneurs of Ukraine, at least 7000 Ukrainian companies were targeted by Yanukovych's "family" across the whole of Ukraine.

One reason for these raids was to raise $1.5 billion for Yanukovych's 2015 re-election campaign and bribing 15 million voters at a rate of $100 per vote. Here's how Andrey Semididko, chairman of the Anti-Raiders Union, described the system, "The raiders operated with simple methods. First, find a profitable company. Then initiate an inspection by the tax [authorities] and, based on its results, start a criminal case. On the basis of the case file, they would make an assessment and the raiders would approach the owners of the company with an offer. Usually there were only a few choices: they could pay a "tribute" of 30-50 percent of the company's profit or give up ownership rights. In this case either part of the company was taken offshore, or the changes in the owners were simply not registered – that is, in law the owners remained the same, but de facto there was a secret ownership change".[132] In fact, the local officials involved would frequently increase "the tribute" in their favor.[133] Over three years, for example, more than $50 million was taken under a tax case from vodka company Nemiroff by shell companies close to the President.

The Presidential term of "proffesor" Yanukovych will be remembered not only for his lack of economic reforms and water-treading between the

European Union or a Customs Union with Russia, but also for his slow speech and numerous stylistic gaffes. He referred to the famous Russian poetess Anna Akhmatova as Anna Akhmetova (Rinat Akhmetov is his godfather), and the famous Russian writer Anton Chekhov as a Ukrainian poet. He believed that the famous Slavic scholar Gulak-Artemovsky was from the Donbas city of Artemovsk. He divided Eurasia into Asia and Eurasia, and speaking to the inhabitants of Kropyvnytskyi he called them residents of Chernihiv. He called Slovakia "Slovenia" and confused Iran with uranium. When negotiating with the President of Turkmenistan he stated that Ukraine had always been on friendly terms with Kazakhstan.

Yanukovych's power "vertical" copied from Putin's Russia seemed to guarantee law and order in the country, and Yanukovych's repeated verbal escapades amused those with enough sense of humor to laugh at the newly minted dictator.

Was Yanukovych meanwhile handing over to his sponsor in the Kremlin? Known for his pro-Russian stance, Yanukovych, the newly minted billionaire businessman and President, suddenly abandoned the idea of a union between Russia, Belarus and Ukraine, and on April 1, 2010, he announced that "the strategic direction of Ukrainian foreign policy is integration with the European Union". It was counter-balanced by the abolishment of the interdepartmental commission on preparation of Ukraine for joining NATO and Ukraine's National Center on Euro-Atlantic Integration, established in 2006 by Yushchenko. In July 2010 he signed into law the abandonment of seeking membership of NATO, and announced Ukraine's non-aligned status.

8

The Turning Point, Minsk 2013

2013 was a relatively calm year in Ukrainian politics. Yanukovych traveled around Europe convincing naïve Europeans that he wanted to join the EU. In post-Soviet Ukraine, this desire was nothing new. All of Yanukovych's predecessors – Leonid Kravchuk, Leonid Kuchma, and Viktor Yushchenko – also planned to get Ukraine into the European Union. At least in theory. There was a practical aspect to consider. Not only Yanukovych, but the President's entire family, the entire government, and the entire Ukrainian elite of oligarchs and hangers-on really did want to be part of Europe, but really only for holidays and in order to check their foreign bank accounts.

Accession to the EU required as a first step the signing of the EU–Ukraine Association Agreement (EU-UAA). Negotiations between Ukraine and the EU on this agreement were launched back in 2007 under Yushchenko. The new agreement was supposed to replace an existing agreement on partnership and cooperation between the European Union and Ukraine and to introduce systemic social and economic reforms in Ukraine and a large-scale adaptation of Ukrainian legislation to EU norms and rules. The text of the agreement did not mention Ukraine's joining the EU as a full member, but it did not deny it the possibility of joining either. The signing of this agreement took Ukraine's relations with the EU to a new level, from partnership and cooperation to political association and economic integration. Many Ukrainians believed, also naïvely, that this meant integration with Europe.

An important element of the agreement was the establishment of a comprehensive free trade zone. This prospect made industrialists closely connected to Russian business very nervous. Russia saw the prospect as a potential threat, because joining the EU was incompatible with joining its own CIS Customs Union, which was dominated by Russia. Accession to the Customs Union meant Ukraine's economic orientation to Russia and subordination of the Ukrainian economy to the Russian economy. Joining the EU meant the orientation towards Europe and subordination of the Ukrainian economy to the European Union.

Russia and pro-Russian "business circles" in Ukraine, such as "Ukrainian Choice" headed by Kuchma's former Chief of Staff Viktor Medvedchuk, the long-time Vladimir Putin's associate and KGB-FSB operative like General Marchuk, were particularly active in this respect. They launched a PR propaganda campaign claiming that the signing of the Association Agreement with the EU would ruin Ukraine's economy because it would lead to a sharp reduction of trade and economic relations with Russia. At the same time, in Russia it was said that the creation of a free trade zone in Ukraine would lead to cheap western goods being smuggled into Russia and hit Russian producers.

Nevertheless, in Ukraine a majority of the population believed in the authorities' intention to follow the path of European integration and supported this idea. Numerous European summits and meetings, consultations, and preparation of the Association Agreement itself seemed to be leading to the inevitable – the prospect of "associated membership".[134] Yanukovych was supposed to sign a Stabilization and Association Agreement (similar to the EU agreements with Albania, Serbia, Montenegro, and Bosnia and Herzegovina), or an Association Agreement between Ukraine and the EU of the type signed by Macedonia in 2001. The only difference being that Kyiv would sign it in two stages: first the political part and then the economic part.

The point of signing this agreement was that Ukraine would undertake political reforms aimed at bringing the country up to European standards. In particular, it was necessary to reform Ukraine's judicial system, including the office of the Attorney General. Ukrainian politicians were especially tempted by the prospect of signing the treaty on the free trade zone and visa-free travel. It was this simplified idea that prevailed. Ukraine would sell its products in Europe duty-free, attracting European industry to Ukraine, while visa-free travel regime would allow ordinary Ukrainians to travel freely in Europe and work there. Joining the European Union seemed like a free ticket to a civilized, well-fed and quiet European life.

The reality was much more complicated. Yes, it would be possible to travel around Europe without visas. But the right to work was still a distant prospect. The European labor market planned to protect itself from Ukrainian guest workers who, according to many, already flooded Europe, especially Italy and Spain, even without Ukraine's accession to the EU. Goods produced in Ukraine had to obtain European "quality certificates" in advance, which cost money. These certificates did not in itself guarantee that Ukrainian goods would be delivered to Europe and freely sold there. For this to happen, the largest Ukrainian producers (there is nothing to say about small ones) had to integrate into European trading networks and obtain the right to sell their goods there. After that, Ukrainian goods, that were up to European standards, would compete with European in a purely commercial sense of the word.

At this point, it might transpire that not all Ukrainian goods were competitive, since many European firms received subsidies from their governments and supplied goods to the market at prices lower than those in Ukraine. Europe was most likely interested mainly in "primary processed" products – metals, grain, fertilizer, and software. Here Ukraine was really competitive.

But even the leading enterprises in Ukraine were struggling to survive, lacking modern marketing and sales markets.[135] Since 1991, while funds were being siphoned off to line pockets of this oligarch or the other, there had been little capital investment in production and equipment was obsolete. The famous Zaporozhye Automobile Plant (ZAZ), producing bottom-range automobiles, could only compete with Mercedes in its home market in Ukraine due to the very low price of its cars. The famous mines in Donbas, where miners died year after because of antedeluvian labor and safety conditions, were untouched by modernization with very few exceptions. By European standards, they probably should have been shut down because of longstanding safety and environment violations. This list of zombie or half-bankrupt enterprises could be extended *ad infinitum*. Over the previous two decades had fallen massively behind in Europe.

In the economic sphere, one of the main conditions for Ukraine's rapprochement with Europe's economy, was the imposition of the rule of law on opaque business practices. But shady business was the feeding ground of Ukraine's clan-oligarchic system of power. The whole state machine, from top to bottom, was built and kept on the kickbacks and bribes. Neither the officials who took bribes, nor the business leaders running Ukraine's multitude of state-related companies who did not pay taxes, were genuinely interested in proper legal and fiscal controls over their shady operations. Only those who were involved in businesses that operated transparently and honestly, and paid taxes to the state on a regular basis, were keen. There were few who belonged to the latter category in Ukraine.

Were the political authorities in Ukraine ready for such a radical step: to destroy the system of bribery and kickbacks for the entire state bureaucracy in exchange for the prospect of membership in the European Union? At the end of 2013 it seemed if not a probability at least a possibility. But the necessary political and economic reforms could take many years, and the time lag of this path depended among other things on the willingness (or unwillingness) of the government and society to move decisively in this direction.

The Commission of the European Union also had its own list of accession requirements: political stability in the country; political consensus of all political parties represented in the Verkhovna Rada; a popular vote through a referendum to join the EU and pursue European integration; real, and not just paper protection of civil rights and freedoms by the Ukrainian legislation adapted to all-European standards; independence of courts, subject to the rulings of the European Court of Human Rights.[136]

As for the economic criteria formulated in the Maastricht Treaty of 1992, the situation was even more complicated and detailed. Ukraine was supposed to become a country with a market economy.[137] In addition, the budget deficit was to be less than 3 percent of GDP, and the government debt was to be less than 60 percent of GDP. Stability of the exchange rate was required.[138] Price stability was defined by yearly inflation, which should not be more than 1.5 percent higher than the average inflation rate of the three EU countries that topped price stability.

Despite these roadblocks, at a conference of the CIS in Minsk, Belarus, in October 2013, Yanukovych still repeated unambiguously that "Kyiv's main priority is to sign the Association Agreement between Ukraine and the EU.

This issue is not up for discussion".

Nevertheless, Yanukovych returned from Minsk a changed man. During a confidential meeting at the conference, Putin – who had assumed the Russian Presidency again – made Yanukovych an offer that he could not (or did not want to) refuse. At any rate, the meeting brought Yanukovych to heel.

Back in Kyiv, Yanukovych suddenly recalled the unbreakable fraternity between the Russian and Ukrainian people and declared extra time was needed to sign the Association Agreement with the European Union. At the same time, Yanukovych and the Ukrainian government began discussing with the European Union the economic package Ukraine would need if it were to join the EU. The figures were astronomical, if not completely unrealistic. Ukraine projected it would lose between $150 to $500 billion in trade with Russia, as Putin would at the very least economically boycott Ukraine (a mild-mannered response) if not impose draconian sanctions (the worst-case response).

Europe could not give Ukraine such an astronomical financial package. Russia stepped into the breach as "saviour" and offered Ukraine $15 billion in loans as well as a significant reduction of gas prices in case of Ukraine's rejection of European integration.

After the Minsk meeting, Prime Minister Azarov began shaping public opinion using a different tune, explaining how bad life would be without Russia and how unclear Ukraine's future in the European Union would be. Much of what Azarov said was true. The Association Agreement did not automatically guarantee accession to the EU. In particular, the EU program "Eastern Partnership" adopted on the initiative of Poland and Sweden was aimed at cooperation with such post-Soviet countries as Armenia, Azerbaijan, Belarus, Georgia, Moldova and Ukraine. The Association Agreement did not imply agreement on EU membership, it was merely the case that a country that did not already have one in place could not hope to be considered for membership of the EU.

Negotiations with European partners to provide Ukraine with such a grandiose financial package went nowhere. Russia's promise of a $15 billion loan led to the first payment of $3 billion. And then the EuroMaidan began.

The word "Maidan", associated with Kyiv's Independence Square, had become a national symbol of freedom and hope. It gave the word a specific though intangible moral and ethical meaning that came to embody the spirit of

Ukraine's peaceful twenty-first century revolutions. These included the "Ukraine without Kuchma" movement of 2000, the "Arise Ukraine" movement of 2002, the "Orange Revolution" of 2004. Perhaps nowhere else in Europe over the past decade have there been as many gentle revolutions as Ukraine.

These Maidans took place not only in the same location, but also according to the same script. 100-200 meters away from Maidan, the people of Kyiv went on with their ordinary lives – grandmothers walked with their grandchildren, mothers and fathers went to work, children went to schools and institutes. Everyone watched the Maidan on television, both in and outside Ukraine. They had different catalysts and different consequences. But they all had one thing in common. They were all driven by the struggle against autocracy, the usurpation of power by certain clans, the disenfranchisement of the people, the all-powerful oligarchy, and most of all rampant corruption.

Nevertheless, until 2014, the Maidan revolutions in Kyiv did not lead to changes in the political system, the mechanisms that shifted oligarchic power around, or the root causes of corruption and bureaucracy. In this sense, these early Maidan were unlike major revolutions of the early twentieth century. Some political parties and oligarchic clans were replaced by others, power was seized by a new group of people pursuing their own economic interests, and the revolutions faded without leading to serious consequences or changes in the lives of the citizens of the country or even the capitol.

The main conclusion that Maidan spectators had gradually come to was that the Maidan was nothing but a symbol, that a Maidan uprising would not accomplish the revolution. It was ultimately a harmless crowd of people in a square, even if that square was in Kyiv and was called Independence Square. But the important thing was still that the political consciousness of Ukrainians was nurtured by these half-hearted, incomplete events.

9

EuroMaidan

For the Ukrainian population at large, Maidan had also become a national hymn, a paradigm – a shared point of view. At the end of 2013, due to Ukraine's failure in signing the Association Agreement with the EU in Vilnius, it re-emerged in a new phrase: "EuroMaidan". The word "Euro" was hugely popular by now, and not only because it represented a stable currency. It was becoming a prefix for many brands, goods and events. EUFA's European Football Championship was called "Euro 2012," so was the name of the European basketball championship "Eurobasket 2014". Even "Euro-fences" were sold (otherwise the same as ordinary Ukrainian or American ones). Mockingly, bad repairs were wryly referred to as "EUrepairs", as house owners were willing to pay more for something mediocre if it involved word "Euro".

In politics, it was from November 2013 to February 2014 that "EuroMaidan" and "AutoMaidan" electrified popular politics, too. How did this come about?

Sensing a change in government direction after the Putin-Yanukovych meeting in Minsk, Yuriy Lutsenko, a former Interior Minister in several governments and one of the organizers of the "Ukraine without Kuchma" and the "Orange Revolution", called on November 13, 2013, on opposition parties to hold mass rallies in support of the signing of the Association Agreement and, in particular, for a rally on 24 November in support of

European integration in Kyiv. New media were used to alert Ukrainians, and an SMS was sent to cell phone users saying: "When you receive an SMS, vote for the EU!"

Lutsenko was ahead of the government by a week. On November 21, 2013, a few days before the EU's "Eastern Partnership" summit in Vilnius of November 28-29, where Ukraine was supposed to sign the agreement, the Ukrainian government dramatically announced that it was suspending the process in a statement by Prime Minister Azarov.

Appeals to gather on Kyiv's Independence Square to protest began circulating on social media. By 10 p.m., more than a thousand people had gathered, demanding that the agreement be signed. Opposition leaders spoke at the rally, accusing the Ukrainian government of derailing its European integration policies.[139] The next day, despite a ban by city officials, protesters began to set up their Maidan tent city (soon some 15 tents and 20 booths were up) like they had for Ukraine without Kuchma and the Orange Revolution protests. Andriy Parubiy, a member of Tymoshenko's party, became its mayor.

On November 22, rallies followed in many other cities in support of the signing of the association agreement with the EU: 2-3 thousand people protested in the western Ukrainian cities of Lviv, Ivano-Frankivsk, Chernivtsi, Rivne, Ternopil and Vinnitsa. Much smaller protests from 50-500 people were held in the eastern Ukrainian cities of Donetsk, Krivoy Rog, Sumy and Kharkiv.

On November 24, Lutsenko's peaceful mass rally took place. According to officials, up to 50 thousand people participated, but according to unofficial data, there were more than 100 thousand protesters, 20 thousand policemen and 40 independent observers and journalists. The protesters spoke in support of European integration under the slogan "For European Ukraine" and announced the beginning of a permanent protest. Speakers included Tymoshenko's daughter Yevhenia who read out an appeal from her mother from Kharkiv prison.[140]

The protesters, who called themselves the "People's Assembly", adopted a resolution demanding the resignation of the government "for betraying national interests", calling for an immediate session of the Verkhovna Rada on November 27 to debate and adopt the laws necessary for Ukraine's EU integration. In addition, the protesters demanded the dissolution of parliament and snap elections, an end to political repression and the release of Tymoshenko, the resumption European integration and the signing of the Association Agreement in Vilnius in two days time. "In case the President refuses to fulfill his constitutional duties and does not sign the agreement," the protesters planned to "seek the impeachment of President Yanukovych for high treason and call on all democratic countries of the world to immediately apply personal sanctions against Yanukovych and representatives of his corrupt regime"; to mobilize all parties, public organizations and citizens who support the European integration of Ukraine to hold protests "until complete victory".[141]

Some demonstrators tried to break through to the central hall of the building where the national government was based and others blocked the passage of government vehicles. In response, several hundred members of Berkut positioned themselves at the entrance, clashing with a small group of demonstrators. They used batons and tear gas, while protesters sprayed gas as well and threw several home-made explosives.

The events of November 24 resonated throughout Ukraine. EuroMaidans were held in all major cities. In Lviv, a rally in support of European integration now drew about 10,000 participants, most of them students from Lviv universities. A much smaller number of participants (from 300 to 500 people) gathered at monuments in honor of Ukrainian national poet Taras Shevchenko in eastern Ukraine – in Kherson, Donetsk, Luhansk, Mykolaiv and Odessa. More than two thousand supporters of European integration also gathered in Kharkiv. Many rallies were held under the slogan: "Yanukovych resign!" In border town Luhansk, the first clashes took place. Many EuroMaidan participants from other Ukrainian cities went to Kyiv to support the EuroMaidan.

In parallel with pro-European integration rallies, in many cities in southeastern Ukraine there were anti-Maidan demonstrations, often organized by local authorities that sided with Yanukovych and opposed the country's European direction. Thus, anti-rallies were held in Donetsk, Sevastopol, Odessa, and Kherson, where participants demanded that Ukraine join the Russian Customs Union. Many demonstrators, in particular miners in Donetsk, were forced to go to the city's central square after their night shift.

A similar "anti-Maidan" demonstration was organized by the authorities in Kyiv.

On the eve of the Vilnius summit, there was relative calm on Kyiv's central square. Everyone expected that the government would listen to "the opinion of the people" and sign the Vilnius agreement. The same opinion was held by the majority of international observers. One or two thousand protesters still gathered in Kyiv itself. But in other cities in the country, the protests all but disappeared.[142] Foreign politicians and OSCE observers visited the Kyiv Maidan. This irritated not only the Ukrainian government but also Moscow, which began accusing the West of "interference in Ukraine's internal affairs".

On November 26, students at a number of universities went on strike. The administrations of the universities of Kyiv and Kyiv-Mohyla Academy released students from their lectures so they could demonstrate. Students from the western regions of Ukraine, particularly from Lviv, Ternopil, and Ivano-Frankivsk, came to support their Kyiv peers. The fact that students began to play an active role meant a broadening of the protestors' social base and indicated that the young and educated part of society wished to see its country integrated into Europe, rather than turning back to the feudal relations of the Russian Customs Union. Pollsters estimated that over 70 percent of Ukraine's youth supported European integration and opposed orientation toward Russia.

On November 28-29, in the capital of Lithuania, in the Palace of the Grand Dukes a two-day summit of the European Union "Eastern Partnership" was held with Azerbaijan, Armenia, Moldova, Ukraine and Belarus in attendance.[143]

Despite Azarov's announcement of November 21 that Ukraine would not sign, Yanukovych went to Lithuania in the hope of convincing his European partners of the need to find a joint solution to the "Ukrainian issue". Yanukovych still said that Ukraine's European course remained unchanged. But in Vilnius few believed this now.

The lengths to which Yanukovych had yielded to Putin became clear that day. He wanted Russia to join the Ukraine-EU negotiations. But European Commission President Jose Manuel Barroso made it crystal clear that there would be no trilateral talks including Russia: "We have already agreed an

Association Agreement with a sovereign country. When we reach a bilateral agreement, we do not allow a third country to interfere in these negotiations. There can be no trilateral format for a bilateral agreement on trade." Barroso was supported by the hostess of the summit, Lithuanian President Dalia Grybauskaite: "The European Union will definitely not do secret deals with the Ukrainian leadership". No one wanted to take an official meeting with Yanukovych on Russian involvement in his country's agreement.

All EU leaders made it clear that they considered Yanukovych's proposal to give Putin negotiation power over Ukraine's population a non-starter. They, however, did give Yanukovych the opportunity to sign on the second day of the summit. He had one more day to make his fateful decision. The heads of EU states and governments, knowing that Yanukovych's officials were still hoping to hear from Yanukovych himself, wanted to hear what the Ukrainian President actually planned to do: if and when Ukraine would sign the agreement; if it would take time out, for how long; if it would haggle for new terms of the agreement, then what they would be. But Yanukovych said little.

On the second day of the summit, the world press was riveted by what was happening in Vilnius. The leaders of the EU, Georgia and Moldova initialed their Association Agreements. But would Ukraine sign it? In Ukraine people were on tenterhooks in anticipation, but no miracle happened. Viktor Yanukovych did not join the other participants and did not sign the agreement.[144]

As soon as it became known in the evening of November 29 in Kyiv that President Yanukovych had not signed, masses of people began to flock to the center of the capital. In return, the government organized its own rally in support of the President's actions, but a much larger number of protesters now gathered on Kyiv's Maidan. Opposition leaders who spoke at the rally called again for Yanukovych's resignation, accusing him of treason, and the protesters passed a resolution to this effect. The government began amassing personnel, including riot squads and other Interior Ministry units, in the center of the capital.

By 4 am on November 30, a large police forces and about 300 riot police were directed into the square. Under the pretext of "preparation for the New Year," the "cleansing" of the Maidan city began. The protesters refused to disperse and resisted the police. When batons and tear gas were used, protesters were forced from the Maidan into the streets adjacent to the square. The Berkut used batons to beat the protesters who straggled and did not spare girls and women. This galvanized the protesters. They started to use bottles, stones, iron bars, and sticks to fight back. Hospitalized protesters were often taken directly from A&E rooms to the police for interrogation. More than 30 people were arrested, but after being given citations for minor offenses, most of them were released.

After the dispersal of demonstrators in Kyiv on the night of November 30, a mass rally began again on Mykhailivska Square, not far from Khreshchatyk Avenue, Kyiv's main street, and EuroMaidan, with over 15 thousand participants. Demonstrators settled in to fight to the bitter end. On the night of December 1, paramilitary street fighters of the "Right Sector", whose leaders had long stayed hidden on the sidelines, joined the protesters. In particular, Right Sector participated in clashes with internal troops and the Berkut units of the Interior Ministry guarding Kyiv's government district, in the seizure of several government buildings, and during the storming of the Presidential Palace on Bankova Street. At the same time, "Maidan Self-Defense" units headed by Maidan mayor Andriy Parubiy were formed. Later it would become clear that the first of three groups of Russian secret-service groups landed in Kyiv in December.

The Right Sector was an alliance uniting activists from a number of Ukrainian nationalist and soccer organizations. The Right Sector carried out its own propaganda, fundraising and recruitment. Along with the "Maidan Self-Defense", they formed the backbone of the EuroMaidan and served as both external and internal security. However, some opposition leaders accused Right Sector of provoking the police and Berkut to act violently against protesters and against random bystanders – who were frequently struck by batons of the police and special forces. In the clashes, both protesters and police officers were injured.

Initially, Right Sector did not lay down demands of its own. Their political independence manifested itself somewhat later, when its leader claimed to be the third party in the negotiations between the authorities and the opposition. The core demands of the Right Sector were on the face of it not very different from the other protesters: immediate resignation of

President Yanukovych, dissolution of the Verkhovna Rada, punishment of heads of security agencies and perpetrators of "criminal orders" that resulted in the murder of about a hundred Ukrainian citizens. The leader of the Right Sector was Dmitry Yarosh, head of the nationalist group "Stepan Bandera's Trident". According to him, the Maidan was a prompt to start a "national revolution," which was to culminate in "the complete removal of the regime of internal occupation and the creation of a Ukrainian national state with a system of all-encompassing national democracy."[145]

On December 1, the government's show of force provoked protesters to seize administrative buildings, in particular Kyiv City Hall, and gave the opposition an excuse to form its National Resistance Headquarters at the House of Trade Unions.[146] The Right Sector made its headquarters at the Dnipro Hotel, which was also in the epicenter of the unrest. Self-defense units began to be formed as people signed up to join them. Opposition leaders called for the formation of regional labor committees to hold a national protest strike, and former boxer and opposition leader Vitali Klitschko called on the people of Lviv to take part in the "For a European Ukraine" march. In response, more than 10,000 people came to Kyiv from Lviv.

Demonstrators began to converge in Kyiv on the central EuroMaidan where a People's Assembly was to be held. A large flag of Ukraine was carried in front of the rally, and more than 100 thousand people gathered on Independence Square.[147] European diplomats, Vice President of the European Parliament Jacek Protasiewicz, former President of the European Parliament Jerzy Buzek, former head of the Polish government, leader of Poland's ruling Law and Justice party, Jarosław Kaczyński, also took part in the demonstration.

During the rally and opposition speeches near the Presidential Palace, there were new clashes between the demonstrators and the police and Berkut guarding it. A tractor was used against the police, which tried to ram the line of Berkut officers. Some of the demonstrators used Molotov cocktails, stones, and metal chains. Two opposition Rada deputies, future President Petro Poroshenko and Oleksandra Kuzhel, arrived at the scene and urged the protesters not to give in to provocations by government-paid "titushkas" (mercenaries).[148] Klitschko tried to calm people down, talking about an attempted provocation by the authorities to break up People's Assembly, and urged demonstrators to return to the square: "I call on everyone to stay on Maidan today… we are doing everything to protect you… we must mobilize everyone in the country and not lose the initiative." He said that "everyone who will stay tonight and tomorrow can get warmed up, get a hot meal and spend the night at the House of Trade Unions."

On the same evening, demonstrators tried to tear down the Lenin monument, but Berkut prevented it. Another opposition leader called for the blockade of government buildings and the central part of the city.[149] More than 165 people, including 50 law enforcers, were injured as a result of the clashes that began. Over 100 people were hospitalized with head injuries and chemical burns to the eyes from the use of tear gas. Mass rallies in support of the Kyiv Maidan began across the country, demanding the resignation of the President and the government, especially Interior Minister Major-General Zakharchenko and Attorney General Pshonka.

"Heating centers" for Maidan participants were set up everywhere, as it was ten degrees below zero. On December 2, protesters seized the October Palace cultural center so that Maidan participants had a place to sleep, get warm and have hot food. On the Maidan, they set up additional hot food and heating stations and medical tents to provide first aid to the injured. People did not go home. On the same day, AutoMaidan, a column of some 300 cars flying Ukrainian flags, tried to break through to President Yanukovych's opulent country residence Mezhyhirya that he rented for $40 a month. They were stopped by the police and Berkut. Then the protesters blocked Kyiv's Mykhailo Hrushevsky Street and the entrance to government buildings so that the civil servants could not get to work. Fixed barricades began to be erected around Independence Maidan and on Mykhailo Hrushevsky Street, both for defense purposes and to immobilize Kyiv's national-government quarter.

Virtually the entire center of Kyiv was now blocked by protesters. Many ordinary residents of Kyiv came to offer help to the mainly young student protesters, providing food, clothing, and medicine where necessary. The government began mobilizing more personnel and additional police and Berkut from other regions to protect government buildings in the capital. Yanukovych and Azarov demanded that the opposition remove their barricade of state institutions in order not to interfere with the work of the government, but these demands were ignored by the protesters, who in turn demanded their resignation.

On December 3, the opposition submitted a draft vote in the Rada of no confidence in the government. But it was not adopted, and the barricade around the Presidential Palace was sealed off on all sides. These events could not but affect the political elite. Well-known politicians announced their withdrawal from Yanukovych's party.[150] Chief of Staff Serhiy Lyovochkin resigned. Significantly, the media, especially television, covered the events on Maidan without cuts or censorship. People all over Ukraine and beyond saw exactly what was happening in Kyiv, the level of mass disorder, and the government's brutality in dispersing demonstrators. A group of enterprising journalists created Public Television which covered the events on Maidan around the clock.

Yanukovych hastily distanced himself from the violent dispersal, saying that he was "deeply indignant" at the actions of the law enforcement agencies. At the same time, he called on the demonstrators to stop protesting: "I reaffirm – we are united in choosing our common European future. Yesterday we completed the Vilnius summit, which showed that we and our European colleagues have a common understanding of the problems that exist and a common desire to work to overcome them", pretending that he was once again ready to consider the question of Ukraine's accession to the EU. But it was too late: he was neither believed nor paid attention to. The revolution in Kyiv had begun. It was impossible to stop it now.

The brutal dispersal of the Maidan participants was viewed differently by official authorities in different regions of the country. The regional councils of the Zakarpattia, Ivano-Frankivsk, Ternopil, and Lviv regions largely condemned the actions of the authorities and revoked the authority of the regional governments; Yanukovych's factions in western Ukraine announced their separation from the national party. The eastern regions, however, supported measures "to bring order to the country." They underlined the right of people to freedom of self-expression, but called on the opposition to refrain from rash actions that could lead to a civil war in Ukraine.

Somewhat different was the reaction of officials in Crimea. Its leadership supported the Yanukovych's policy to suspend European integration, speaking out against "the actions of destructive opposition political forces," calling on the Azarov government in Kyiv to "restore order" and, if necessary, "declare a state of emergency." Its State Council called for "all efforts to preserve Crimea as a territory of stability and interethnic harmony and to strengthen friendly relations with Russia."

Some Ukrainian diplomats, including Ukraine's representative to the UN Yuriy Sergeyev – as well as representatives of the Ukrainian diaspora in many European countries, US, and Canada – also condemned the actions of the authorities. Hoping to appease the opposition and save the situation, Yanukovych accepted the resignations of the Kyiv Interior Ministry chief Valery Kornyak, as well as the Interior Minister himself, Major-General Zakharchenko. The latter was forced to apologize to the public for the abuse of power by the police and Berkut.

However, Yanukovych's power was slipping. Throughout December, rallies in support of the Kyiv protesters continued uninterrupted across the country. The OSCE commission which met in Kyiv at that time brought along deputies from the EU's European People's Party to the Maidan, who spoke in support of the opposition. Catherine Ashton, First Vice-President of the European Commission, and Victoria Nuland, US Assistant Secretary of State, met with President Yanukovych and conveyed to him the European and US views on the need to resolve all issues in a peaceful manner. Victoria Nuland appeared on the Kyiv Maidan the next day and handed out bread and cookies to the protesters, which looked very comical, since the protesters had plenty. US politicians could not understand that it was not food that the protesters needed, but real US support in the fight against the hated party-oligarchic regime.

As Nuland was feeding the "needy", Azarov's government agreed to negotiate with the opposition on condition that they lift the barricade of the government's offices. But the opposition held firm and insisted on his resignation and release of protesters arrested by the police.[151] During the same period, a group of activists led by a deputy from the nationalist Freedom (Svoboda) party demolished a monument to Lenin in Kyiv's Bessarabskaia Square erected there in 1946. This served as a kind of signal to the removal of monuments to the leader associated with the Soviet regime and Russia in many cities of Ukraine. The campaign of demolition of Lenin monuments was popularly called "Leninfall", but in some places, for example in border town Kharkiv, city authorities did not allow the demolition of his statutes (later the governor of the Kharkiv region, though, would have the monument dismantled).

On the evening of December 7, Yanukovych caved in and held the first round of talks with opposition leaders, who demanded early Presidential Elections in addition to their previous demands. A compromise was not reached, but a dialogue had started. On December 19, the Verkhovna Rada ordered the release the protesters who had been arrested in a resolution. On December 22, another People's Assembly was held on Kyiv's Maidan, which decided to create the "Maidan People's Front", whose leadership included the leaders of the revolution and well-known political figures, artists, and Maidan activists. Well-known Russian opposition activists Ilya Yashin and Konstantin Borovoy were also present at the Assembly.

Yanukovych had executed Putin's Minsk script in Vilnius. How would the Russian President respond to being cheated of having a Ukrainian President he controlled?

10

The Mysterious Return of the "Banderites"

The term "Banderites" originally referred to the ideology of the Organization of Ukrainian Nationalists (OUN), headed by Stepan Bandera.[152] His supporters were called "Banderites" and fought for Ukraine's independence against several foes. In the 1930s, its Ukrainian Insurgent Army (UIA) fought against monopolization of western Ukraine's economy by Poland, then against the Soviet occupation of Ukraine (1939-1941), and then against the German occupation during World War II. Given that theirs was a struggle against an overlord, the term came to refer to Ukrainian underground nationalism. Ukrainian nationalists used this word with a plus sign, while the opponents of a Ukrainian identity used it with a minus sign.

During the lifespan of the USSR, "Banderite" became the accusation that was attached to anyone who showed even the slightest Ukrainian feelings, regardless of their attitude toward Bandera himself. The last armed resistance to Soviet rule recorded by Soviet law enforcement agencies was on April 14, 1960. The group of three was led by someone called Maria Palchak. Two of the insurgents shot themselves while being arrested. She was convicted, served many years in Soviet camps, was released, and returned to Ukraine.

After Ukraine gained its independence, the heroization of Bandera was given a new lease of life. Many streets in cities in western Ukraine were named after him and Bandera monuments were erected. In 1995, the Lviv regional council made a decision on recognizing Bandera's soldiers as an army and its veterans as fighters for freedom of Ukraine. Numerous political parties of supporters of Bandera's ideology and views also appeared. The most popular was the "Ukrainian People's Rukh (Movement)". But after generations of stigma "Banderites" continued to split public opinion. Some saw them as enemies of the independent Ukraine that had just been achieved.

A national commission of experts appointed by the Ukrainian government in 1997 was to authenticate Banderite history. But the commission's report was only made public after Viktor Yushchenko came to power in 2005. Banderites were described by the commission as fighters for freedom, and veterans of OUN and UIA were equated with veterans of World War II. Public reaction to the report's conclusions remained mixed, and both World War II veterans and members of the movement were unhappy. This discontent prompted another exceptional step by Yushchenko. He posthumously conferred the title of "Hero of Ukraine" on the movement's leader Stepan Bandera.[153]

"Substitution of ideas" being one of the main tools of Russia's government's propaganda war in and outside Ukraine, the label "Banderite" was thus the perfect candidate to mold Ukrainian public opinion and prop up Yanukovych's regime – after Putin had finally been able to turn him into his puppet in Minsk. As the stand-off between Yanukovych and the Ukrainian population heated up, Russian propaganda once again latched on to this historical term to taint Ukrainians' desire to dismantle the country's oligarchic mesh of business and political power. In eastern Ukraine this propaganda was constantly repeated by pro-Russian activists, insinuating that every supporter of EuroMaidan was a dangerous extremist. A Banderite pamphlet presciently observed in 1948, "We, the sub-Soviet people, must understand that as long as the imperialists of Moscow – white or red, Tsarist or Bolshevik – dominate the territory of the [Ukr]SRR, they will always dream of dominating the world".

Regardless of Bandera's mainstream rehabilitation or the historical truth of his extremism, Bandera's brand was hardly a general battle cry inside Ukraine. Only nationalist activists adopted "Banderites" as their honorific when they joined mainstream EuroMaidan under the Right Sector banner led by Yarosh. Before Right Sector, he was the leader of "Trident", a successor party dedicated to Bandera[154]

11

Civil War

On New Year's Eve 2014 and during the snowy Christmas holidays, the revolution did not leave Maidan. However, the number of activists decreased. Many students had to prepare for their winter exams, although in many ways they had already passed the main test in their lives. At the same time, the central authorities, in order to defuse the conflict and dial down the criticism for the state violence during the EuroMaidan, adopted a law on December 19, called "On the removal of negative consequences and prevention of prosecution and punishment of persons in connection with the events that took place during the peaceful assemblies".

The bill was debated and passed on the same day by the Rada. It was supported by an overwhelming majority of representatives of all parliamentary factions, with the exception of Moroz's Socialist party. It was decided to exempt from liability people who participated in protests and mass events from November 21, 2013, and up to the moment when the law came into force. The Rada also stated that all criminal and administrative cases opened in connection with the Maidan events were to be closed, new ones could not be opened, and those already arrested were to be released.

It made little difference as Yanukovych's regime had lost its credibility. On January 12, 2014, another People's Assembly was held, which brought together up to 100,000 people. AutoMaidan protesters were on duty near Yanukovych's Mezhyhirya residence and held their own rally. Two days earlier, protesters had attempted to block the courthouse where protesters were being tried, which again led to clashes with the police and Berkut. Influenced by these events, on January 16, the government parties in the Verkhovna Rada adopted a series of amendments to public-order laws by a show of hands, without any debate of the texts by deputies. Yanukovych signed off on these emergency amendments the next day, Saturday January 17. However, as they had not been debated the opposition dubbed them "dictatorship laws" and called January 16 a "Black Friday".

The January 16-17 laws contained a number of new restrictions and increased criminal liability for violations relating to participation in peaceful protests. In particular, the amendments covered: blocking opposition websites "on the decision of experts," the responsibility for the installation of tents, stages and sound equipment at rallies organized without the permission of the authorities, the prohibition of being at demonstrations in masks and with weapons, the need to register political organizations financed from abroad. What was considered "from abroad" was left to the discretion of the government:

- Berkut and enforcement officers who commit crimes against Maidan activists are exempt from criminal liability;
- written charges need not to be provided to the suspect of violations, witnesses are sufficient for conviction;
- a person can be convicted *in absentia*;
- Verkhovna Rada deputies can be deprived of immunity, and consent to their arrest does not require investigation by a parliamentary sub-committee but may be given in a plenary session;
- the state can prohibit access to the internet;
- failure to comply with restricted access to the internet a fine of 6,800 hryvnia, and for failure to comply with the "official orders" of SBU employees a fine of not less than 2,000 hryvnia;
- driving in a convoy of more than five cars revoked the driver's license for two years;
- blocking access to buildings up to 6 years;
- setting up tent cities, stages and sound equipment without police permission up to 15 days;

- contempt of court – up to 15 days;
- disorderly conduct in groups 2 years imprisonment; mass disorderly conduct 10 to 15 years;
- gathering information about Berkut, judges, etc, 3 years;[155]
- operating a media agency without registration – confiscation of equipment and products, plus a fine.[156]

The reaction to these new regulations was mixed, both in Ukraine and in Europe. Some European leaders, particularly the British and German foreign ministers, stressed that these laws "limited the personal freedom of citizens and alienated Ukraine from Europe." The Council of Europe's Venice Commission (EU countries and the former USSR states minus Russia and Belarus) deemed them "consistent with European practice." Either way, in Ukraine, Yanukovych's adoption of the new "draconian measures" triggered a new, even stronger wave of discontent across the country.

One of the parliamentary hawks in Yanukovych's party who initiated these changes argued that they were in full compliance with American and European norms, and that the adopted laws were the implementation of European standards in Ukraine.[157]

On January 19, a crowd gathered for another People's Assembly and demanded the creation of a "People's Government" and early Presidential Elections. The protesters tried to break into the Verkhovna Rada to demand that the deputies cancel the "dictatorial laws" and, moving along Mykhailo Hrushevsky Street, began to storm Kyiv's government quarter. The police and Berkut blocked the demonstrators' way and clashes broke out again. The demonstrators threw stones, fireworks and Molotov cocktails at the security forces and set several trucks on fire as the police used water cannons.

On January 20, law enforcement officers beat up about 30 journalists who were covering the events, which caused a new wave of discontent. Vitaly Klitschko, one of the leaders of the opposition, again met with Yanukovych in the evening and urged him to remove Berkut and squads of "titushkas" (thugs) financed by the government. The President promised to set up a government commission to resolve the conflict. Meanwhile, soccer fans in several cities united to protect civilians from rampaging "titushkas", who often beat innocent bystanders rather than protesters.

Yanukovych's own position was growing precarious. His opposition called on the police and Berkut to take the side of the people, which they did in western regions of Ukraine. President Yanukovych, meanwhile, called on Arseniy Yatsenyuk, opposition leader of Tymoshenko's parliamentary party (the largest after Yanukovych's), and asked him to become Prime Minister, but Yatsenyuk declined.

Government brutality intensified and the first Maidan victims, killed by gunfire, fell – although it remained unclear who was to blame. About 50 people were seized and taken to an unknown destination. A video was made of the police forcing one of the protesters to strip naked in the freezing cold, while taking selfies with him. This footage of police torture caused outrage not only in Ukraine, but around the world. Waves of protest in Ukraine swept through all regions and solidified the hatred of the Yanukovych regime. In western Ukraine – in Lviv, Lutsk, Rivne, Ternopil, Chernivtsi, and Ivano-Frankivsk – regional state administrations were seized. Protesters forced governors to resign in some regions. Attempts to seize authorities were made in Cherkasy, Zhytomyr, and Poltava. In Kyiv, barricades began to be once again erected on Mykhailo Hrushevsky Street; a number of ministerial buildings were seized.

On January 24, representatives of the European Union and the opposition again met with the President to resolve the crisis. Yanukovych promised not to prosecute the protesters and to give them amnesty. Vitaliy Klitschko managed to persuade people on Kyiv's Maidan and Mykhailo Hrushevsky Street to maintain a truce for the time being while negotiations were taking place. Given his popularity among the people, the well-known boxer was widely used by the opposition to gain wide support for the EuroMaidan during the most critical days in January and February.[158]

On January 28, there was a breakthrough. Having been undermined by Yanukovych who had offered the role of Prime Minister to the leader of Tymoshenko's opposition party, the first political casualty was the Azarov government.[159] As Yanukovych was trying to save the government and Azarov promised to reshuffle his ministers, a cornered Azarov himself resigned and soon fled the country.[160] It was after Azarov's resignation that parliament promptly cancelled most of the laws adopted on January 16 against the EuroMaidan, under pressure from the mass protests in Ukraine and public outcry abroad. While doing so, the Rada, trying to preserve face, criminalized the denial or justification of Nazi crimes and the desecration or destruction of monuments built in memory of fighters against Nazism. However, seizures of government buildings and rallies in support of EuroMaidan continued throughout the country, including central, northern, eastern, and even southeastern Ukraine.

In parallel with the rallies in support of EuroMaidan, pro-Russian activist groups began to be organised in cities in southeastern Ukraine, calling for the protection of their territories from nationalists and extremists. For example, the pro-Russian youth movement in Odessa began forming a "People's Squad," a "Bulwark Square" squad in Kharkiv, and a "Night Wolves" biker squad in Sevastopol. Sevastopol and Crimea politicians called for "restoring order in the country and the declaration of a state of emergency," urging local governments to form their own self-defense units to protect the peninsula's population, leave Ukraine, and create a federal state of Russia Minor. Crimean officials went further. If the government in Kyiv did not take effective measures, they were ready to assume sovereign power over the peninsula.

Indecision plagued the government side. In parliament, Yanukovych's party insisted on introducing a state of emergency, but neither Yanukovych nor parliament agreed, fearing an escalation of tensions that were already "heated" to the extreme. Secret negotiations (fueled by financial contributions from Ukrainian oligarchs) began in the corridors of the Rada and led to the defection of some of the deputies from the crumbling government alliance to the opposition. Meanwhile, the Maidan elected the "People's Rada" at its own Assembly on Kyiv's Independence Square. Similar "Radas" began to be elected in the western regions of the country. Further cracks in the Interior Ministry's law enforcement apparatus began to appear. Some police units including officers of SBU's anti-terrorist "Alpha Units" announced their switch to the Maidan side.

On February 1, EuroMaidan leaders Klitschko and Yatsenyuk attended a conference in Munich where they held a series of meetings with US Secretary of State John Kerry and European leaders, who declared their support for the opposition and willingness to provide financial assistance to

Ukraine to overcome economic difficulties. A round table was held in Kyiv to which all former Presidents of Ukraine – Leonid Kravchuk, Leonid Kuchma and Viktor Yushchenko were invited. President Yanukovych, while agreeing to a dialogue (on condition that the rebels lift the barricade of government buildings) and under pressure to compromise, branded the protests extremist and equated the demonstrators, who were fighting for European integration, with the Ukrainian nationalists.

Meanwhile, seeing that Yanukovych was losing ground fast, Moscow applied more pressure and said it would delay giving Ukraine another tranche of the $15 billion loan pledged in Minsk, stressing that the next one would depend on the formation of a new government. At the same time, the Kremlin brazenly called on the Ukrainian opposition to abandon its "campaign of ultimatums and threats" that "contradicted the opposition's commitment to democracy and European values".

On 7 February 2014, the Winter Olympics opened in the Russian coastal city Sochi. The eyes of the world were on Russia, and Putin did not want anything to detract from the games' global success after having spent a record-breaking $50 billion on them. It was another revealing moment about Yanukovych's relationship with Putin. Yanukovych decided that his presence at the Olympics was a more important event than the dismal situation in Kyiv and sorting out relations with the protesters. Of course, in Sochi he not only waved his country's flag from the rostrum of official guests, but also held "political consultations" with Putin regarding the situation in back home and the next tranche of the $15 billion loan that Moscow, contrary to personal assurances to Yanukovych, had stopped paying. Putin had already made different plans and was fanning the chaos in Kyiv that turned Yanukovych into a spent force.

Vitaliy Klitschko now called on parliament to return to the Constitution of 2004, which proclaimed the transition from a Presidential-parliamentary to a parliamentary-Presidential form of government. This proposal was supported by Yatsenyuk, the leader of Tymoshenko's party, who said that he would accept the post of Prime Minister after all if the country returned to the 2004 Constitution. Yatsenyuk said that the government would be made up of representatives of opposition parties and Maidan activists.

It is worth noting that Tymoshenko herself, who was still in prison in

Kharkiv, appealed to her party to reject a return to the Constitution of 2004 and prepare instead for the Presidential Elections, in which she saw herself as the main candidate after leaving prison. Tymoshenko expected that she would be the voters' favorite and become Ukraine's next President and preferred to enjoy the same power as Yanukovych.

The EuroMaidan, however, wanted the 2004 Constitution. The European Parliament adopted a resolution on the situation in Ukraine that called on the European Union to begin preparing targeted sanctions on the foreign travel, assets, and real estate of Ukrainian officials, parliamentarians, and oligarchs responsible for the use of force against protesters and the deaths of opposition activists.

In Kyiv, meanwhile, a scandal erupted in connection with the leaking of a telephone conversation between Assistant Secretary of State Victoria Nuland ("Nuland-gate") and the US Ambassador to Ukraine. It became clear from the conversation that the US was betting on Yatsenyuk as the new Prime Minister. There was nothing unexpected about this in itself. Nevertheless, it led to complications in the relations between opposition leaders Yatsenyuk and Klitschko. The former boxer refused to take part in forming a government (unless he became deputy Prime Minister) as he focused his efforts on his own Presidential Elections campaign. However, Tymoshenko's release from prison and her announcement of her participation in the Presidential race folded Klitschko's cards.[161]

On February 18, the day of the Verkhovna Rada session in which opposition deputies tabled their demand for a return to the 2004 Constitution, nationalist Right Sector and the Maidan Self-Defense militia, wearing masks and carrying bats, held a warning rally outside to put pressure on its deputies. On Kyiv's central Maidan, some local residents said they wanted to clean up the accumulated garbage in the city center, proposing "For a Clean Kyiv". But the protesters suspected that this was an attempt by the authorities to remove the barricades, and representatives of Maidan Self-Defense dispersed them, while their leaders urged all Ukrainians to enroll in self-defense units and organize Maidan in the eastern regions of Ukraine. This dispersal of locals and call for arms, in turn, was latched on to by pro-Russian organizations, which began campaigning against Right Sector and the Maidan in Kyiv.

Clashes with protesters resumed. Law enforcement officers blocked the demonstrators' on their way to the parliament. They, in turn, started throwing stones and Molotov cocktails at the police and Berkut, and trucks blocking the path of the demonstrators were set on fire.

In parliament itself Yanukovych's party tried to respond to delay a return to the 2004 Constitution by proposing that a commission look into it. The opposition disagreed and blocked the rostrum; whereupon its deputies left the assembly. Deputies of the Yanukovych-supporting Socialist party were also prevented from getting to the Rada's rostrum. As a result, the opposition's draft resolution was duly lodged, and the mood in the Rada calmed down. However, clashes continued in the area surrounding parliament. The Military Museum, which had been turned into a government "emergency center", was seized and the office of Yanukovych's Regions party was set on fire, in which one of its employees was killed.

The events that followed marked a sudden, steep escalation of the crisis. Law enforcement forces began aggressively to push the protesters back to the central Maidan in order to free government offices and an "Anti-Terrorist Campaign" began to clean up the quarter, which lasted almost a day. During the day, fire was opened and 25 people were killed, more than 350 were wounded, 200 of which were hospitalized.

Leaders of the nationalist Freedom Party called on residents of the western regions of Ukraine to go to Kyiv and support the demonstrators. In response, the authorities blocked the possible movement of traffic along the country's main highways toward the capital. Trains were cancelled and could only pass through Kyiv in transit to other destinations, with passengers looking on in amazement at the empty platforms of the Kyiv railway station. The broadcasts of one of the central television channels were suspended.

Protesters seized government buildings in Dnipro, Mykolaiv, Kherson, Poltava, Chernihiv, Khmelnytskyi, Zhytomyr, and in the regions around these cities. Monuments to Lenin were destroyed in a resumption of "Leninfall", though some of them had been dismantled in advance by supporters of the Socialist party and hidden. In a concession, the authorities did not issue criminal charges for the destruction of the monuments because "there was no crime because these monuments were not cultural heritage". Seventy monuments and busts of the leader of the revolution were demolished and dismantled. In eastern Ukraine attempts to destroy Lenin monuments were also made in Kharkiv, Luhansk, Donetsk, and Zaporizhzhia, but local authorities prevented their demolition.

Klitschko and Yatsenyuk called again for early Presidential and Rada elections to prevent further escalation and appealed to Yanukovych to meet, declare a truce, withdraw the Berkut from Kyiv, and recall the police presence on the streets. Having agreed to negotiate with the opposition, Yanukovych demanded an end to the armed resistance of the demonstrators, who by the evening of February 18 were hemmed in on the central EuroMaidan by riot troops and Berkut. Two streets were left open to herd the withdrawal of people from the square. After that, the security forces proceeded to clean up the square itself. Yatsenyuk and Klitschko had their meeting with Yanukovych on the night of February 18-19; however, it did not lead to any results. They made mutual accusations and did not reach a compromise.

In the morning, the protests resumed. Demonstrators in Kyiv occupied the Main Post Office, the Conservatory, and the State Committee for Television and Radio. They began to seize arms depots and build barricades on Mykhailo Hrushevsky Street, leading to the Verkhovna Rada. The Museum of the History of Kyiv, which contained weapons and was under the protection of security forces, was looted during the night. In the meantime, the authorities began to erect concrete barriers near parliament, and the 25th Airborne Brigade was summoned to the capital from Dnipropetrovsk to reinforce the security of the arms depots.

At the same time, the SBU announced an "Anti-Terrorist Operation" (ATO) across Ukraine. A fire broke out in the Trade Union Building, where the central headquarters of the uprising was located, killing more than forty people. In almost all western regions of Ukraine, protesters resumed seizures of offices used by the regional administrations, the SBU, the Interior Ministry, and the Attorney General. An enormous number of documents and office equipment were destroyed. Ukraine was on fire.

On February 20, despite Yanukovych's concession to hold early Presidential Elections, the protesters, armed with whatever they could, including guns, began pushing government troops away from the city's EuroMaidan toward the Verkhovna Rada, Government House, and the

Presidential Palace. Panic broke out and more casualties fell on both sides. Demonstrators began throwing Molotov cocktails and cobblestones at Berkut and police officers. Law enforcement forces began to retreat towards the government quarter, firing rubber bullets. A meeting between Right Sector leader Yarosh and President Yanukovych also yielded no positive results. The President suggested that Yarosh agree to the non-use of force by his Right Sector, but the latter refused, saying that Ukrainians would stand their ground to the end.

It was on this day that the government irretrievably lost control when live ammunition was used in cold blood. From the rooftops of the government quarter, snipers started shooting at the demonstrators. The sudden escalation turned the EuroMaidan from a protest movement into a full-blown civil war. On that ill-fated day, some hundred people were killed by gunfire, protesters as well as policemen. The day would later be commemorated as the Day of the Hundred, and the dead were awarded the posthumous title of Hero of Ukraine to mark their place in national history.

The news of these terrible events went around the world. Later everyone began to discuss what had happened and hypothesize who had fired what and from where. Some people said that the shots came from the roof of the Kyiv Conservatory, others said from the roof of the House of Trade Unions, and still others said from the roof of the Ukraina Hotel. The SBU and the Interior Ministry on the one hand, the Right Sector and the Maidan Self-Defense on the other blamed each other for the bloodshed. Russian special services and even the United States were suspects. Some suggested the involvement of the oligarchy which had their own "special forces" and were interested in bringing down business rival Yanukovych.

An important fact to take into account here is that the shooting of demonstrators and security forces took place on the day before the government and the opposition had expected to come together. There was a settlement agreement that everyone had been waiting for and which was thought to be the basis for a peaceful solution of the situation and a gradual, consistent resolution of the conflict. The signing of the declaration was aborted as the "Kyiv snipers' case" was filed with other unsolved murders. In 2015, at the first anniversary of the momentous day, however, more would become clear about who ignited the powder keg.

On February 21, talks between Yanukovych and opposition leaders to resolve the political crisis in Ukraine and end the mass bloodshed were held.[162] The talks were mediated by Germany, Poland, France and Russia.[163] It resulted in a resolution by the opposition and the government, witnessed by the foreign observers: to restore the 2004 Ukraine Constitution, instigate constitutional reform to adjust the balance of powers between President, government and Rada, hold Presidential Elections, and investigate the recent violence.[164]

Putin's envoy Vladimir Lukin, however, refused to countersign the resolution on behalf of Russia, explaining it as follows: "Moscow decided not to witness these agreements for a very good reason – as a matter of fact, the situation that is the subject of this agreement is not very clear"; it "does not detail the forces and persons who should implement all this". Russia proved to be consistent in its inconsistency. Later, when Yanukovych, having fled Ukraine, was in Russia, the ex-President remembered the agreement and insisted that it be implemented. At that point, speaking from Russia, Lukin's signature on the document would have helped him immensely. But it wasn't there.

However, after the agreement was announced on Kyiv's Maidan, Right Sector, Maidan Self-Defense, and AutoMaidan expressed their dissatisfaction with the results and the slow pace of political reforms. They insisted on the immediate resignation of the Yanukovych (a demand that had not been part of the February 21 resolution), the dissolution of the Verkhovna Rada, and punishment for the heads of Ukrainian law enforcement agencies who had ordered the shooting of demonstrators. Right Sector leader Dmitriy Yarosh called the February 21 resolution "another whitewash" and refused to abide by it.

On the night of February 22, Maidan Self-Defense and Right Sector units completed their occupation of the government quarter. Maidan activists now controlled the Verkhovna Rada, the Presidential Palace, Government House, and the Interior Ministry. More than a hundred policemen, who defected to the side of the protesters, and former soldiers who had fought in the Soviet Army in Afghanistan came with service-issue weapons to Kyiv to protect the EuroMaidan. In a number of western regions, police and Berkut units also sided with the protesters. Many police units in Kyiv now patrolled the capital alongside self-defense units. One by one, the police chiefs began to resign: the head of the Kyiv police left, and significantly the military leadership of the General Staff of the Ukrainian army resigned in protest against the involvement of the armed forces in the internal conflict. The self-defense units, together with the militia, had taken complete control over the capital.

12

Change of Power or Oligarchs?

On the morning of February 22, the Verkhovna Rada began its session at the usual time of 10 a.m. However, there was no Speaker. Speaker Volodymyr Rybak, a deputy from Yanukovych's Regions party, had resigned. So had the First Deputy Speaker, a deputy of the Socialist party.[165] Their resignation letters were read out by Ruslan Koshulynskyi, Second Deputy Speaker and a member of the nationalist Freedom Party.

Having learned about the resignation of the Speaker and his First Deputy, and that Yanukovych himself had quietly disappeared from Kyiv, the opposition went on the attack. Along with Yanukovych, his loyal acolytes – Attorney General Pshonka, Interior Minister Zakharchenko, and Treasury Minister Klymenko – had also fled the country.[166] The night before, behind-the-scenes negotiations had been held in the Verkhovna Rada resulting in a number of deputies from Yanukovych's Regions party, almost all independent deputies, and even a few communists joining the opposition.

With a quorum of the Verkhovna Rada's 450 deputies in attendance, the opposition first seized legislative majority and then Ukraine's executive powers. About 240 deputies supported these resolutions. Just before lunch, Oleksandr Turchynov, one of the leaders of Tymoshenko's Fatherland party, was elected as the new Speaker of parliament. The Rada also passed a resolution of censure, stating "that Mr Yanukovych has vacated his constitutional duties, threatening the governance of the state, the territorial integrity and sovereignty of Ukraine, and the mass violation of citizens' rights and freedoms." Presidential Elections were promptly scheduled for May 25, 2014. The Verkhovna Rada also announced the return to the 2004 Constitution and appointed Speaker Turchynov as the country's Acting President in order to maintain a tight leash on the country's most powerful executive office.

Opposition party deputies demanded other stringent measures, including the abolition of the Socialist Party. Yanukovych's Regions party and the Communists remained silent throughout. A new government and new Interior Minister and Attorney General were appointed in order to swiftly restore order in the country.[167]

On February 22, Tymoshenko was released from prison and immediately flew to Kyiv. The next day she appeared before the EuroMaidan, hoping to be greeted as a triumphant figure. But it could not be called a triumph. Tymoshenko was greeted with ambivalence: by some with joy, by others with distrust. The Maidan princess of 2004 did not become the EuroMaidan queen of 2014.[168] Some suggested she ought to retire from politics, while others advised her to fight for the Presidency, which was more to her liking.

The new government laid all the blame for the country's chaos on the law-enforcement branches and withdrew Interior Ministry officers from Kyiv. Next, the widely-loathed Berkut riot police, accused of exceeding its authority, was in fact abolished and withdrawn. Some of the Berkut officers fled to Crimea or defected to Russia, taking Russian citizenship (they were later redeployed by Russia to foment unrest in eastern Ukraine). Virtually the entire leadership of the Interior Ministry, both centrally and locally, was fired. Of course, this led to quiet neglect by the rest of the police of their immediate duties. The police, called to protect public order, worked to rule, quietly watching from the sidelines as representatives of various political formations beat each other up in the squares of various cities.

The events in Kyiv clearly scared Yanukovych's party, which on February 22, on the initiative of Kharkiv governor Mykhailo Dobkin, decided to convene a rally under the banner of "Ukrainian Front", which was attended by deputies of local councils in southeastern Ukraine and Crimea, mostly from the Regions party.[169] In addition, governors of neighboring Russian regions (Belgorod, Kursk, Voronezh, and Rostov) and a delegation from the Russian State Duma attended the rally as guests. The "Ukrainian Front" was held in the Sports Palace in Kharkiv, surrounded by supporters of EuroMaidan, who were shouting "East and West together!", "Out with the Gang!", "Kharkiv, Rise Up!", and so on. It proved to be a tumultuous setting.

Yanukovych, who had both left Kyiv and his wife of forty-three years in Donetsk, showed up in Kharkiv with his new girlfriend. He planned to speak at the rally and lead a march from eastern Ukraine to Kyiv. In the end, he did not attend in person. He did send a video address to the people of Ukraine in which he reminded them that he was still the legally elected President of the country and would not sign any decisions of the Verkhovna Rada that had been issued in his absence – something the Rada had not asked Yanukovych to do given his flight from the capitol.

Contrary to expectations, no sweeping statements about Ukraine as a state were made at the Kharkiv rally. A non-binding resolution that was passed by those in attendance did not even use the words "autonomous regions" or "federalization" of Ukraine. It boiled down to: "given the events of the last days in Kyiv, local self-governments take responsibility for ensuring order on the ground until the restoration of constitutional order and legality, as well as the legitimization of the new government". This did not stop Kyiv from accusing the rally of separatism because the resolution questioned the legitimacy and constitutionality of the central government.

The organizers of the congress were clearly nervous, rushing the speakers, and urging delegates to keep in mind the hostile crowd who had gathered for the rally near the Palace of Sports. Governor Mykhailo Dobkin as well as Kharkiv Mayor Gennady Kernes, the leaders of Kharkiv, disappeared, bewildering their guests from Russia. A couple of days after the event, they reappeared, explaining their absence by urgent business trips. Soon after, Dobkin was fired and put under house arrest; Kernes was charged with a number of crimes (which he denied). Then he, too, was put under house arrest. In late April, during a bicycle ride, Kernes was attacked. He was taken to the hospital with a severe bullet wound and then transported to Israel, where surgeons saved his life.

Yanukovych, meanwhile, having assured his people in his video messages that he would be with them "until death," tried to leave Ukraine together with his new girlfriend. But Ukrainian border guards would not let him leave when he tried via Kharkiv, Donetsk and then Luhansk. Then Yanukovych left for

Crimea, from where he was "escorted" to Rostov-on-Don, Russia. This city became his temporary foreign residence as the Russian government had expressly forbidden Yanukovych to go to Moscow. From late February to April, he appeared at press conferences in Rostov and made all kinds of statements about the situation in Ukraine, meanwhile calling on Russia to "restore legitimacy" in his country. But Yanukovych had already become a lame duck, perhaps the reason why it was repeatedly reported in the press that he was dead.

On February 27, the Verkhovna Rada inaugurated Arseniy Yatsenyuk as Prime Minister.[170] In his address, Yatsenyuk said that the country was in danger, the Treasury was empty due to the previous government, but the path towards European integration would be unshakeable.[171] The new Ukrainian government – which was not recognized by Russia, but was recognized by Western European nations and the US, as well as the large Ukrainian diaspora abroad – began to make its first decisions. Only four people had government experience and the 21 ministers were carefully balanced across all the parties who had taken part in the opposition to Yanukovych. Tymoshenko's Fatherland party claimed the largest number of ministers, seven in all. [172]

Having subsequently passed "approval" through the people's "purgatory" – the EuroMaidan – the government zealously set to work. The main task was to patch up the holes in the state budget created by the previous government. The $3 billion tranche given to Russia to the Yanukovych government was running out, and Russia had no intention of extending the remainder of the $15 billion loan to the new government. Then the Ukrainian government turned to the US and EU for help. The International Monetary Fund agreed to provide the bulk of a $17 billion facility if Ukraine complied with certain political and economic conditions.

Yatsenyuk also appealed to the US and EU to block the assets of the Yanukovych family and other representatives of the former Ukrainian government abroad, but there was no discussion of returning these funds to Ukraine. An initiative to do so foundered as none of the oligarchs had the slightest interest in this.

It begs the question: which clans controlled Ukraine on the eve of Russia's covert military campaigns in Crimea and Donbas?

The Donetsk clan

After the ousting of the Yanukovych clique, new political forces backed by the oligarchs came to power. In fact, they were the same oligarchs who had previously supported both the old government (openly) and the opposition (covertly). Their calculation had always been that you have to be friends with the ruling majority and support the opposition minority, because if the government falls, the opposition you support will come to power, and your economic interests will still be taken care of. "Down with the old oligarchs – long live the new oligarchs!" might apply elsewhere but not in Ukraine because the oligarchs remained the same, even if political power changed hands. A number of oligarchs had stable seats in the Rada: the 20 richest members of the Ukrainian Parliament had a combined wealth of $8.6 billion.[173]

The roots of this unhealthy mix of economic and political power went back to the 1990s era of independence and the distribution of state property among Ukraine's main players – former Presidents and Prime Ministers, heads of special services and law enforcement ministries. Their main purpose was to improve their own well-being. The combined wealth of the oligarchy was estimated at more than $83 billion and the top "influencers" of Ukrainian politics and its economy were and remained the Donetsk and Dnipropetrovsk clans[174].

Despite the fact that about 50 percent of the country's metallurgical industry, almost the entire coal mining industry, heavy engineering and energy companies are concentrated in Donbas, the national government in Kyiv, with few exceptions, was dominated by the Dnipropetrovskis. They had been part of Mount Olympus since Soviet times. Nevertheless, they had to worry about the Donetsk clan.[175] The latter skillfully used the miners' trade unions, the strongest in the country, and the political forces represented by the Communists.[176]

It was only after Yanukovych and his associates came to power that the Donetsk people managed to grab power in Kyiv at last.[177] All key positions in the Presidential administration, the government, the parliament, the security services, the prosecutor's office, the center, and the regions were filled by representatives of the Regions party. Oligarchs Rinat Akhmetov and Dmitry

Firtash became the backbone of Yanukovych's regime.

The leader of the Donetsk clans was Akhmetov, without whom not a single appointment or removal of the highest positions in Ukraine took place. He was Ukraine's richest oligarch and the key sponsor of Yanukovych's Regions party, with a fortune estimated at $22-25 billion in 2012 (according to Bloomberg, he was the 26th richest man in the world that year).[178] Several clan members held important political roles. Akhmetov's friend and business partner Borys Kolesnikov was a former Deputy Prime Minister and former Infrastructure Minister.[179] As Deputy Prime Minister and Infrastructure Minister Kolesnikov was responsible for the preparation of EUFA's Euro 2012 in Ukraine.[180] The main soccer clubs in Ukraine, however, were bought out by that time, and Kolesnikov, a passionate hockey fan, became the owner of hockey club Donbas.[181] Kolesnikov shared Ukraine's confectionery market with opposition deputy Petro Poroshenko and they had factories both in Ukraine and Russia. Brothers Andriy and Serhiy Klyuyev were also representatives of the Donetsk clan. Both were Regions' deputies of the Verkhovna Rada, and Andriy became Yanukovych's First Deputy Prime Minister, Head of the NSDC, and briefly Chief of Staff at the height of the 2014 political crisis until Yanukovych's flight from office.

The "Yanukovych family"

Of course, a businessman who becomes a high-ranking official and continues to run his own business at the same time is liable to be accused of dishonesty, and often is. But then what can we say about the politician who becomes a big businessman precisely when he occupies a high government position, especially when it is the highest executive office, the Presidency of the country? Viktor Yanukovych became such a businessman during his Presidency. According to the assessment of Anders Aslund, a senior researcher at the Peterson Institute for International Economics in Sweden and a former economic advisor to the Ukrainian government, the net worth of the Yanukovyches stood at $12 billion in 2013.

The "President's family" consisted not only of Yanukovych's sons (who actually ran the "family business". According to the Interior Ministry, more than 50 banks were involved in the money laundering of the Yanukovych clan. The multistorey office of the "Yanukovych family" was located in the center of Kyiv. It was where its money laundering was carried out. Serhiy Arbuzov – who became First Deputy Prime Minister and started his career under the patronage of his mother, the CEO of Bank Donechchina and later Governor of Ukraine's central bank – played an important role in this chain.

The "family" included some lucky friends. A young friend of the President's son, Serhiy Kurchenko, at the age of 28, after graduating from two universities, moved from Kharkiv to Kyiv and instantly became a billionaire, buying up Ukrainian businesses and assets: enterprises, stadiums, soccer clubs. The twenty-something businessman consolidated about 55 companies in the gas industry that were registered in Kharkiv and Crimea within "his" Gaz Ukraine. Gaz Ukraine, with a turnover of more than $10 billion, now controlled 18 percent of the Ukrainian gas market. It goes without saying that Tymoshenko, Ukraine's "gas princess," felt even less happy in prison as she saw her gas companies move to a new owner. But other businesses were also being scooped up. For example, the "FC Metalist Kharkiv" soccer club and stadium were taken away from Oleksandr Yaroslavskyi, a Kharkiv businessman.

Later Kurchenko changed his strategy and created a group of companies called "East European Fuel-Energy Company" acting jointly with Russian Lukoil and Sibneft to buy in Ukraine and abroad (particularly Germany) a network of gas stations and refineries. To suppress the media, Kurchenko, on the orders of Yanukovych's son, bought up the assets of the United Media Holding group, founded by another Kharkiv resident, Boris Lozhkin. The latter had merged his business with Rinat Akhmetov. In effect, the Yanukovych family were taking part of the business from their own sponsor oligarch, Akhmetov.

When Yanukovych copied Putin's model of the Presidency, he realized, like Putin, that in order to strengthen his personal power he needed to limit the influence of the opposition, as well as that of his own supporters in the Regions party and business colleagues, even if they had been his own sponsors and partners. Wielding power like Putin, Yanukovych started with the most promising oligarchs, by ousting, pushing them aside, expropriating, and buying at low prices some of the businesses of Rinat Akhmetov and Dmytro Firtash.[182] Serhiy Kurchenko and similarly capable young businessmen were used for these raids. Indeed they managed to build an entire chain of firms to resell other people's businesses and launder money received from the state budget. Of course, this model of extortion could not have existed without the Attorney General, the Interior Minister and the SBU turning a blind eye. These people became members of the Yanukovych family. Attorney General Pshonka and his son collected "tribute" in the form of bribes and "kickbacks" from businessmen. Ukrainians, with their laconic humor, noted that the main business quality of a Ukrainian businessman is not "selling", but "kickbacking". But only people close to the ruling elite could expect kickbacks. In this sense, Interior Minister General Zakharchenko and SBU Head Oleksandr Yakymenko were also members of the "family," tasked with finding businessmen willing to pay tribute.

It became clear to Ukrainian oligarchs that the Yanukovych family was engaged in "lawlessness", at any rate that "sensible" arrangements could no longer be reached with Yanukovych.[183] An undeclared war against the President and his cronies began within the Donetsk clan that had once been loyal to Yanukovych. As one researcher wrote in 2012, "the steep strengthening of the Yanukovych family clan, infringing on the interests of billionaire oligarchs, will lead in 2013 to a sharp aggravation of relations in Ukraine and predictable public confrontations with the aim of trying to remove the Yanukovych clan and its closest cronies". He was preternaturally accurate in his predictions.

In autocratic countries, such as Ukraine and Russia, businesses closely linked to government officials flourish until the government collapses. It is no coincidence that as soon as Yanukovych left Ukraine, the leader of Yanukovych's Regions party in parliament hastened to make clear that his party had "nothing to do with the Yanukovych family" and distanced himself instantly from his one-time patron.

The "businessmen," who bought themselves protection under the "roof" provided by government officials try, while in power, to quickly become rich, move their capital abroad, divide it up, and hide it under other people's names. They haven't got much time until they are replaced, and they know it. While Kuchma, Tymoshenko, Yanukovych were in power, their entourage became fabulously rich, knocking the financial base out from under the feet of their opponents or even putting them in jail. The example of Tymoshenko (in

Russia, Mikhail Khodorkovsky) was the most illustrative in this sense. Everyone understood that her case was political. That the now ruling Yanukovych family was taking her business was no less obvious. Whether or not Tymoshenko had really committed crimes was completely irrelevant.[184]

Dnipropetrovsk Group

This was the power base of Yulia Tymoshenko. The Dnipropetrovsk clan, unlike the Donetsk clan, was formed back in the time of Leonid Brezhnev, Russia's leader as General Secretary of the CPSU Central Committee, and a native of Dnipropetrovsk. This clan occupied the leading party and political positions both in Moscow and in Kyiv which at one-time gave the small region far-reaching international power. In the 1960s and 1970s a joke was popular in Moscow about the three stages of Russian history: "before" Petrovsky (Peter the Great), Petrovsky and "Dnipro"-Petrovsky. More than half of the cadres of the Ukrainian party and nomenklatura authorities were from the region.[185] Whereas the Donetsk people relied on the mines and metallurgical plants, the Dnipropetrovsk people relied on the military-industrial complex of the region.[186]

Luckily for the leaders from Dnipropetrovsk, Kuchma, who was part of their clan, became President in 1994 and restored his local peers to national importance. By the end of 1996, the Dnipropetrovsk clan dominated all branches of state power. It was through this formerly Communist-turned-business network that the energetic, attractive and ambitious Tymoshenko built up her video business in Dnipro.[187]

A special role among the Dnipropetrovsks was played by Pavlo Lazarenko, former governor of the region. Appointed Prime Minister in May 1996, Tymoshenko was appointed under him as Ukraine's leading gas CEO. Lazarenko's was a cautionary tale of too much greed. He began to form his own group in the government, controlling the country's fuel and energy complex.[188] After Kuchma sacked him, Lazarenko joined Kuchma's opposition, created his own party, Unity (Hromada), and in 1998 was elected to the Rada and hoped to run for President himself.[189]

As we saw at the beginning of the book, it led to his fleeing the country to the US, hoping to receive political asylum. Instead he ended up in jail, charged with extortion, money laundering and fraud on the evidence supplied by his political opponents in Ukraine who now controlled the government. He was released only in 2003 after paying $86 million in bail.

Lazarenko remained under house arrest from 2003 until 2009.[190] On August 25, 2006, he was sentenced to nine years in prison and a $10 million fine. A little later, a judge decided to reduce the amount of proven financial abuse by about $5 million. The most scandalous accusations – relating to the activities of Tymoshenko's gas company – were dropped from the US charges during the time when Tymoshenko was Prime Minister.[191] Even in jail, Lazarenko never gave up and tried twice to run in local elections in Ukraine in absentia.[192]

Tymoshenko, Lazarenko's former underling, carried on after him. She continued to control the activities of the UESU and created her own political faction, Fatherland, replacing the Unity party, which collapsed because of Lazarenko's arrest. Probably the most powerful position of the business clan was held by Tymoshenko's group. Having ceaseless ambitions, she was not afraid to challenge Yushchenko.[193] When she became Prime Minister she regained her gas empire.

No one was as adept at Russian politeness as Yulia Tymoshenko, who could negotiate with everyone and everything. For all the charm of her nature, she could not compromise, neither in business nor in politics. In this, she resembled only one person – the Prime Minister and President of Russia Vladimir Putin. Both had the same principle of exchanging opinions: you come in with your opinion, and you leave with mine. For this reason, the main task of the Donetsk people who came to power under Yanukovych was to destroy Tymoshenko's gas empire and compromise her as a politician.[194,195]

13

The Invasions of Crimea

In November 2013, the political leadership of Crimea came out in support of the Yanukovych Presidency and Azarov's government and expressed "concern" about the opposition's actions threatening the political and economic stability of the country. Just a day after the EuroMaidan crackdown in Kyiv, on November 21, Crimea's autonomous State Council, its local parliament, supported Yanukovych's decision to suspend the signing of the EU Association Agreement and urged the population of the peninsula to "strengthen ties with Russia".

In early December, the Crimean parliament and administration adopted a series of appeals to the Ukrainian leadership, demanding that order be restored in the country and a state of emergency be introduced. Separatism was expressly discussed by Crimean authorities. On December 3, the Presidium of the Crimea's State Council suggested that the Ukrainian President consider Ukraine joining the Russian Customs Union. Pro-Russian organizations – particularly the Russian Bloc party, whose ranks included many FSB agents, called for the formation of autonomous self-defense units on the peninsula and, in particular, in Sevastopol to protect the city and in the "event of a *coup d'etat*" to secede from Ukraine. Sevastopol's Coordinating Council had already called for the creation of a federal state of autonomous Malorossiya ("Russia Minor") with a political orientation towards Russia.

For many years, the idea that Crimea is a Russian State and that the peninsula rightfully belongs to Russia was promoted to Crimea's local population. What is the historical background, though, of the peninsula? Even the broad outlines of Crimea's history are not commonly known locally, let alone Ukraine at large, as it was a subject that fell under USSR propaganda until 1991 and remained politically sensitive thereafter.

Crimea's history

Crimea's ethnic mix is historically a patchwork of people. The most ancient population of Crimea are the Cimmerians, who inhabited the northern Black Sea coast in the eighth through seventh centuries BC. After the invasion of the Huns (375 BC) and the fall of the Bosporan Kingdom, starting from the fourth through fifth centuries AD, the dominion of the Roman (Byzantine) Empire was gradually established. In subsequent centuries Crimea was seized by the Khazars and then the Armenians, who had formed a number of colonies during the twelfth through fifteenth centuries.

From 1239, Crimean territory conquered by the Mongol-Tatars (the "Kipchaks") became part of the Golden Horde, and from the middle of the 15th century the Genoese were at war with the Christian-Orthodox principality of "Theodoro" (or "Gothia") over the coastal lands of the southern Crimea, inhabited by Goths, Greeks, and Alans from Persia. At the same time, eastern-Crimean Tatars coexisted peacefully with the Genoese, trading with its coastal factories (a Genoese fortress controlled Sudak). During this period, many Circassians settled in eastern Crimea from the north Caucasus (today Russia, then Ottoman lands).

By now, the population of the Crimean peninsula consisted of a wide range of ethnicities: Kipchaks, Goths, Greeks, Alans, Armenians, and even Russians who settled in the cities. Slightly earlier, before the defeat of the Khazar Khaganate in the tenth century, there were the Qaraites, who practiced Judaism, some of whom, together with the Tatars, later moved to Lithuania. Their descendants continue to live in Lithuania and the Grodno region in Belarus.

The population inhabiting the so-called Crimean Yurt (Homeland) increasingly sought independence from the Khans of the Golden Horde, whose power began to weaken by the beginning of the fifteenth century. With the support of the Lithuanian principality and the local Crimean nobility, an independent Crimean Khanate was established in 1441, headed by its first khan Haji Giray I, who ruled the Crimea until 1466.[196]

From 1478 up to 1774 the territory of Crimea became a protectorate of the Ottoman Empire. The Ottomans kept their garrisons and a bureaucratic apparatus in the Crimean Khanate. The Girey dynasty ruled the Khanate, and the power was transferred from one relative to another quite often, as a result of intrigues, murders and coups.

Having a certain independence within the Ottoman Empire, the Crimean Khanate served as a buffer between the empire's heartlands and the Grand Duchy of Moscow, conducting constant devastating raids on Russian lands and stealing slaves which were sold in the slave markets of the East. Claiming the Volga and Astrakhan on the Caspian Sea, Crimean Khans even dared to attack Moscow, burning it down in 1571 taking fifty thousand Russians as prisoners. In fact, until the times of Peter the Great (with some interruptions) Russia paid tribute to the Crimean Khans, who could rely on military support from the Ottoman Sultan.

Islam Girey III (1644-1654) coincided with the era of Hetman Bogdan Khmelnytsky and the incorporation of his Cossack territory in eastern Ukraine into Russia – the "real" Malorossiya (Russia Minor). Girey III rendered military assistance to Khmelnytsky's Kozaks during in the War of Independence against Poland. Through him, Khmelnytsky conducted secret though fruitless negotiations on the Hetmanate becoming a protectorate of the Ottoman Empire instead of Russia.[197]

Crimea's political direction turned on July 21, 1774, with the Treaty of Kuchuk Kainarji. Having lost a devastating war, the Crimean Khanate was released by the Ottoman Empire and became a protectorate of Catherine the Great, who installed Shagin Giray as Khan (1777-1782, 1782-1783). The Sultan paid her 4.5 million rubles and ceded the northern coast of the Black Sea (the north Caucasus), along with two important ports and more remote territories.

Crimeans did not warm to Russia's protégé who tried to reorganize the administration of his Khanate on a Russian last. Even his brothers rebelled against him. Finding himself overthrown, Giray turned to Russia for help to regain his throne. Catherine the Great had been waiting for this moment and sent Prince Potemkin to suppress the uprising. Thereafter, she forced Giray to abdicate and annexed Crimea to Russia in set of moves that Putin would emulate 250 years later.[198]

In 1802, Crimea was subsumed under the newly formed Taurida Province of the Russian Empire, which included three mainland counties and five counties of the peninsula. This province existed until the end of the Russian Revolution and Ukraine's Civil War in 1921. But earlier, as a result of the Crimean War of 1853-1856 against an alliance of France, Britain, Italy and the Ottoman Empire, Russia lost the right to keep a fleet on the Black Sea and have military arsenals on the Black Sea coast, though it managed to keep a number of Crimean cities, in particular Sevastopol.

After the February and October revolutions of 1917, Crimea was not part of the newly formed Ukrainian People's Republic from the start. However, after Hetman Skoropadsky came to power in Ukraine and Ukraine was occupied by German troops, Crimea did fall under Ukraine, and under the Brest Treaty of 1918, Soviet Russia recognized Crimea as Ukrainian territory.[199]

The civil war meant there were numerous changes of "White" and "Red" governments in Crimea. Of the latter, both a Soviet Socialist Republic of Tavrida and a Crimean Soviet Socialist Republic were proclaimed. Even so, Crimea was the last territory held by the White Army under the command of General Baron Peter Wrangel. On the night of November 8, 1920, the commander defending Crimea, General Alexander Kutepov could not hold back the attack, and the Red Army broke through to the Crimea with heavy losses.[200] After the seizure of the Crimean Peninsula, the Bolsheviks carried out mass arrests and shootings in Crimea. According to estimates of Soviet historians in the period from November 1920 to March 1921, from 52-56,000 people were executed. According to foreign historians it may have been twice that number.

In October, 1921, the Crimean Autonomous Soviet Socialistic Republic (CASSR) was formed as part of Soviet Russia (RSFSR).[201] At the end of 1922 the formation of the Union of Soviet Socialist Republics (USSR) was proclaime, whose main republics were Soviet Russia and Soviet Ukraine. However, even after 1922 there were small territorial changes. Thus, the

Ukrainian Donetsk Province included the Taganrog District. It only became part of Russia in 1925. Putin never mentions this

During World War II ("The Great Patriotic War"), new tragic events took place in the Crimea. In May-June 1944, the Crimean Tatars, Armenians, Bulgarians, and Greeks were compulsorily deported from Crimea by the Soviet government after accusations of collaboration with the Nazis. The autonomy of the Crimean Soviet Socialist Republic was abolished at the end of the war and almost all Tatar, Greek and Bulgarian settlements were given Russian names. In June 1946 Crimea became a province of Soviet Russia, with navy base Sevastopol a separate administrative unit.

1954, the transfer of Crimea to Ukraine

The transfer of Crimea from Soviet Russia to Soviet Ukraine is surrounded by numerous and often contradictory legends. The reality is more prosaic. 1954 was the 300th anniversary of Ukraine's Cossack relations with Russia. The Communist Party and the Soviet government decided to mark the glorious anniversary by presenting Ukraine with a fraternal gift: the handing back of Crimea. It was an early example of "Substitution of Ideas", i.e. separating historical facts from their relevance. In 1754 the Hetman's counterpart was a Romanov Tsar, whose descendants the celebrants had assassinated – a fact not otherwise part of the festivities. The idea was Nikita Khrushchev's, Secretary of the USSR (1953-1964) and a native of Ukraine, who as Communist Party leader of Ukraine (1944-1947) had first thought of it.

On January 25, 1954, the meeting of the Presidium of the Supreme Soviet of the RSFSR, chaired by Georgy Malenkov, duly approved the gift with following wording: "Taking into account the commonality of the economy, the territorial closeness and close economic and cultural ties between the Crimea region and the UkrSSR, the Presidium of the Supreme Soviet of the RSFSR decides to transfer the Crimea region from the RSFSR to the UkrSSR".[202]

The reasons for the transfer of the Crimea to Ukraine were not just a celebration of legal casuistry. They were dictated by economic expediency. After the compulsory deportation of the indigenous peoples of Crimea in

1944 – Tatars, Greeks, Armenians and Bulgarians, who led a mostly agricultural way of life and were used to growing crops in Crimea's arid steppe conditions – the settlers drawn from Russia's interior had struggled. Their attempt to grow traditional potatoes and cabbage was not a success. They had no experience of farming in such hostile conditions, and they did not know how to take care of the fields and vineyards, nor were there many who were drawn to this frankly rather thankless labor.

Most Russians settled in Crimea in order to spend their retirement warming their bones in the Crimean sun. Accustomed mainly to complaining, the Soviet settlers wrote about the poor conditions, lack of housing and food as the region was becoming more and more desolate. In addition, during that period, the construction of the enormous (for that time) north Crimean water canal from the Kakhovsky water reservoir on the Dnipro river had started. It was more convenient to carry out the financing of such large-scale hydraulic works within the framework of one Soviet republic than have endless cross-border turf fights between bureaucrats of two republics.

In March 2014, Vladimir Putin engaged in some historical substitution of his own to justify annexation. He claimed that the sole initiator of the transfer of Crimea to Ukraine "was Khrushchev personally", who was acting on "the desire to gain the support of the Ukrainian *nomenklatura* or to make up for his guilt for organizing mass repression in Ukraine in the 1930s." In 1954 Khrushchev could not take such dictatorial decisions on his own. After Stalin's death on 5 March 1953 Khrushchev was embroiled in a power struggle with Malenkov, which he only won in 1955. Khrushchev could not have made that decision on his own. In any case, none of the decisions regarding the transfer of Crimea carry Khrushchev's signature and nor did Putin aim to join a historical debate.[203]

In July 1990, after the Declaration of Independence of Ukraine, the latter withdrew from the USSR, together with Crimea, and there were no protests about it in Russia. The fact of the cession of the Crimea region was later confirmed by bilateral Russian-Ukrainian agreement of November 19, 1990, by which the parties renounced their territorial claims, and was fixed in treaties and agreements, witnessed by the governments of the Commonwealth of Independent States (CIS).

In February 1991, based on the results of the referendum, the Autonomous Soviet Socialistic Republic of Crimea (as part of Ukraine) was restored. After signing the Belovezh Accords to dissolve the USSR on December 8, 1991, a cautious Leonid Kravchuk, the first President of Ukraine, asked Yeltsin, just in case, "What shall we do about Crimea?" – "Well, take it!" replied Yeltsin. So Crimea was established as part of Ukraine through a referendum of its own population, and Russia affirmed that it was part of Ukraine at least three times: in 1954, in 1990, and in 1991.

There was some pushback among Russia's Communist elite. After the end of the USSR on 26 December 1991, President Boris Yeltsin was held to account by a pro-Communist parliament, Russia's Supreme Soviet (restyled "State Duma" after 12 December 1993 when the RSFSR itself became today's "Russian Federation"). On May 1, 1992, Russia's Supreme Soviet adopted resolution N 2809-1, which declared "null and void from the moment of adoption" the February 5, 1954, decree of the RSFSR's Council of Minister's that transferred Crimea to the UkrSSR. With hindsight, the 1991 Supreme Soviet found it to be "in violation of the Constitution (Fundamental Law) of the RSFSR and legislative procedure". Even so, their resolution N 2809-1 clarified that this issue should be resolved through interstate negotiations between Russia and Ukraine with the participation of the Crimean Autonomous SSR and on the basis of the will of its resident population, a stance Russia's deputies clarified a few days later in an appeal to their Ukrainian peers.[204]

The history of sovereignty in modern Crimea

On May 5, 1992, Crimea's State Council proclaimed the Republic of Crimea, a sovereign state. The following day, its Constitution was adopted, which defined the Republic of Crimea as a democratic state, and Sevastopol as a city with special status from other cities but otherwise as an integral part of sovereign Crimea. On May 13, Ukraine's Verkhovna Rada suspended the decision of Crimean State Council as contrary to the Constitution of Ukraine, and on May 21, Crimea's State Council voluntarily withdrew its resolution of May 5.

The issue of Crimea's sovereignty was thus temporarily resolved, although the alternative name – the Republic of Crimea – began to coexist along with the Crimean Autonomous SSR (CASSR).

In 1993, there was a renewed attempt to establish the Republic of Crimea with the creation of its own Presidency, assumed by a deputy of the "Russian Bloc" party. He reinstated the 1992 Constitution of May 6, 1992, by decree. In September 1994, the Verkhovna Rada renamed CASSR as the Autonomous Republic of Crimea and on March 17, 1995, it repealed a number of laws passed by Crimea's State Council and abolished its Presidency.[205] By way of compromise, a new constitution of the peninsula, adopted in 1995, established its autonomous status within Ukraine and delegated the right to Crimea's State Council to adopt certain laws. In October 1998, a new version made Crimean autonomy fully compliant with the Ukrainian Constitution.

After the revolution in Kyiv and Yanukovych's flight from the country, Putin surreptitiously invaded Ukraine and took Crimea. Russia already had troops stationed at its Crimean military bases, but it now entered the territory with additional operatives and held a referendum at gunpoint (from the "managed democracy" rulebook developed in the Russian Federation).[206] According to counts tallied by Russian officials, 82 percent of voters supported both Crimea's independence and its annexation to Russia. According to independent experts, however, no more than 50 percent of voters showed up for the referendum (in some regions of Sevastopol the figure was indeed as high as 80 percent) and fewer than 30 percent voted for annexation to Russia.

What was striking was the swiftness with which events unfolded. The referendum was held on March 16, the results were announced on March 17, and on March 18, the signing of documents about the annexation of Crimea into the Russian Federation took place in the Kremlin. Ordinarily, it would have been impossible to do all this so quickly (even the UkrSSR took eight days to accept the RSFSR's gift), not to mention the fact that Russia, for example, did not hold a referendum on the admission of Crimea to the Russian Federation. The Russian government was clearly in a hurry to admit Crimea to the Russian Federation under the false flag of a "popular" vote before protests of the international community and Ukraine, which was in the throes of the May election of a new President.

Crimea's clamor for "independence" and its subsequent "popular" agreement to relinquish that same "independence" by annexation to Russia was thought out, planned and detailed in advance. A giveaway sign of Putin's hurry to occupy Crimea was the premature casting a medal "For the Return of Crimea," the reverse side of which indicated the date of the operation: "February 20 to March 18, 2014". On February 20, President Yanukovych was still in power in Ukraine. On that day that demonstrators in Kyiv were massacred that would bring down his regime in subsequent days. Putin pretended that his decision to enter Crimea came only on February 22, after the "overthrow of the legitimate President of Ukraine Viktor Yanukovych" (who fled precisely to Crimea, and from Crimea to Russia), covering up the plans of the invasion. A Crimean referendum was on no one's lips on 20 February.

Sixty years later: Russia's seizure of Crimea

In early 2014, the Crimea, of course, was in an unenviable position, looking like an open wallet. While Ukraine had few troops, Russia already had naval bases and a total of more than 4,600 military infrastructure facilities in Crimea, enabling it to lock down the peninsula. The presence of a huge number of villas and luxury mansions in this most famous resort of the former Soviet Union created an additional incentive for Russian oligarchs, officials, and army generals to swoop while the iron was hot. Numerous Crimean health retreats and resorts could be privatized by Putin's clan or given to the Russian *nomenklatura*.

Under Crimea's territory there were also huge deposits of oil – 10 oil fields with reserves of 47 million tons; gas – 27 gas fields with reserves of 165.3 billion cubic meters; 7 gas condensate fields with 18.2 million tons. In addition, there were 5 more gas fields and 3 gas condensate fields on the Black Sea shelf; 6 gas fields on Crimea's Azov shelf. Ukraine's government had estimated the potential revenue of shale gas on the Crimean shelf at $40 billion. There were other raw materials: iron ore, mineral salts, stone…

Even so, the economic benefits paled in significance to imperial, political and geopolitical ones. The occupation of Crimea by the Russian army in March 2014 was also the first stage of "Operation Novorossiya" in President

Putin's grand plan to recreate the Russian Empire.

Any serious strategic plan always consists of numerous steps. One such steps was to bring Ukraine under Russia's dominion. Another was to do the same with Belarus. In both cases, they would leave the Treaty on Non-Proliferation of Nuclear Weapons so that Russia had a proxy-nation from it could launch nuclear weapons, and bully others, while pretending that it had nothing to do with the decisions of a "sovereign" nation. It would mean that the population of these nations would bear the brunt of any nuclear retaliation, while removing Russia's own territory as an immediate target. (Already a large part of this plan had fallen into place in 2022. On February 27, 2022, 65.2 percent of votes counted in Belarus were in favor of its dictator Lukashenko's proposal to change the constitution so that it could station Russian nuclear weapons once again.) Next was the capture of the Baltic states.

There are other steps, ones which we can only guess at. For example, quite a few Russian officials started talking about Transnistria (a breakaway part of Moldova), which is impossible to get to except through Ukraine. Ukraine's accession, under Putin's original plan, could take place in stages or at one time. It was only a question of technology and military capabilities: Many factors were unclear: the level of resistance among Ukrainians, the level of outrage in the world, the scale of sanctions against Russia, the degree of readiness of Russian soldiers to kill Ukrainians, and the degree of readiness of Ukrainians to die for their country.

Unexpectedly for Putin, Ukraine itself, and the world, Ukrainian politicians surrendered Crimea without so much as a fight. In March 2014, it was not immediately clear whether this was good or bad, and what signal it sent to all parties involved in the conflict: the aggressor – Russia, on the one hand, and Europe and the United States, on the other. On one thing everyone agreed. They saw the bloodless surrender of Crimea as Ukraine's weakness and as Ukraine's tacit acceptance that Crimea was "an ancestral Russian land".

However, this "signal" served the world and Putin poorly: the Russian President now had no doubt in his mind that the rest of Ukraine would surrender. On the heels of its unexpected success, the Russian government began organizing pro-Russian uprisings in eastern Ukraine, demanding eferendums at regional level on the annexation of the eastern Ukrainian egions to Russia. It was assumed that under the influence of the unrest in astern Ukraine, Kyiv would agree to hold referendums in the eastern egions of the country; that Russia would recognize the results of the eferendums if they were in favor of Russia, or would not recognize them if hey were in favor of Ukraine. In either case, Russia could then introduce roops into Ukraine's eastern regions under the pretext of protecting the ights of the Russian-speaking population, as had previously been done in Crimea. The Russian General Staff then planned to move its armies into outhern Ukraine toward Odessa, advancing from Crimea and the east, cut Jkraine off from the Black Sea, reach Transnistria, and announce the reation of a new state that had never before existed on the map: Novorossiya.

14

False "Russian Spring"

During the EuroMaidan, both in Kyiv and in Eastern Ukraine, there were demonstrations calling for the reining in of the oligarchy and the overthrow of the Yanukovych regime. But over time the slogans of the demonstrators in southeastern Ukraine began to change, although the region's population remained the same. After the loss of Crimea in March 2014, people in southeastern Ukraine began talking about the "Banderite" menace. There was some basis for this. There were numerous remarks by the nationalist Freedom party and representatives of the Right Sector, who declared that, after taking Kyiv, they would go on to take the east.

In truth, these nationalist parties neither took the capital nor went on to "take" eastern Ukraine. In the May Presidential Elections, the Right Sector candidate won 0.7 percent of the vote (by way of comparison, the Jewish oligarch Vadim Rabinovich won 2.27 percent of the vote and turned out to be more than three times as popular). Yet, southeastern Ukraine started to become a base for fighting against the "Banderization" of Ukraine, and this political awakening began to be referred to as the "Russian Spring."

The specific event that triggered the "Russian Spring" was the Verkhovna Rada's hasty repeal on 23 February, 2014, of Yanukovych's regional languages law, which had made it possible for Russian-speaking Ukrainians to use Russian as an official language in southeastern Ukraine and Crimea. This imprudent decision by the Rada detonated latent partisan discontent, and initially this discontent spread throughout Ukraine – and conveniently for Russia – as a movement calling for the defense of the Russian language and the Russian-speaking population from the "Banderites entrenched in Kyiv."

In addition, EuroMaidan supporters in Kyiv and western Ukraine had begun a movement of occupying regional administrations, toppling monuments of Lenin (erected throughout the country by the Soviet regime and which still had not been removed), dismissing governors and mayors of cities from their posts, and vigilante justice and beatings, such as the tying of the governor of Volhynia to a whipping post. These actions were not considered fair by people in the eastern regions, although, prior to this moment in time, Yanukovych and his Donetsk clan were not regarded with much fondness in eastern Ukraine either.

It was against this background that a "process of unification" of south-eastern Ukraine – which began on February 22, 2014 in Kharkiv, at a meeting of local government officials – spread through the Kharkiv, Donetsk, Luhansk, and Zaporizhzhia regions. Radical elements in the southeast now also started occupying regional administrations and buildings belonging to the security services and law enforcement agencies. Outwardly, the protests and unrest were a mirror image of analogous protests in the western part of Ukraine. But their thrust was different. At a conference in Kharkiv, demonstrators urged local authorities to take control over the regions, and this was seen by Kyiv as separatism.

Supporters of this eastern movement now began to be called "separatists," although strictly speaking neither during the conference itself, nor during the first demonstrations in Kharkiv, Donetsk, and Luhansk, were there any calls for separatism. These calls for separatism began to be heard later, after young combative people arriving from Russia – mostly from the Belgorod, Voronezh, and Rostov regions of the Russian Federation, which border on Ukraine – began to mingle among the demonstrators.

Gradually, the situation began to ignite and spin out of control. There were mutual clashes. Aggression came less from EuroMaidan supporters than by from pro-Russian activists, who were well prepared for such aggression. The participants in the fights came predominantly not from pro-Russian social associations, but from such organizations such as Kharkiv's "Oplot" (Bulwark) whose ranks were made up of youths trained in combat sports, who knew how to use both fists and baseballs bats. These organizations usually spread to other regions, for example, to Donbas, joining local self-defense units, which were reinforced by Russian troops deployed to southeastern Ukraine from Russia and Crimea.

In reality, this "Russian Spring" was nothing other than a Russian diversionary campaign carried out by Russian security services in Ukraine, latching on to local discontent, with the aim of destabilizing the political situation. From February 2014, three tactics were deployed: local Russian operatives and agents; local pro-Russian "separatists" and "militants"; and sabotage experts from special forces units of the GRU and the FSB, who in Soviet times had been sent to Africa and Latin America to foment revolts and civil wars.[207] Now they could use their mother tongue, which made the sabotage experts' work much easier and made fighting with them much more difficult for Ukraine's law enforcement agencies. The interim goal of the "Russian Spring" was to unleash an information war, provoke ethnic, religious, and regional clashes, so as to create conditions for the introduction of Russian troops into Ukraine with the aim of occupying initially a part of Ukraine, and then its entire territory. The final political and geopolitical goal of the operation was the abolition of Ukraine's sovereignty.

The demonstrations in the southeast assumed a more and more anti-government character. Calls for the overthrow of the "Kyiv cabal" were constantly heard (Russian propaganda teams had skillfully put this term about), as well as calls for the annexation of southeastern Ukraine to Russia. The nature of the demonstrators changed as their ranks swelled with mercenaries from Russia, retired soldiers and officers from Crimea, local pro-Russian "militants" hired from among the local population for money, and even criminals, released from prisons.

While in their initial stages the civic demonstrations in southeastern Ukraine were peaceful in nature, now the "demonstrators" led by Russian security services agents turned into organized military factions, armed and financed by secret sources. The suspicion fell, on the one hand, on Russia, and on the other hand, on former Ukrainian President Yanukovych and his people, who were hiding in Russia.

The propaganda war unleashed simultaneously by the Russian media against Ukraine was breathtaking in its gross distortion. Yet it turned out to be highly effective, particularly because prominent Russian cultural A-listers took an active part in this propaganda war on Russia's side.

As a counterweight to this, their Ukrainian counterparts appealed to Russian colleagues and friends to "show respect for the aspiration of Ukrainians to continue building their state on a legal foundation after the fall of the corrupt" Yanukovych regime, which was "stained with the blood of its own people." "We are no fascists, no extremists," they stated in their appeal. "We have an overwhelming desire to live in a free country. We call on you to support the Ukrainian people's right to defend its independence and to help to stop the war between the friendly and brotherly Russian and Ukrainian nations, to stop Russia's military invasion of Ukraine's territory!"

Putin's plans   *leaked how?*

Before the overthrow of Yanukovych's regime, few people in Ukraine imagined that Russia might launch a military invasion. Neither its military nor its elite foresaw this danger. The situation changed after the Russian occupation and annexation of Crimea. Now a Russian invasion of continental Ukraine looked like a real possibility. Yekaterina Gorchinsky, the editor-in-chief of the *Kyiv Post*, published a leaked Russian document entitled "On the Crisis in Ukraine." It contained a plan for the occupation of Crimea, obtained from a reliable source, which had been developed by Russia's Security Council. It made provisions for the annexation to Russia of Crimea, eleven Ukrainian regions, and Kyiv:

> First, only the full annexation to the Russian Federation of the Russian regions of Ukraine, namely Crimea and the regions of Luhansk, Donetsk, Zaporizhzhia, Dnipropetrovsk, Chernihiv, Sumy, Kharkiv, Kyiv, Kherson, Nikolaev, and Odessa, can guarantee peace, security, *The Producers Hitler song* and prosperity to their inhabitants and secure the reliable protection of Russia's interests. Second, this objective may be realized only by establishing control over the Mother of Russian Cities, the capital of Ukraine, the Hero City Kyiv. *Only conquest can bring peace*

The document had been prepared long before the start of the unrest in eastern Ukraine and Russia's occupation of Crimea, since it contained provisions for the suppression of the EuroMaidan and the dissolution of the Verkhovna Rada, with all power passing into Yanukovych's personal control. Russia planned to use the "period of chaos" for its own political interests, intending to "neutralize the most prominent representatives of the Banderite opposition" and to take "stabilizing measures" aimed at creating favorable conditions for Ukraine's participation in integration with the CIS, while removing from power those who believed that Ukraine should join NATO and the EU.

When were such plans hatched? As early as April 2008, invited to the NATO summit in Bucharest, several months before the Russian invasion of Georgia but after Yanukovych was dismissed by then President Yushchenko as Prime Minister, Putin had stated that Ukraine was a failed state and that many Ukrainian territories, which had been attached to Ukraine by Russia during different historical periods, should return to Russia. At that time, all those present at the summit, including American President George W. Bush, took Putin's remark as a joke. The only person not laughing was Andrey Illarionov, former economic policy advisor to President Putin. On his blog, Illarionov posted an article entitled "Plan for Military Actions Against Ukraine," written by a Russian expert who had for many years worked for Russia's Defense Department.

The third President of Ukraine, Viktor Yushchenko, was also convinced that a "Russian plan" for Ukraine was to put an end to Ukraine's existence an independent state, and insisted on European integration as soon as possible as the only possible means of avoiding war and preserving Ukraine's sovereignty. He warned about this on February 21, 2014, well before the annexation of Crimea. "The development of the Russian scenario, which consists... [of] the escalation of the conflict... [and] the formation of a puppet government, must be brought to a halt at once," Yushchenko stated. "A permanent European Union mission should be established to facilitate Ukraine's return to European integration as a guarantee of the preservation of its territorial integrity, as a guarantee of the return of peace and stability, and as a guarantee of the further enactment of reforms in all spheres. Ukraine must take steps toward Europe by approving a policy of political association with it, establishing a free trade zone, and introducing a visa-free transit regime; at the same time, the EU must impose financial sanctions and other constraints on the organizers of the terror against Ukrainians."

But for the most part, the failure to appreciate the seriousness of the Russian leadership's plans for Ukraine was global. Most politicians, analysts, experts, and specialists on Russia and Ukraine believed that Putin would not dare to annex Crimea. After the occupation of Crimea, many assumed that the Kremlin would limit itself to recognizing the "independence of Crimea" and possibly its inclusion in the Russia's Customs Union, but still would not go so far as to annex it, let alone to launch a military invasion of southeastern Ukraine.

Putin did exactly what he had said he would do in 2008. He annexed Crimea and went on to the next stage: dispatching GRU and FSB special units to Ukraine in order to organize "self-defense forces" there. Here is one of the first Russian letters of instructions to Ukrainian "separatists" and southeastern "militants" (read, in both cases, Russian operatives):

1. Do not leave buildings that have been occupied, but reinforce and hold them. At night, there should be no fewer than 1000 people, armed and entrenched, in each building-encampment. Men should be in units; women should supply provisions and medical supplies. Organize round-the-clock sentries, form armed rapid response groups.
2. In the regions, "cut off" local SBU offices. Occupy buildings, shut down communications, put facilities out of service. The Kyiv SBU office must lose regional support. SBU is enemy no 1; it must be cut off by any means possible; its agents must be exposed.
3. Occupy local television studios and start your own broadcasting. Most importantly: preserve technical access to the network. If the reporters run away, do anything you like – show YouTube clips, read the news. Most important: broadcast your own information.
4. Do not call for referendums, instead organize them. Establish election committees, demand that official election committees provide lists of voters, arrange with printers to print leaflets. Accept help from the official authorities in Donetsk, who were also in favor of a referendum; but do not cede the initiative to them.
5. Go to the mines and campaign for support. Thus far, this is a

revolution of young people and old people. Everyone else is working, drinking beer. The mines must switch to a regime of strikes until the situation has been fully decided. In the event of a reunification with Russia, work stoppages will be fully compensated. ⚡

6. Enter into contact with "The Legitimate One" [President Yanukovych]. Let him do at least something useful – appoint people's representatives as bosses [governors] of the Donetsk and Luhansk regions. *annoyed at him*

7. Spread propaganda among the police to get them not to intervene and not to carry out orders "to protect" governing bodies that are loyal to the junta. Forbid them to engage even in passive defense. They shouldn't meddle.

8. Block Internal Troops units. Encourage conscripts drafted as part of the mobilization to go over to the side of the people in an organized fashion.

9. Unlock the border with the Russian Federation in at least a few districts. On the western borders of southeastern Ukraine, on the contrary, establish pickets and do not let anyone from western Ukraine come in.

It is evident that important strategic decisions in Russia today (if not all decisions) are made not collectively, but individually by Putin, for whom his own interests and the interests of his inner circle are paramount. At the same time, it appears that Putin has no strategic plan. More precisely, his plan consists in taking over all the parts of the "Russian world" that the international community will allow to be taken over. But where this "Russian world" begins and where it ends is something that no one in Russia today knows, including President Putin. The concept is transgressionary – it will morph into some other expansionist idea once "all Russians" are gathered behind his borders.

The Empire returns

When the Russian army occupied Crimea, it might have seemed to many that the world had gone mad. But it was not the whole world that had gone mad, and not even all of Russia: only the relatively small group of people who ruled this country. Of course, once one calmly and objectively analyzed everything that was going on, it became clear that this group of people had also not gone mad. In the clinical sense of the word, they were perfectly sane. But they inhabited a different mind space, one that had long disappeared in Europe.

The older residents of eastern and southeastern Ukraine also lived in a different dimension. Cut off in 1991 from both Moscow and Kyiv, they now attempted to return to a long-gone Soviet Union, assembling with red banners around Lenin monuments. They did not understand that Putin's Russia was not the old USSR that they had known since childhood, but an altogether different kind of state, in which the wild laws of the market prevailed. They tried to go back to a bygone age of Communism.

In part, neither the current leaders of Russia not the residents of southeastern Ukraine were to blame for all this. Soviet era Communist culture vanished suddenly in 1991, without explanation. Meanwhile, the people who ruled Russia had grown up before 1991. In their past lives, almost all of them had been members of the CPSU: some had been part of the Komsomol (the youth branch of the CPSU); others had worked for the KGB or the GRU. These organizations had a very particular character. The people who belonged to them were carefully chosen, and their work in these agencies left a deep impression on their personalities. These people never thought that the Soviet Union was "bad" – nor was it, to them. They sincerely believed that the Soviet Union was "good," and that some evil power (most likely the United States) in 1991 had ruined this wonderful country in which they played such a well-organized, comfortable role. *esp recall 1990s econ decline ↦ nostalgia*

After 1991, several attempts were made to bring Russia back to the state in which it finds itself today. The August 1991 Moscow Putsch itself was the first attempt at such a return to the past. The second attempt took place in October 1993, when Russia's Supreme Council, dominated by Communists, tried to overthrow President Yeltsin by impeaching him, organizing sabotage, and calling for an uprising. The third attempt was made in March 1996, when the head of Yeltsin's Security Service (and a former bodyguard of Yuri Andropov), General Alexander Korzhakov, the head of Russia's Ministry of Security (the successor agency to the KGB), Mikhail Barsukov, and their protege, Deputy Prime Minister Oleg Soskovets (thought of as the future President of Russia); tried to cancel or postpone the Presidential Elections by declaring a state of emergency.

The plan to declare a state of emergency owed its existence to the fact that all Russian public opinion surveys indicated that the Presidential Elections of 1996 would be won by Gennady Zyuganov, the candidate from the Communist Party, and not Yeltsin. To avoid losing power in 1996, the Yeltsin administration provoked the Chechen war before the election (in time, this war began to be called the "First Chechen War," as, in 1999, it was followed by a "Second" one). The war was supposed to serve a pretext for declaring a state of emergency and canceling or postponing the election. After that, according to their plan, General Korzhakov had to find a way to remove Yeltsin: to force him to resign, to replace him with Oleg Soskovets, and to create a Russia like the one that exists today.

However, in 1996, the Russian security services were unable to take over the government: Yeltsin with his astonishing intuition understood that Korzhakov represented a threat, and accepted the helping hand that was offered to him by Russia's oligarchs, foremost among them Boris Berezovsky (who gave Yuri Felshtinsky, co-author of this book, unrestricted access to his papers and other sources of this time in Russian history). Then, in 1996, Yeltsin went ahead with the election, called off the still undeclared state of emergency declaration from March, and fired Korzhakov, Barsukov, Soskovets. Whether honestly or dishonestly, he beat Zyuganov in the election by a slight margin and in return for this victory, he handed over the rule of Russia to the oligarchs – until the next Presidential Elections of 2000.

In 1999, Russia's security services began a new assault on the Kremlin's top position. This battle was won by Putin. It could have been won by the architect of the First Chechen War, Sergei Stepashin, or by Yevgeny Primakov, the former head the Russian secret service. All three came from the security services. All of them were considered by Yeltsin as potential successors to him as President of Russia. On the political chessboard of the Kremlin in 1999, the pieces were positioned in such a way that no matter what move was made, the outcome was the same – checkmate: in all cases, a member of the ex-KGB would become the next President.

When Vladimir Putin, the former head of the FSB (as the former federal intelligence service was now called), became President in May 2000, many in Russia and abroad were unhappy because he was Yeltsin's man – or Abramovich's – or Berezovsky's – or Voloshin's man – or the oligarchs' man. But no one was unhappy about Putin's appointment because he was from the KGB. In the political chess game of 2000, however, this was the most important element. And when Putin began to create a "power vertical," emasculating the Council of the Federation, taming the parliament, changing the Constitution, establishing rigid centralization, abolishing a system of local elections (which may not have been absolutely free, but were at least not controlled by the Kremlin), and finishing off the independent media, no one quislings could understand why he would need to do all this. But they let him. In February 2022, this at last became obvious for all to see: he needed to do it all for a new twist in the history of Russia, for the rebirth of the Russian empire. Because he could not launch the country into this without having first become a dictator.

Great effort was put into creating an ideology for "the people," for how can "the people" be ruled without an ideology? After all, the Soviet Union, in the opinion of Putin and his inner circle, rested on two pillars: Communist ideology and the KGB. Among those who spoke to the need to create a new ideology was the Kremlin's main ideologue and political operative, Vyacheslav Surkov. He was unable to come up with anything new, although he tried very hard. When Dmitry Rogozin, an undisguised Russian "fascist with a human face," began his rise through the ranks and was eventually appointed as Deputy Prime Minister in charge of the military industry, a clear new ideology took shape: the ideology of Russian fascism.

Now even the President of the multi-ethnic state – which the Russian Federation had always been – began to say without embarrassment that he was a Russian nationalist and that to be a nationalist in Russia was good and commendable. Not a "patriot," but specifically a "nationalist" – someone who is the diametrical opposite of a pre-1991 Communist. If we put this nationalist idea together with another one of Putin's admissions – that his own greatest personal tragedy was the collapse of the USSR in 1991; and if we add to them Rogozin's appointment as head of the defense industry, with Putin's puppet Dmitry Medvedev overseeing the government's financial policies and allocating more and more budgetary resources to the modernization of Russia's army; then we will come up to the line that Russia crossed in when it began taking back territories lost by the Soviet Union in 1991.

Putin is preparing for the hundred-year anniversary of the start of the First World War by starting the Third World War. And not at all because he is crazy. By no means. The fact is that everyone in the KGB thought just as Putin thinks. The people with whom Putin has surrounded himself – Sergei and Viktor Ivanov, Igor Sechin – are exactly like him. They have only now finally "made it" in life; only now do they finally understand what they've been living for, why for so many years they licked the boots of democrats like Leningrad (St. Petersburg) mayor Anatoly Sobchak, or populists like Boris Yeltsin, or oligarchs like Boris Berezovsky, Roman Abramovich, and Mikhail Fridman.

"Back to the empire" – that is the slogan of the initial stage of the Third World War, the battle over Ukraine. Today, the whole world is embarrassed by this word. "Empire," today, sounds proud, but criminal – forcing a population to give up its sovereignty at gunpoint. Russia is once again proud of it, as it was proud of it before and after 1917.

To judge by Russian television, after 2014, eastern Ukraine is Russian territory, temporarily occupied by a Nazi enemy, and Russian cultural figures, writers, journalists, are quite prepared to kill the "Ukrainian occupiers." Orwell's "Two Minutes Hate" (from his novel *1984*) are child's play compared to the coverage of Ukraine in the Russian media. And yet the words pouring off the screen were from leading opinion makers, "artists," "masters of their genres", not just news programmes. On his television show Replika (on Russia-24), the famous Russian writer Alexander Prokhanov vividly described how Ukrainians "will disembowel pregnant Russian women" (a literal quote) if they are not conquered. Channel One, which broadcasts practically to the whole country and is the main source of information for Russia's population, talked of Ukrainians crucifying Russian children.

On all Russian television channels, there was a propaganda war going on. If one knew nothing about what was happening in the world and viewed only Russian television, then one knew that there was a certain odious country called Ukraine, ruled by a junta, and that the despicable, self-proclaimed government of this nasty country was maltreating the oppressed

Russian population. There is another country called the United States, and some kind of strange association called the EU, which, although they are not as vile as Ukraine, are also despicable and dishonorable. They are constantly doing harm to the benevolent and humble Russian Federation – a neighboring state whose heart bleeds both for the Russians living in Ukraine and for the hapless, foolish ordinary Ukrainians, who have ended up under the control of the junta and the "fascists," referred to as "Banderites"; and these Ukrainians (whom Russia is in addition kindly subsidizing to the tune of billions of rubles per year) do not want to understand that it would be better for them to submit to Russia and to forget about independence – well, "Nazi"-rule really. This is broadcast in Russian, 24 hours a day, 7 days a week, by the special news channel Russia-24, and 22 percent of Ukrainians, mainly Russian-speakers in the east, watch it. At the same time, Russian TV (called *obv lie!* RT to make it less immediately obvious that it is Russia's channel) additionally broadcasts in English, to the whole world.

It is remarkable that, in contrast to 1938-1939, everyone knows everything. US and European leaders, forever trying to avoid economic problems in their own countries, everyone understood that Russia was aggression against a smaller neighboring state; and that its actions are the spitting image of Hitler's and Stalin's machinations. Everyone understood that the "insurgency" in eastern Ukraine was organized by Russia. No government needed the invasion of 2022 to have this explained to them.

The international community of course never recognized the petty scam that was Russia's annexation of Crimea, or its blood-thirsty military attack on eastern Ukraine; and indeed, Russia has no support from a single state. What is happening is not about Ukraine, and the issue not whether Ukraine was good or bad, whether this or that government was or was not corrupt, and whether Crimea or eastern Ukraine really wants to become a part of Russia or whether it wanted to remain a part of Ukraine. The cause of all that is going on lies in Moscow and in Putin's regime. And all grievances should be addressed to Russia alone.

As in the First World War, as in the Second World War, the offensive side believes that the victim will surrender and that there will not actually be a war. This is what Austria-Hungary believed in 1914, retaliating against Serbia for the assassination of the archduke; this is what Germany believed in 1939, laboring under a vision of all ethnic Germans united within the borders of a single state. This is what is believed today by FSB Lieutenant Colonel Putin, President of Russia, and his FSB Generals Sergei and Viktor Ivanov, and all the other men in uniform who are now in command in Russia and who have taken it upon themselves to unite within a new empire the whole "Russian world," for the sake of which they are now hatching a new war: to make the planet recognize the greatness of Russia, just as Europe once had to recognize the greatness of Germany, or Asia and the United States – the greatness of Japan.

Experts in Europe, the United States, and Russia, are beginning to speak of war as something perfectly likely, casually alluding to nuclear weapons as well. This would be a war provoked for the sake of protecting a "Russian world," which does not exist and has never existed: the greatest numbers of Russians were killed in Russia by Russians themselves. Starting in 1917, when the Bolsheviks came to power, the regime killed tens of millions of people.

Russians have once again reached the edge of a cliff: they are once again being sent to war. Only now it is not Lenin, not Stalin, and not even Brezhnev, but a group of colonels and generals from the KGB-FSB, who have taken over Russia.

15

"Substitution of Ideas" as a Dance to War

Having annexed Crimea, Putin thought it would be just as easy to invade Donbas, where he hoped to be supported by pro-Russian Ukrainians in the region. Special military detachments led by career officers of the secret services were deployed by him to Donbas. Georgia, Crimea, Donbas – three times a charm.

One such officer was Lieutenant Colonel Igor Girkin (known under his alias as "Strelkov") of Russia's military intelligence, GRU, who had previously been involved in secret combat operations in Bosnia and Herzegovina, Transnistria, and many other hotspots. Girkin was appointed as chief saboteur and the commander in chief of the troops stationed in the breakaway republics in eastern Ukraine. His task was to recruit as many local residents as possible into these so-called "people's armies." Hiding its armed forces under the cover of this false banner, Russia began its military interference in this part of Ukraine, although the Kremlin categorically denied this chain of command when challenged.

Propped up by these covert Russian military units and at the instigation of FSB agents, officials in a number of areas in Luhansk and Donetsk regions proclaimed themselves to be the government of "people's republics." A similar attempt by the Russian special services to declare the formation of a "Kharkiv People's Republic" was unsuccessful, however. Kharkiv's population resisted the proclamation of a quasi-republic, and officials of Kharkiv defied the encroachment of Russian authority on their city. This defiance was not forgotten. Putin was to take barbaric revenge after the start of hostilities of February 24, 2022, subjecting Kharkiv's civilian population to punishing rocket and artillery shelling.

Having captured the city of Sloviansk in north Donetsk, Russian units led by Girkin found themselves surrounded by Ukrainian troops who outnumbered them. In order to cover themselves, the Russian troops used a human shield of Sloviansk residents, as Girkin himself later admitted. This was not an isolated incidence. It was Russian policy handed down by the President. Putin himself said the following in connection with the occupation of Crimea: "Let anyone from among the [Ukrainian] military try to shoot at their own people, behind whom we will be standing. Not in front, but behind. Let them try to shoot women and children." It was Putin himself who urged Russian troops and pro-Russian separatists to use Ukrainian civilians as human shields.

Ukrainian troops overwhelmingly outnumbered Russian troops and equipment by the beginning of July 2014. Curiously, however, their commanders allowed Girkin's Russian military saboteurs to withdraw from Sloviansk, and to fall back and invade regional capital Donetsk in the south, which the Russian forces occupied instead. Those who were part of the "Anti-Terrorist Operation" (ATO), the name the Ukrainian government gave to resisting Russia, claimed that they never received orders to obliterate the Russian troops that withdrew from Sloviansk and moved into Donetsk, even though the Russians used vehicles they had seized from Ukrainians. Given their strategic superiority, Ukraine's air and ground forces could have wiped out Girkin's troops and that might have been the end of the "liberation" of Donbas by Putin. Whether this was stupidity or betrayal remains an unexplained mystery to this day. Yet there were many such instances during the Russian infiltration of Donbas – the area of Luhansk and Donetsk.

In Kyiv, the country's leading politicians were divided among themselves and may either have been unable or unwilling to fight the annexation of Crimea and Russia in Donbas – perhaps fearing the personal consequences of such decisions. Acting President Oleksandr Turchynov, Speaker of the Verkhovna Rada, was advised to appoint General Vitaliy Radetsky as

Defense Minister, a post he had held from 1993-1994 under President Kravchuk. His candidacy was supported by the Head of the SBU, Ihor Smeshko. Turchynov was no stranger to the contradictory currents in Ukraine's national government; he had been the first civilian to head the SBU under Yushchenko.

However, the Acting President stuck to the coalition agreement which stipulated that the Ministry of Defense belonged to the nationalist Freedom Party, which, for its part, nominated its party member Admiral Ihor Tenyukh. Tenyukh claimed that he pleaded several times with Turchynov to allow him to start combatting the Russians in Crimea, but was repeatedly turned down. He served from February 27 to March 25, 2014. and then resigned days after the annexation of Crimea, stating that he could not perform the duties entrusted to him. He was also afraid of being made politically responsible for the loss of Crimea on the one hand and the desultory military response on the other.

Such was the political toxicity of the post that the country's political leadership failed to find a heavy-weight defense minister between March and October 2014. General Mykhailo Koval, previously Deputy Commander of Ukraine's border control, held the post from March 25 to July 3. Valery Heletey was appointed from July 3 to October 14. He was a policeman as well as the former head of security of the newly elected President Petro Poroshenko. During his short tenure, he received the rank of Colonel General and solemnly swore in front of Rada deputies that the next Ukrainian victory parade would be held in Sevastopol.

Finally, as the country's need of professional military leadership grew, a senior expert finally accepted the job. General Stepan Poltorak, who had previously headed the Interior Ministry's National Guard, managed to last five years as minister from October 14, 2014, to August 28, 2019, when the newly-elected President Vladimir Zelensky relieved him from his post.

The revolving-door appointment of defense ministers and their modest professional caliber did not help to boost morale among the Ukrainian military. In 2014, the Ukrainian army itself could hardly be called an exemplary force in any case. It was half-armed and half-trained after twenty five years of peace following the collapse of the USSR and further weakened by Yanukovych's military reforms. Its success in Donbas was based on the heroism of individual Ukrainian army units, which often acted in isolation, without coordination from central military command, and, of course, on the heroism of the volunteer battalions, which bore the brunt of the war in Donbas. To thank as well were the efforts of private Ukrainians themselves, who sacrificed their personal savings to pay for bringing the army back to fighting condition.

Ukraine's political elite had always been more acutely aware than any other nation that Vladimir Putin had been traumatized by the collapse of the USSR, as he himself had repeatedly stated. That under him the strategic objective of the Russian Federation was the restoration of the Russian Empire. That his idea was ideologically draped around the concept of a Russian world where all Russian speaking people are united within a single state, instead of Soviet Communism uniting the world. That Putin never viewed Ukraine as a territory deserving its own statehood or Ukrainian people as an established nation.

Nonetheless, Kyiv had been caught off guard by familiarity. This was not entirely surprising. After EuroMaidan, the Ukrainian oligarchs – or so they thought – would, as before, re-arrange themselves around whomever was the new President to fight for a larger share of Ukraine's economy through Ukraine's ritual abuse of state power. Putin would restart the tug of war with the new President to kick the Association Agreement again into the long grass. Everything would be different but the same. Besides a defensive militarily build-up in eastern Ukraine aimed at Russia could equally provoke Putin – on whom Ukraine relied for gas supplies – as Ukraine's Russian-speaking officials and media in the area which might perceive it as an attempt at intimidation. Nor did Putin have a standing border army poised to suppress Ukraine.

They overlooked that the loss of Yanukovych as Putin's President had created an an alternative. Finally, Putin had the "Georgian" option available in Ukraine, as a result of the seething civil unrest. He could exploit it to occupy border regions where the secret services had their strongest foothold: Crimea (where Russia even had troops on hand at its Crimean navy bases), Luhansk and Donetsk. With minimum effort, these regions could be occupied as "independent" territories as Ukraine's central government was paralyzed by chaos and oligarchs played each other off against one another in a version of financial musical chairs. It was in Russia's interest now to fan the flames.

And that is what happened. When incumbent President Yanukovych signalled he would hand over power to the opposition, Russian special services, supported by their agents in Kyiv, instigated first the shooting of peaceful protesters, then the evacuation of Yanukovych via Crimea to Russia. This had the added advantage that in Russian exile Putin could force Yanukovych to finance Russia's secret-service operations in Donbas from the billions the ex-burglar had accumulated during his Presidency. We established that this is what happened with Yanukovych through two separate sources of Michael Stanchev, co-author of this book.

Despite the power vacuum in Kyiv one thing happened. The danger of the Russian invasion and subversive activity of the Russian operatives and troops inside Ukraine made it impossible to do nothing for long. On March 17, full mobilization of the army was order for the first time in contemporary history. Did Russia foresee this, or, if they did, discount it as irrelevant? They must have. It meant that Ukraine's full military capability, such as it was, became a factor in Putin's move to grab border regions under the cover of separatism.

By this time "separatists" had seized a number of government buildings in Donetsk and Luhansk regions, as well as the cities of Sloviansk, Lyman, Yenakijeve, Mariupol, Horlivka, and several others in order to organize "official" referendums. Unsuccessful attempts to seize government buildings and hoist the Russian flags were also made in Kharkiv, Dnipropetrovsk, and Zaporizhzhia. The confrontation between supporters and opponents of the referendum on secession in Odessa on May 2, 2014 ended in a fire that killed dozens of people (in 2022 the investigation into the tragedy was still ongoing).

The Donetsk and Luhansk People's Republics ("DPR" and "LPR") proclaimed their independence on April 7 and April 28, amid mass unrest from the local population but with the direct support from the Russia Federation. Tellingly, Abkhazia and South Ossetia, the "autonomous republics" occupied by Russian forces invading these formerly Georgian territories in August of 2008, were instructed to recognize their Ukrainian equals. No one in the international community recognized them, except

Lukashenko's Belarus, al-Assad's Syria, and other dictators in Nicaragua, Sudan and Central Africa Republic). In Ukraine, the DPR and LPR were called "so-called republics," which held "so-called referendums", when on May 11 the nominal leaders of these mini-states announced what they claimed were the counts of local plebiscites in favor of secession from Ukraine.

On May 25, 2014, Ukraine's snap Presidential Elections were won by Petro Poroshenko, the one-time rival of Tymoshenko's under the Presidency of Yushchenko. He won 54 percent in the first round against Tymoshenko's 13 percent as runner up. Poroshenko's main election promise was that he would end the stand-off with Russia within two to three weeks of taking office. He had given voice to the hopes of Ukrainians at large that the political and military confrontation would soon end, bringing to an end the civil unrest.

The very next day, on May 26, Ukraine under its new commander in chief, launched its largest "Anti-Terrorist Operation" (ATO) against Russian forces on Ukraine's territory, using airpower and paratroopers. Ukrainian troops forces retook Donetsk Airport, which was held by its fighters, nicknamed "cyborgs" for their resilience, for 240 days.

On June 20, carrying out his election promise in part, Poroshenko did announce a unilateral cease-fire on the part of the Ukrainian armed forces, although there was no real cease-fire, as the "separatists" continued baiting Kyiv with continued shelling, causing casualties among Ukrainian soldiers and civilians. Poroshenko's decision lasted no more than 10 days. The unilateral ceasefire from the Ukrainian side caused mixed reactions among the Ukrainian military and politicians, so on July 1 the ATO-war resumed and two days later Poroshenko appointed his former body guard as Defense Minister. The oligarchy likely had a formidable hand in the resumption of the ATO-war against Russia. Substantial holdings of Rinat Akhmetov's were in Donbas and, as his businesses were now in the DPR and LPR, a different kleptocracy threatened them – the Russian one rather than the Yanukovych family. By 2022, he was worth a "mere" $4 billion, having lost as much as 80 percent of his net worth.

On July 2, Ukrainian troops entered Luhansk, but were forced to leave the city as early as July 6. However, on July 5, Sloviansk, Kramatorsk, and

Artemivsk (since rechristened Bakhmut) were liberated from Russia's forces "defending" the "separatists".

Throughout July and August 2014, there were fierce battles, with varying degrees of success. Cities changed hands. In August, the Russian Federation changed tactics and balled its forces into a fist near Luhansk deploying several battalion-tactical groups of the 76th Pskov Airborne Assault Division's airborne regiments, as well as the 61st Marine Brigade, with the support of tanks, which gave them the upper hand.

On August 29, several Ukrainian volunteer units entered Ilovaisk, south of the city of Donetsk, but met stubborn resistance from Russian-backed forces. When the fighting became widespread, Russian troops intervened directly and, as the Ukrainian soldiers attempted to withdraw from Ilovaisk, they were surrounded by the Russian army. It turned into the Ukrainian army's largest defeat since the start of the ATO-war. One and a half thousand troops were encircled.

Having finally gained a decisive military victory, Russia mobilised a large-scale invasion force of regular Russian army into eastern Ukraine, which allowed them to seize a number of districts in the Donetsk region without local opposition and move close to harbor city Mariupol.

The Minsk Agreements

The defeat became the main reason for the signing of the first Minsk Agreements in a ringing historical echo of Imperial Russia. Meeting on not very neutral territory in Minsk, Belarus, Ukraine was represented by former President Kuchma (who had not yielded in 1999 to KGB plant General Marchuk), Russia by its Ambassador to Ukraine, and, on the LPR and DPR side, by their titular heads Igor Plotnitsky and Alexander Zakharchenko.[208] A cease-fire was agreed on September 5, 2014. According to its protocol, parties agreed to stop hostilities on the same day, as well as to monitoring and verification of the non-use of weapons by the OSCE, who acted as neutral observer to the negotiations.

Russia stipulated that Ukraine pass a law "On Temporary Order of Local Self-Government in Certain Areas of Donetsk and Luhansk Regions" (ORDLO) which devolved power to these areas. The Verkhovna Rada passed it on September 16, 2014. Ukrainian authorities planned to hold elections in Donbas on December 7. The law introduced a special procedure for local self-governance in the occupied areas of Donetsk and Luhansk regions and prevented Ukrainian authorities from prosecuting anyone who had taken joined its forces in the new "autonomous" territories.

ORDLO's wording on national language was carefully balanced. It gave every resident of Donbas the right to determine what language they consider their native language: Ukrainian or Russian (or, technically, any other). However, Ukraine set preconditions: withdrawal of illegal armed units and military equipment from Ukraine; guarantees of freedom of expression of; independent observation of elections, including representatives of international organizations; non-interference in the electoral process; observance of the principles of political pluralism and freedom of political campaigning.

And so the Minsk Agreements never truly led to a ceasefire. The withdrawal of illegal Russian military never took place and the ceasefire was repeatedly violated by both sides. Ukraine as the violated party was interested in adhering to the agreements in good faith, but Russia, the aggressor, had no real intention of giving up its campaign of provocation. As before, the foreign "separatists" stationed in Donbas constantly taunted the Ukrainian side, remaining a constant source of irritation with shelling and, when Ukraine responded, planted a seed among the Donbas civilian population that Ukraine was literally acting against them. The only clause in the agreement that was periodically implemented was the prisoners' exchange, although this was never "all for all" principle. Neither did the Minsk Agreements succeed in adopting a program for the economic revival of Donbas and the restoration of the region's commerce. Nor was there any dialogue about the future of Donbas.

None of this mattered to Russia. Putin's real objective was to use his victory to suppress any discussion of Crimea under the agreements. In this he succeeded and as of 5 September, the Annexation of Crimea to the Russian Federation was a *fait accompli* through its exclusion from the endlessly spun-out talks in Minsk.

At a February 2015 summit, Germany and France joined the negotiations and a new set of measures to implement the Minsk Agreement were agreed in order to de-escalate the conflict. These documents were approved by a special UN resolution of February 17, 2015, which, although advisory in nature, urged the parties to implement them (and implicitly sanctioned the status quo by accepting the silence on Crimea).

Known as Minsk-2, it was once again signed by the three sides. As new points, it included an immediate and comprehensive ceasefire from 00.00. (Kyiv time) on February 15, 2015; the detailed withdrawal by both sides within 14 days of all heavy weapons to an equal distance from the line of contact to create a 50 km wide security zone; for artillery systems of 100 mm caliber and above to create a 70 km wide security zone; for multiple launch rocket systems Tornado-S, Uragan, Smerch and tactical missile systems Tochka (Tochka U), a 140 km wide zone. All this was to be monitored by the OSCE mission using its trusted capabilities.

Point 4 of the agreement was the real bone of contention: to begin a dialogue on the procedure for local elections in accordance with ORDLO and future governance of the DPR and LPR. The Ukrainian side insisted on holding these elections after the withdrawal of "foreign" (Russian) and other illegal military combatants from the territory of Ukraine. Kyiv undertook obligations to restore social and economic relations with the territories occupied by separatists, including payment of pensions and other payments to the population of these areas, and resumed taxation there within the legal framework of Ukraine.

Kyiv also insisted on the restoration of full control of the state border of Ukraine throughout the conflict zone by the Ukrainian border guards. Border control was to begin on the first day after local elections in certain areas of the Donetsk and Luhansk regions and end after a comprehensive political settlement of the conflict by the end of 2015. Ukraine considered the "state border" to be the existing administrative Ukrainian-Russian border, which had been delimited and demarcated earlier, before the occupation of Donbas, while the Russian side considered the line of contact in the conflict zone as the state border. The Ukrainian side agreed to hold elections under ORDLO only after full control was established over the entire territory within the old administrative boundaries, which the Russian side categorically did not agree to.

Russia wanted further concessions under its continuing aggression. The

OSCE was not given access to the DPR and LPR so it could not verify what was happening on the occupied territories after the agreement. Also Minsk-2 contained a paragraph that stated: "the constitutional reform in Ukraine and the entry into force by the end of 2015 of the new Constitution", involving as a key element the decentralization of the state structure of Ukraine, i.e., the actual recognition of the autonomy of the DPR and LPR, and the passing into law of ORDLO.

Of course, conducting constitutional reform and adopting a new constitution was an internal matter of Ukraine. However, under pressure of the defeat at Ilovaisk, President Poroshenko felt forced to agree to the inclusion of these points into the Second Minsk Agreement, not understanding that by doing this he made the entire set of agreements Minsk-2 unimplementable. Now Moscow had the right to demand fulfillment of Minsk-2, signed by Poroshenko, while accusing Ukraine of failing to comply with its obligations under the agreements.

Poroshenko did understand perfectly well that behind all this was Russia's attempt to interfere in the internal affairs of the Ukrainian state; Russia's desire to maintain pro-Russian armed forces under the guise of local militia; and Russia's intention to determine the appointment of prosecutors and judges loyal to the DPR, LPR and Russian authorities, while maintaining Donbas at the expense of the Ukrainian taxpayer.

On 20 February 2015, the anniversary of the EuroMaidan heroes, Poroshenko made a bombshell claim during a meeting with relatives of the dead. The background to his official statement was that, on January 24, 2014, his predecessor Yanukovych had appointed a new Chief of Staff, Andriy Klyuyev. As described above, in 2004 Klyuyev was an energy minister under Yanukovych as Prime Minister and captured on tape discussing the logistics of a covert operation that was a carbon copy of the second assassination attempt on Orange Revolution leaders Viktor Yushchenko and Yulia Tymoshenko following the poisoning of the former. Klyuyev enjoyed a first-hand working relationship with Vladislav Surkov, Putin's Special Advisor on Ukraine as well as Abkhazia and South Ossetia, the two regions that had declared "breakaway independence" from Georgia after being occupied by Russian forces. Surkov had arrived in Kyiv on 20 February 2014, the day of the mass killing of The Hundred civilians and officers.

Rus kills

At the commemoration, President Poroshenko said, "The leadership of the Security Service of Ukraine informed me that [SBU anti-terrorist] Alpha fighters interrogated by the agency testified that Russian Presidential Aide Vladislav Surkov directed the organization of a group of foreign snipers on the Maidan." There were also on-going phone conversations between Yanukovych and the Russian security services that the SBU had intercepted.

The Head of the SBU, Valentyn Nalyvaichenko confirmed the evidence that Putin's Ukrainian point man Surkov was behind the slaughter and that three groups of Russian secret-service agents had arrived in Kyiv from December 2013 to February 2014, ostensibly to educate Ukrainian law enforcement on the dispersal of mass demonstrations. Nalyvaichenko identified his sources, saying his SBU officers "gave us concrete information [under interrogation] about the positions of foreign sniper groups that were targeting both protesters... and Interior Ministry police officers."

A week later, on Russia's state Channel One, Vladimir Putin personally responded to the accusation. Pleading that the order could not have come from him, Putin called it "complete, utter nonsense," and that it was "so far from reality that I have no idea where it would come from." He added, "I would ask [others] to be more attentive when using data acquired by my Ukrainian colleagues".

West appeases

Instead, however, of giving Ukraine support, the West and the US looked the other way as had happened with Georgia in 2008. Ukraine was being isolated in one of the most costly mistakes in foreign affairs made in the twentieth first century.

In order to appease Russia, the West and the US put pressure on Ukraine, demanding with Russia that Ukraine stick to the Minsk Agreements, even though realizing that Russia, for its part, had no intention of doing so. This misguided and short-sighted policy could not lead to an end to violence, but only made further expansion of Russia's territory and escalation of violence a matter of time. In history, lessons are learned the hard way.

After the traumatic experience of Crimea's annexation and the ATO against covert Russian forces, under Petro Poroshenko first real steps were finally made to align Ukraine's military with NATO standards and bring the army under control of civil leadership. Poroshenko set this in motion alongside a massive (for Ukraine) investment to upgrade military equipment.

President Zelensky developed this policy further by identifying Russia as a security threat to Ukraine and refining interoperability with EU and NATO forces. Whether it was enough, or too little too late, lies in the balance after the invasion.

Having executed the Georgian option for Ukraine, Putin dropped his facade. The Kremlin no longer called Ukraine a brother nation while twisting arms behind the scenes to stop its leaders from joining NATO or embarking on a path towards membership of the EU and extorting it otherwise. Having tried for decades to control Ukraine's Presidency behind the scenes, Putin had succeeded in preventing Ukraine from turning – like 1990s-run-down Poland had – into a formidable economy of 40 million-people and a military gorilla on its doorstep. But he had failed in his main objective – this was Putin's "Ukraine complex" – and the gloves remained off.

Using round-the-clock propaganda channels that monopolize the Russian media, Putin's government continued to shape an image of Ukraine in Russia as its enemy threatening the independence and security of the Russian state. Ukrainians who were active in the Maidan were denigrated as "Banderites". At the same time, Ukrainian leaders and military officers were depicted as Nazis to insinuate that they had gained illegal control, and the new territories he wanted were referred to as Novorossiya. None of it made historical sense, but that didn't matter. Through "substitution of ideas", Putin created a narrative that identified Russia as the savior of the peaceful Russian-speaking people living in Ukraine who were being suppressed by evil actors.

This now served as the informational and ideological basis on which the Kremlin's military strategy against Ukraine was built. Putin himself joined the misinformation war aimed at Russians. In speeches and "historical articles"[209] he claimed that Russians and Ukrainians were "one people" with "one faith," discounting the existence of Ukraine as a state equal in independence and sovereignty. An important element in the confrontation between Russia and Ukraine were the economic, and trade wars between the two countries. To justify his aggression, Putin used the "recognition of the legal status of Crimea" on the one hand and Ukraine's cooperation with NATO on the other. The latter allegedly threatened Russia's security and the status of the Russian language in Ukraine.

Later, prior to the invasion of Donbas, those arguments were supplemented by the "threat from NATO" in case Ukraine was accepted into its ranks, arming the Ukrainian army and "strengthening Nazism" that "threatened the security" and even the "territorial integrity" of the Russian Federation. They were all things, of course, which his annexation of Crimea and "separatist" campaign in Ukraine's Donbas had intentionally accelerated. As he had already created a territorial dispute, there was no chance that NATO, a defensive alliance, would invite Ukraine as a member.

Over eight years the Kremlin had poisoned Russian minds towards Ukrainians suggesting that Ukraine's Russian-speaking citizens cried out for a patriotic battle to save them. On February 21, 2022, the exact day on which Yanukovych "surrendered" (according to Putin) his Presidency in 2014, and four days before attacking Ukraine, Russia fired the starting shot. Its Duma officially recognized the sovereignty of the Donetsk and Luhansk People's Republics from Ukraine, ignoring forceful protests from Ukraine's President Zelensky. This recognition occurred against the backdrop of an unprecedented concentration of Russian troops along the Russian-Ukrainian and Belarusian-Ukrainian borders, and it became apparent that his army was ready to attack as we had predicted. The day after the "Defender of the Fatherland Day" concert at the Kremlin Palace, on February 24, 2022, Putin addressed the Russian people and announced the start of a "special military operation" against Ukraine and that it was already on its way.

16

Do Russians Want War?

In 1961, a Russian pop song asked, "Do Russians Want War?" The rhetorical answer was supposed to be "No!" after hearing the lyrics which reminded the listener of the losses during "The Great Patriotic War" (World War II), Russian women, and Elbe Day when Soviet and American troops met amicably in 1945. It was performed in Italy, Belgium, France, Switzerland and in the UK in the Royal Albert Hall.

Generalizations are always risky. Nonetheless, we cannot avoid making generalizations in this book. Do Russians want war? With the caveat that not all Russians want war, and that in fact many Russians do not want war, we must recognize the fact tha the situation in Russia was one in which the majority of Russians agreed to support their government as it embarked on the road to a major war. Russians (a majority of them), discovered that they wanted to be feared – unexpectedly for Europe, and unexpectedly for themselves, too – just as Soviet soldiers had always been feared in Europe. The invasion of Ukraine 2022 was a logical next step.

Lessons from WWI and WWII Putin never learned

After the First World War ended and the conditions of the peace agreement were being discussed, American President Woodrow Wilson proposed quite lenient terms of surrender for Germany. But France and, to a somewhat lesser degree, Britain categorically insisted on (and obtained) very severe terms, which guaranteed, as it seemed to everyone at the time, that Germany would never be able to recover economically and to become the cause of a new war in Europe. That is how the Treaty of Versailles came about in the form in which we know it. Years will pass. Volumes will be written about the fact that the Second World War began precisely because of the Treaty of Versailles, which was humiliating for Germany, and because of the unrestrained appetite of France, which sought to prevent the revival of Germany at any cost. In many respects, the authors of these books were likely right.

So, the first reason for Hitler's rise to power in Germany was the Treaty of Versailles, which humiliated Germany and paved the way for the rise of nationalism and the ascent of the National Socialists. The second reason was an unshakeable conviction on the part of the right-wing, conservative part of the German population and the army that Germany had lost the war because of a "stab in the back" – such was the term that appeared in Germany at the time, and this stab in the back of the German army had come from revolutionaries: Communists. The supporters of this view were right in some respects. The revolutionary uprisings in Germany in the fall of 1918, which brought about the German "November Revolution," certainly weakened the positions of the German army and government, which, by the end of 1918, were already not very strong.

It should be added here that Germany's Social Democrats had drawn lessons from the history of the Russian Revolution of 1917. While in Russia the Social Democrats – the Mensheviks and the Socialist Revolutionaries – united with the Bolsheviks to oppose a "counter-revolution" that was largely a figment of their own imagination and gave up power to the Bolsheviks as a result, in Germany the Social Democrats joined with the army, i.e. with the counter-revolution, and squashed the Spartacists-Communists. As a consequence, it was the German Social Democrats who came to power in Germany on the wave of the crushed revolution of 1918 and not the Communists.

It was a difficult lot that fell to the democratic governments of the Weimar Republic of 1919-1932 (because of the lost war and its consequences, and because of the unfulfillable financial-economic terms of the Treaty of Versailles). As a result – with Germany enjoying absolute freedom of the press throughout the 1920s – German democracy turned out to be compromised by the Social Democrats themselves, to whom the population and media, ascribed responsibility for all economic ills.

But the most important reason for the Nazis' rise to power was a third one: the nationalist question. In the case of Germany, this issue may be divided into two strands: first, the rebirth of the German nation, the unification of all Germans within the borders of a single empire; and second, the fight against world Jewry, above all with Jews in Germany. When the Nazis, to fuel the flames of anti-Semitism, pointed to the "stranglehold" of Jews on Germany and Austria, they found enough arguments to make their case. The intellectual elite of Germany and Austria (doctors, lawyers, financiers, businessmen, the creative intelligentsia) to a very large extent consisted of Jews.

There were also ancillary reasons that facilitated the Nazis' ascent. In the Comintern (the international organization run by the CPSU), Stalin had proclaimed the German Social Democrats to be the main ideological enemy of the international Communist movement.

One should consider this fact carefully. The German Social Democrats in the Weimar Republic were teetering under the burden of the financial-economic conditions of the Treaty of Versailles. It might seem that it would have been natural for the Soviet Union to support this weak democratic government in view of the new, growing threat of extreme nationalism in Germany – a threat, incidentally, that was not merely theoretical, but quite real. In Italy, the fascists had already come to power. Thus, grounds to see fascism as a real threat existed. According to the Communist dogmas of Marx and Lenin, furthermore, Nationalism was the sworn enemy of international Communism.

Nonetheless, Stalin forced the German Communists to unite with the Nazis in opposing Germany's Social Democratic government. If the Communists had supported the Social Democrats, they would have had a majority in the Reichstag (the German parliament), and Hitler would have never been able to come to power, because he came to power not as the result of a revolution or coup, but legally. But Stalin gave the German Communists exactly the opposite instructions: they had to use all their power to support the Nazis and, together with them, to come out against

Germany's Social Democratic government.

Stalin's strategy with respect to the revolution in Germany differed both from the straightforward approach of Marx and Trotsky, who expected the German working class to rise up, and from the anti-French plans of Lenin, who sought to push the Germans to create a "front on the Rhein." Stalin wanted to destroy all centrist political groups and to leave Nazism and Bolshevism as opposing forces. He rightly believed that the main power of the world revolution was the USSR, and that the other international Communist parties played an auxiliary role.

Within the framework of such a program, during the period 1929-1939, all efforts of Soviet foreign policy and the Comintern with respect to Germany were aimed at undermining the Weimar Republic, directly supporting the Nazis' strikes, and fomenting armed conflicts with the Republic. According to Stalin's thinking, Hitler in Germany, and in Europe as a whole, had to play the role of the "icebreaker of the revolution," clearing the way for the Communists. Therefore, from 1933 on, Stalin's goal was to form an alliance with the German militarists and Hitler, and the strategy of a "united front" in Europe in 1934-1939 was for Stalin merely a cover for a policy of preparing an agreement with the Nazis.

If Stalin had planned to form an alliance with Britain and France against Germany, he would have conducted open talks with Germany and secret talks with France and Britain. But Stalin wanted to form an agreement precisely with Hitler. Therefore, he conducted open talks with Britain and France, and secret ones with the Nazi government. This was the background against which Europe was shaken by a blow that historians would later compare only with the beginning of the Second World War: the Munich Agreement.

The Munich Agreement was signed by France and Britain in order to prevent a war. This was a last, desperate attempt by France and Britain, who sacrificed Czechoslovakia, to appease Hitler and to preserve peace in Europe. By 1938, the situation that had developed in Europe was catastrophic for the Western democracies. Mussolini was in power in Italy, Hitler in Germany, Franco in Spain. Austria no longer existed: as a result of the "Anschluss," it had become a part of the German empire. In Portugal and Hungary dictators were in power.

Formally, there was a treaty between France, Czechoslovakia, and the USSR. In the event of a German attack on Czechoslovakia, the Czechoslovak government could request military assistance from France and the USSR. And all Soviet history books describe in detail exactly how the Soviet Union was prepared to offer this assistance, how many divisions the USSR had, how many airplanes and tanks stood at the ready...

But in September 1938, no one wanted and no one was prepared to go to war over Czechoslovakia: not France, not Britain, not the Soviet Union, not even Czechoslovakia itself. Edvard Beneš, the President of Czechoslovakia, did in fact send Stalin a telegram at the critical moment, formally requesting that the Soviet Union offer such assistance under the treaty. But Beneš did not receive a response to this telegram in time. The Soviet government delayed its response. Soon, Beneš sent another telegram informing Stalin that Czechoslovakia had accepted the terms of surrender and was no longer seeking military assistance from the Red Army.

It is clear that the Soviet government had no intention of going to war with Hitler over Czechoslovakia at that time. Stalin had entered into talks about military assistance for Czechoslovakia exclusively in order to obtain Poland's permission for access to the Czechoslovak border. The occupation of Poland was Stalin's obsession after losing against Poland in 1920. Stalin's anti-Polish complex comes close only to Hitler's virulent anti-Semitic complex and Putin's Ukraine complex. The Poles understood Stalin's hatred well and did not grant permission to Soviet troops to pass through Poland, since it was obvious to the Poles that once the Red Army entered Poland, it would never leave. This was a lesson drawn from the history of Russian-Polish relations. France, Britain, Czechoslovakia, and the Soviet Union exerted pressure on the Poles, but the Poles refused to allow Soviet troops to enter.[210] The brutality of 22,000 Polish officers massacred in cold blood by Soviet troops a few years later proved them right. (In 2022, the reports of criminal barbarity against Ukrainian civilians by Russian soldiers is a direct consequence of Putin's Ukraine obsession.

The Soviet Union did not, in fact, have a border with Germany, France, or Czechoslovakia. But why were France and Britain – which throughout the 1920s had insisted on the observance of the terms of the Treaty of Versailles – not prepared to declare war against Hitler in 1938 in response to he Nazis' demand that Germany be given the Sudetenland, a part of Czechoslovakia that was populated largely by ethnic Germans? Why was it necessary to agree to a "partition" of Czechoslovakia?

First and foremost, because Britain and France were not prepared to appear as aggressors, as we would say today, before their voters. Europe was not ready to start the Second World War in 1938 over Sudetenland Germans, that is ethnic Germans who lived in Czechoslovakia and wished to be annexed to Germany. Nor, indeed, was Europe ready to start a war over Hitler's occupation of the remaining part of Czechoslovakia in March 1939. Why go to war when Czechoslovakia itself was surrendering without resistance?

This is the point at which we should go back to Stalin's foreign policy plans and to the man he thought of as the "icebreaker of the revolution," Hitler. In March 1939, Hitler was not risking a major war. He knew that no one would start a major war over Czechoslovakia. Indeed, he no longer believed in a major war at all. With the occupation of Czechoslovakia in March 1939, he had resolved all of the foreign policy problems that the Reich faced. That is to say, all but one: the destruction of European and world Jewry. Ethnic Germans were united within the borders of the empire. Germany's economy was on the rise. Over time the terms of the Treaty of Versailles had ceased to exist (Hitler had simply stopped adhering to them). The property of German Jews had been confiscated. They themselves had been deprived of all rights, banished from the Reich, or arrested and sent to camps.

It was at this moment, when Hitler had obtained everything he wanted for Germany, with little foreign blood spilled, that Stalin invited him to the negotiating table. This invitation was both unambiguous and symbolic. On May 3, 1939, Vyacheslav Molotov, the head of the Sovnarkom (the USSR's government) and a Russian by nationality, replaced Maxim Litvinov – a Jew, with whom Hitler would have never sat down at the negotiating table due to his visceral anti-Semitism – as the People's Commissar for Foreign Affairs.

The replacement of Litvinov, a Jew, with Molotov, a Russian, was a signal sent by Stalin to indicate his readiness to begin serious talks with the German government. This signal was understood, the invitation was accepted. Hitler, of course, knew about Stalin's Polish obsession and the Soviet government's endless demands that the Poles give the Red Army access to pass through Polish territory. Hitler knew that Stalin wanted Poland. Therefore, Hitler could not attack Poland without first reaching an agreement with Stalin concerning the division of Polish territory.

The upshot for Poland of the pact that Hitler and Stalin formed in August 1939 was that Soviet and German troops would simultaneously attack Poland's borders and erase the Polish state. Germany would again avoid a major war since, with the USSR taking part in the division of Poland, France and Britain would not risk fulfilling the terms of their mutual assistance agreement with Poland, and would not come to Poland's help. Instead, they would follow the Czechoslovak precedent.

In August 1939, when after the occupation of Czechoslovakia in March 1939 it seemed to Europe that there might be no major war with Hitler, Stalin unleashed the Second World War. The fact was that Stalin knew very well why he was signing a Soviet-German non-aggression pact with Hitler, along with a secret protocol that stipulated which countries would fall under the USSR's sphere of influence.

By August 1939, the Soviet government had a choice. Stalin could have signed a mutual assistance agreement with France and Britain. In keeping with such an agreement, if Germany attacked France – and this was the only great power that Germany could attack, since it had no borders with Britain or the USSR – the USSR and Britain would have to come to France's aid. Without Poland's permission for the Red Army to pass through Polish territory, the Soviet Union realistically could not in any way help France and Britain.

To be sure, the Soviet Union could have maintained amicable neutrality. But this was all that Stalin could have done. The signing of such a mutual assistance agreement between the USSR, France, and Britain would have resulted in Hitler not attacking either France or Poland. Because given the existence of such an agreement between France and the Soviet Union, Stalin would have had to declare war on Germany. This was not a risk that Hitler could take in August-September 1939.

Stalin risked drawing the Soviet Union into a war with Hitler's Germany as early as September 1939, which would have been undesirable. Therefore Stalin had a different plan for his foreign policy. A completely secure plan

He could sign no agreement with France and Britain and he could sign no agreement with Hitler. In this case, September 1939 would have looked somewhat better for Hitler.

In the first scenario, the Soviet Union would find itself in a state of war with Germany if Hitler attacked Poland and France. In the second scenario, the Soviet Union would remain neutral. Then Hitler would have had to occupy all of Poland and come up to the Soviet borders of August 1939, which would have created for Hitler the risk of new military conflicts, this time with the Red Army, and the beginning of a war on two fronts. It was difficult to imagine that Stalin's Soviet Union and Hitler's Germany – two aggressive states headed by capricious, paranoid dictators – could coexist in peace for long. To avoid sharing a border with the USSR, Hitler could occupy only western Poland and turn eastern Poland into a buffer zone. How long such a "buffer" state might last was not clear. But at least, both in the event of the appearance of a shared border with Germany, and in the event of the creation of a buffer zone in eastern Poland, the Soviet Union could for some time not take part in the big European war and watch from the side as Hitler crushed the rest of Europe.

Of course, the main risk for Stalin was that Hitler might not begin a major war in Europe at all. In September 1939, as far as Poland was concerned, he might limit himself only to solving the "Danzig problem." The "Danzig problem" consisted of the fact that the region around Danzig was populated by ethnic Germans. Hitler sought to reunite them with Germany. This required not only the transfer of Danzig to Germany, but also the creation of a German-national road – called the "Danzig corridor" – to connect Danzig with the rest of Germany.

Obviously, in order for these Polish territories to be transferred to Germany, it was necessary to obtain Poland's consent. But Hitler had already obtained a successful outcome in Munich, and he planned to play out the same scenario with Danzig as he had with the Sudetenland and its population of ethnic Germans: first, to threaten France, Britain, and Poland with the possibility of a major war and to use this threat to obtain Danzig and the corridor; and then, to accuse the Poles of failing to comply with certain terms of the agreement, to enter Poland on the pretext of defending the interests of ethnic Germans in Poland, and to occupy western Poland.

Ultimately, Poland would have still had "its" September 1939, but it would have come not in September 1939, but later, say, in 1940-41.

Hitler was planning on occupying western Poland without a major war. After all, didn't Britain, France, and the Soviet Union allow him to occupy Czechoslovakia in 1939? Why should Poland be any different?

Why then, with such a plan, did Hitler still need a non-aggression pact with Stalin?

Hitler feared that Stalin, despite not having any mutual assistance treaty with France, would enter the war, cross the border of Poland (with or without the Poles' consent), and open up an eastern front against the German army. Such a scenario would have been extremely disadvantageous and dangerous for Hitler. Consequently, Hitler could not undertake such an enormous risk in September 1939. Without signing a non-aggression pact with Stalin, Hitler could not begin a war against Poland. Hitler could begin such a war only if Stalin, for his part, would promise not to support France and Britain and not to open a second, eastern front against Germany. For Hitler, it was absolutely imperative to have a non-aggression agreement with the Soviet Union prior to beginning offensive action against Poland.

Clearly, the price for an agreement that was so advantageous and indispensable to Hitler was Germany's consent to allow the Soviet Union to occupy a number of eastern European countries. On August 20, 1939, hurrying to resolve the Polish question, Hitler wrote a letter to Stalin in which he unequivocally stated that he planned to attack Poland and was therefore interested in signing a non-aggression agreement as soon as possible. Hitler asked Stalin for permission to send Ribbentrop to Moscow at once in order to sign a non-aggression pact and a secret protocol detailing the division of spheres of influence in eastern Europe. Stalin agreed.

For all the drawbacks of the Munich agreement of 1938, and despite the validity of all the epithets that we now bestow on this agreement when we call it "cowardly", "treacherous", and so on, the Munich agreement was signed by Britain and France in order to preserve peace, while the Soviet-German treaty was signed by Hitler and Stalin in order to begin a war. This was why Hitler was in a hurry. And it was in order to help Hitler to start a war in Europe more quickly that Stalin agreed to receive Ribbentrop in Moscow at once.

On August 23, Ribbentrop flew to Moscow. The Soviet-German non-aggression agreement and secret additional protocol were signed on the same day. In essence, the protocol gave Russia the Baltic States, eastern Poland, Finland, and Bessarabia (today Moldova and west Ukraine). Hitler did not ask Stalin to agree, for example, to the German occupation of France, Belgium, the Netherlands, and other European states. Hitler needed Stalin to agree only to war with Poland. Even during this period, Hitler still assumed he was avoiding a major war. He discussed this topic with Mussolini during a meeting on April 15-16, 1939, shortly after the occupation of Czechoslovakia. That was when the heads of the two states agreed on a date for the start of a major war: not before 1943. It was still August 1939.

On August 31, Molotov made a long foreign policy speech before the Supreme Soviet of the USSR. On September 1, the day when Germany invaded Poland, this speech was published in *Pravda*. The gist of the speech was that yesterday fascist Germany had been an enemy; today, it is a friend.

Stalin could have stopped the Second World War. All that he would have had to do was to sign a mutual assistance pact with France and Britain and to renounce his own plans to take over Poland or eastern Poland. Stalin would have had to do nothing more to prevent Hitler's further aggression and a major war in Europe. But Stalin had the opposite objectives: to unleash the Second World War, to force Hitler to get involved in a major war, to use this Trojan Horse to ride into Europe, both East and West, and to conquer it. And the unsuspecting Hitler fell into the trap set by Stalin. On September 1, he attacked Poland. On September 3, during the day, first Britain and then France declared war on Germany.

On the evening of September 3, the German government sent its first urgent classified telegram to Moscow with the request that Russia start military actions against Poland as soon as possible. Why?

First, the Germans were suffering losses. Of course, these losses, as it later turned out, were immeasurably small in comparison to those of the Polish army, but all the same, for the first time in the whole history of Hitler's aggression in Europe, the Germans were suffering losses, numbering in the thousands. Second, it was important to the Germans to prevent a situation in which the Polish army could retreat to the east, into the Soviet sphere of influence, which the Germans could not enter under the terms of the non-aggression agreement with the USSR. Third, Hitler wanted to demonstrate to Poland, and to Britain and France, that Stalin in this war was an ally of Germany, not an ally of democratic Europe.

There is another consideration that is of great importance. If Stalin had attacked Poland on September 1 or 2, it is possible that Britain and France might not have declared war on Germany at all, but that they would have done the same as with Czechoslovakia. However, this would have meant that no major war would have begun in Europe. Germany and the USSR would have reached a shared border in Poland, which they now both occupied.

It is clear that, under those circumstances, the next major war would have been a Soviet-German war, not the Second World War. Therefore, Stalin did what he did. He waited for Germany to attack Poland. This was his first move. He waited for France and Britain to declare war on Germany. This was his second move. He waited for the German government twice to send him urgent requests to attack Poland. And only after the second request did he graciously agree to begin military actions.

On September 3, 1939, the world did not yet understand what the Second World War was going to be and how it would unfold. The First World War was well remembered by everyone. It had ended only 20 years earlier, and most of the survivors of that war were still living. Those who had been 30 years old in 1918 were 51 in 1939.

During the First World War, Great Britain lost about one million people; France lost 1.7 million. France's losses were catastrophic, and France was in no state to win a second time at such a cost. The history of the Second World War showed that France was ready to surrender, but not to fight. In 1939, France had only one goal: not to lose people in a new war. This goal was realized successfully, in part. During the Second World War, the French lost fewer lives than in the First: approximately 568,000 people or 1.35 percent of the population (as opposed to 4.3 percent in the First World War).

Britain was in a far better position. Britain was an island, inaccessible for Germany. France knew that it could not and would not fight Germany alone, therefore it waited for Britain to declare war on Germany first before declaring war itself. Britain declared war on Germany in the first half of the day on September 3. France declared war in the second half of the same day.

But Britain, although it had declared war, also had no intention of starting a war. It, too, did aim to bring another nation to heel without regard to the human cost to its population. And in fact, in this sense Great Britain achieved its goal. It lost half as many lives in the Second World War as in the First: approximately 450,000 people.

By the evening of September 3, 1939, staggering possibilities opened up before Stalin. He could simply do nothing, as in August, and not invade eastern Poland. In this case, he would leave Hitler one-on-one with the Poles, the French, and the British. Of course, knowing what we know now about Hitler's barbaric plans with respect to all mankind, this would have been ignoble on Stalin's part, but in terms of the interests of the Soviet state and even in terms of Stalin's personal foreign policy plans, such a solution might have been advantageous. Hitler would have had to fight with Poland. Many thousands of Germans would have been killed. A military campaign against Poland would have taken some time. France would not have been able to watch the extermination of the Poles for long without beginning military actions against Germany. After this, Britain would have also been forced to intervene to the extent of its capacities. To be sure, at that point Britain's capacities were limited, since it had no land army for an invasion, while its air force was in an embryonic state. But on the seas, the British navy reigned supreme. This was not insignificant.

If we do not idealize Stalin but consider him an evildoer worthy of Hitler, then we can see that a non-interventionist approach described above would have also led to an outcome that was advantageous for the USSR. Stalin would be pulling Europe into the Second World War, i.e. realizing his insidious plan of the "icebreaker of the revolution." He would obtain everything except eastern Poland, since he risked having the Germans occupy it out of military necessity. Once they had taken over the territory of eastern Poland, the Germans might not leave it again, and the new Soviet-German border would now lie along the old Soviet-Polish border of 1939. The price for such a possible – only possible, not inevitable – relinquishment of eastern Poland to Germany was that the Soviet Union would not participate in Hitler's German campaign and that it would preserve its military neutrality in the war that would begin in Europe.

There were also other options. Stalin could have argued that the declaration of war by France and Britain against Germany changed the international conditions under which the non-aggression pact between Germany and the Soviet Union had been signed, and that the Soviet government was annulling this agreement along with its secret protocol. Naturally, Hitler would have been forced to regard such a move as hostile with respect to Germany, with all the attendant consequences. Such a claim would have meant that, already in 1939, the Soviet Union would enter the world war on the side of Poland, Britain, and France. But the same claim might have forced Hitler to renounce his plans to occupy all of Poland, or just western Poland, and to seek an opportunity to settle the conflict that had begun as soon as possible, for example, with Italy acting as an intermediary. In other words, Stalin might have prevented the Second World War even after September 3, 1939.

But Stalin had no plans of stopping the German invasion of Poland and putting out the fire of the Second World War which had only just begun to spread. On September 5, 1939, in response to Ribbentrop's query, Stalin confirmed that he was reserving the right to eastern Poland, but that he would not attack it as yet, even if the Germans might sporadically cross over into the Soviet sphere of influence for a short while.

Why did Stalin make this particular decision? First, in the event of a Soviet invasion of Poland and a rapid Soviet-German occupation of this country, the Second World War might have ended as quickly as it had begun and been limited to the disappearance of Poland from the map. This was, in fact, what Hitler had counted on. Second, Stalin made the decision not to attack Poland at once so that the Poles might resist the Germans longer and better, and consequently, so that they might suffer greater losses. The longer the Poles fought the Germans, the weaker would be their resistance to Soviet aggression. Third, if Poland had been already swallowed up by the USSR and Germany during the first days of September, would it have been worth starting a major war over this *fait accompli*? Finally, Stalin was in no hurry to enter a war, but wanted to allow the Germans, too, to suffer the greatest possible losses in Europe and to get drawn into a world war as part of Stalin's overall strategy of transforming Germany into the "icebreaker of the revolution."

Stalin planned to start an advance into eastern Poland only after German troops captured Warsaw. At that point, the Soviet government would declare that Poland – that "monstrous offspring of the Treaty of Versailles," as Poland would be called in a speech by Molotov – had collapsed, and that the Red Army was entering Poland to "defend the Ukrainians and Belarusians" who lived there. On September 14, Molotov demanded that the Germans capture Warsaw as a precondition for the Red Army to begin military actions against Poland.

But there was one delicate point: the threat that Germany, having captured Warsaw and western Poland, would agree to a truce with the Polish government. Then the old problem would once again rear its head: the threat that the Second World War would fizzle out before becoming a major war. Therefore, on September 10, the Soviet government informed Berlin that it would begin military actions against Poland if the Germans, for their part, promised not to form a truce with the Poles. On September 13, Ribbentrop assured Stalin that "the issue of the need to form a truce with Poland" was "not being considered" by the German government.

In September 1939, Hitler hoped that the fuse of war would quietly smolder until he himself was ready for new, active, offensive operations in the west. This hope of Hitler's obtained fully. France and Britain were not ready – either militarily, or politically, or psychologically – to start a major war over Poland. They were prepared to declare war, but not to fight one. Stalin hoped that both sides would get bogged down in a war in the west and that the Soviet Union would meanwhile be able to achieve its foreign policy objectives within the framework of its secret protocol with Germany. This calculation also proved correct. The French and British governments expected that, following the occupation of Poland, Hitler's next aggressive move would be an eastern campaign, not a western one. This hope came true, although with a time lag of almost two years, on June 22, 1941.

In this way, the foreign policy predictions of all of the great European powers came true. But the situation that emerged from the realization of these predictions, which politicians in each country regarded as most advantageous to their side, turned out to be disadvantageous in the extreme for each of its participants.

We will say no more about Poland, which was sacrificed under these calculations. Poland simply ceased to exist. France and Britain, seeking to delay their entrance into the war for as long as possible and hoping to gain time, consequently gave Germany and Italy a temporal advantage in preparing for a serious military campaign in 1939-1941, against all of democratic Europe.

From a military point of view, the operations conducted by the German army between September 1939 and the summer of 1941 should be considered brilliant. By the summer of 1941, continental Europe was entirely captured by Germany and the Soviet Union. For its protection, the British Empire could count only on its navy and on the steep coast of the English Channel. It had no forces that could put up an active resistance on land.

In this whole scheme, Hitler and Stalin made only one geopolitical misstep, which at the same time became Britain's only success: in the course of the military operations, a shared border was created in Europe between the German empire and the Soviet Union. Now Hitler confronted the problem that he needed to have foreseen and avoided, because it inevitably led to a military collision between two states, two regimes, two dictatorships.

In November 1940, Molotov arrived in Berlin for a new round of talks. The talks were difficult. Molotov demanded that Germany agree to let the Soviet Union take over Finland (which had successfully defended its independence during the winter war of 1939-1940); to occupy Bulgaria, to "establish a base for the land and naval forces of the USSR in the Mediterranean region of the Bosphorus and the Dardanelles on the basis of a long-term lease"; and even to launch a joint Soviet-Italian war against Turkey, under certain conditions. In addition, the Soviet government insisted that Hitler's Axis-partner Japan give up its oil and coal concessions to the north of Sakhalin, the island wedged between Japan and the USSR.

In response, Hitler proposed that the Soviet Union join the Tripartite Pact between Germany, Italy, and Japan, formed in Berlin on September 27, 1940. The Germans drafted an agreement between the Tripartite Pact states and the USSR. It included two secret protocols with a long list of the aggressive intentions of the USSR and Germany. In particular, Hitler agreed that the "main territorial interests" of the USSR "lie south of the territory of the Soviet Union, in the direction of the Indian Ocean," and that "Germany, Italy, and the Soviet Union will work jointly to replace the current convention regarding the regime of the Straits, signed in Montreux, with a new convention. The new convention would grant the Soviet Union unrestricted passage through the Straits at any time for its navy, while all other countries, with the exception of the Black Sea states, as well as Germany and Italy, would in principle relinquish the right of passage through the Straits for their military vessels."

Molotov's demands that Germany yield Finland, Bulgaria, and a base in the Bosporus and the Dardanelles were ignored by Hitler. On the evening of November 25, 1940, Molotov summoned the German ambassador, Schulenburg, and handed him a response to the German offer. The Soviet government was ready "to accept the draft of a pact between four states pertaining to political cooperation and mutual economic assistance," but with serious amendments. German troops must immediately leave "Finland, which according to the agreement of 1939 belongs to the Soviet area of influence"; the Soviet area of influence must also contain Bulgaria. "During the next few months, the Soviet Union's security in the direction of the Straits must be guaranteed... with the establishment of a base for the land and naval forces of the USSR in the region of the Bosporus and the Dardanelles on the basis of a long-term lease." Germany also had to recognize that "the area to the south of Batumi and Baku in the general direction of the Persian Gulf" was "the center of the Soviet Union's territorial ambitions," while Japan had to relinquish its claims to coal and oil concessions in the north of Sakhalin Island. The Soviet government also insisted that Turkey join the pact between the four states, and in the event of Turkey's refusal to do so "Italy and the USSR jointly," on the basis of a new, separate agreement, must employ "military and diplomatic sanctions" against Turkey.

Hitler had proposed two secret protocols. Stalin proposed five secret protocols: a third secret protocol between Germany and the Soviet Union regarding Finland; a fourth secret protocol between Japan and the Soviet Union regarding Japan's relinquishment of all claims to old and coal concessions north of Sakhalin; a fifth secret protocol between Germany, the Soviet Union, and Italy recognizing the fact the Bulgaria was geographically located within the security zone of the Black Sea borders of the USSR and that the formation of a mutual assistance agreement between the Soviet Union and Bulgaria was a political necessity.

Hitler could not have given a more eloquent response to the Soviet demands of November 25, 1940 than the one he gave: on December 18, he signed Directive No 21, the plans for Operation Barbarossa, authorizing the invasion of the Soviet Union. Of course, the Soviet government did not know about this order. But Hitler's rejection of the demands of November 25 was certainly known. Soviet-German relations had reached an impasse. There were German troops in Finland, Bulgaria, and Romania, i.e. in the zone that Stalin considered his own. A military conflict between the USSR and Germany was inevitable.

But was Germany ready for war with the Soviet Union? We know that Germany was not ready for this war (because Germany lost the war). During the fiscal year 1938-1939, Germany spent 15 percent of its national income on its armed forces – approximately as much as Britain. Hitler did not want to expand the German military at the expense of the wellbeing of the German people. This could have caused a drop in his popularity. In the Soviet Union, during the third Five Year Plan (1938-1942), 26.4 percent of the budget was designated for military needs, but in reality every year more and more was spent on the armed forces. In 1940, 32.6 percent of the budget went to the military, while in 1941 the designated amount grew to 43.4 percent.

With hindsight, we are used to viewing June 22, 1941 as Hitler's greatest mistake. But it is evident that the offensive operations of the summer of 1941 were for him the high point of his military career. Germany's war against the USSR was a tactical, rather than a strategic operation on Hitler's part. Hitler did not regard the Soviet Union as a serious adversary. He planned to crush the Red Army in several months and from a military point of view he accomplished this task. He did not seek the help of an important potential ally – Japan. Given the general tension in Soviet-Japanese relations during all of the 1930s, it is likely that Hitler would have succeeded in persuading the Japanese to attack the USSR from the east. But this did not happen, and no second front against the Soviet Union was opened by Japan. Certainly, Hitler had made a miscalculation. He underestimated Stalin and the Soviet Union.

Stalin's operation to mislead Hitler and foment a war in Europe was so grand in scale that not even the greatest defeats of the Red Army in the summer and fall of 1941 could break his triumphant offensive spirit. Soviet troops still entered Berlin and established a Communist system of rule in eastern Europe. It just happened four years later than planned. And since Stalin, unlike France and Britain, did not need to win with "the least amount of bloodshed," but sought victory "at any cost," Soviet losses in the Second World War were not even tallied by his government.

Some seventy-five years later, the world again found itself on the threshold of a Third World War because of Russia's ambition to revive its empire. In connection with this, we ought to recall the first sentence of the speech delivered by Vyacheslav Molotov, People's Commissar for Foreign Affairs of the Soviet Union, on June 22, 1941, the day when Germany attacked the USSR:

> Today at 4 o'clock a.m., without any claims having been presented to the Soviet Union, without a declaration of war, German troops attacked our country, attacked our borders at many points and bombed from their airplanes our cities: Zhitomir, Kyiv, Sevastopol, Kaunas and some others.

Empires take a long time to build, but fall apart quickly. After 1991, not one of these cities fell under Russian rule. The Soviet Union, which had won the war, lost these territories when the empire created by Stalin collapsed. In the end, Stalin's policies toward Germany and Europe in 1939-1941 turned into a catastrophe for the USSR itself, which fell under the weight of insurmountable imperial problems. And this is the main history lesson that ought to be remembered by Putin, who is pulling the world into a Third World War.

Russian gas as a weapon of mass destruction

After suffering crushing defeats in the Second World War, Germany and Japan, which had been completely ruined by the destructive bombings of the Allies, in a remarkably short time restored their economic might and in only a few decades came to dominate the top of the world economy, without the help of Panzer divisions or the Luftwaffe, without aircraft carriers and kamikazes. But in order to recognize the obvious, these countries had to go through the lessons of cruel military defeats.

The Soviet government did not have to wait for crushing defeats in a major war. Neither the occupation of eastern Europe, nor support for the regimes of distant socialist countries such as Cuba or Vietnam and the war in Afghanistan, prevented the dwindling of Soviet influence in the world and the collapse of the USSR's economic system. As in the case of Germany and Japan, military might was no guarantee for political and economic dominance. It only created the mystique of a superpower. In 1991, the CPSU relinquished power as easily as it had seized it in 1917. Soviet political influence over Europe – based as it was on a military presence and military force – ended with a crushing defeat for the USSR, comparable to the defeat of Germany and Japan in the Second World War.

It seemed for a while that, like Germany and Japan, Russia had learned its lessons from this defeat. After a decade of instability between 1991 and 2000, Russia presented itself to the world as a leading economic power, whose might was now determined not by tank divisions or by warheads aimed at Western Europe and the United States, but by oil, gas, and other raw materials, exported to the whole world. It turned out that exerting economic influence was more effective and cheaper than using military pressure. Russians became wealthy tourists associated with money, not with AK-47s; not aggressors and occupiers, but profitable clients, buyers, investors, spending money that had been earned from the sales of Russian raw materials.

Nonetheless, Russia's new persona was not without its complications. Russia's main problem lay in its absolute lack of democracy. The Yeltsin years had brought the market economy and freedom to Russia, but they had failed to create the rule of law: genuinely democratic institutions that could guarantee civil liberties, an independent and uncorrupt judiciary, or government agencies that protected Russia's citizens. Not without help from Yeltsin himself, who had compromised himself with two Chechen wars and corruption scandals, a former officer of the KGB, Putin, came to power in Russia. The elderly Yeltsin handed over the rule of the country to him just as the elderly Hindenburg had handed over the chancellorship of Germany to Hitler.

After obtaining absolute power, Putin stopped caring about public opinion, deprived the public of any say on questions that concerned the governing of the country, the foreign and domestic policies of the state. The degree of the disconnect between the voters and the Kremlin leadership, overwhelmingly populated by former members of the KGB, was now absolute. Citizens' opinions stopped interesting Putin, since elections were rigged, while the media was wholly subjugated to the state. The parliament, Russia's courts and law enforcement agencies, in Moscow and around the country, were controlled exclusively by the Kremlin.

Unaccountable to the people, Russia's leaders, brought up within the bulwark of the KGB, reverted to the old Soviet method of military pressure. In 1999, the Russian army for a second time invaded Chechnya. In August 2008, Russian troops crossed Russia's border and invaded Georgia. For this invasion, they made use of a tactic very similar to Hitler's. They claimed that they were defending the interests of fellow citizens residing outside the borders of the empire. Hitler defended the rights of Germans in Austria, the Sudetenland, and Danzig in this way. The Russian government defended the rights of Russian citizens in Abkhazia and South Ossetia.

This was the first time that the new Russia used its army for foreign expansion, and the action went unpunished. In this way, a dangerous precedent was established, and, as Russia's economic power grew, the temptation for the Russian government to use the army against a weak adversary waxed instead of waned. For all countries bordering on Russia, the risk of a military invasion became an absolute reality.

By contrast with a classic military intervention, which the world witnessed in 2008 when Russian troops invaded Georgia, in Ukraine the Russian leadership is combining military operations with economic pressure. There is something unexpected (and cynical) about the fact that the occupation of Ukraine by Russia is accompanied by the simultaneous demand that Ukraine pay Russia billions of dollars for past, present, and future deliveries of Russian gas to parts of Ukraine that have not yet been occupied. And indeed, to those parts which have been occupied, too, since Russian gas was delivered to Crimea, and to the Donetsk and Luhansk regions.

It is clear that the government of Ukraine is largely to blame for accepting the absurd game Russia was playing. Greed on the part of Ukraine's powerful oligarchs had a lot to do with it. It refused to recognize (and to explain to the population) that Russia had declared war on Ukraine, that Kyiv's indignant lamentations about "perfidious" attacks by "terrorists" on Ukrainian regiments were the height of naivete, that talks about new terms for gas deliveries are a diversionary maneuver by the Russian leadership; that very soon deliveries of Russian gas to Ukraine would be stopped in any case, under one pretext or another, and that in such a situation the whole question should be formulated in a different way: Ukraine must present the Russian government with a bill for its military actions against Ukraine, in particular, for the annexation of Crimea. Until the Kremlin has paid this bill and until Crimea has been returned to Ukraine, all talk about Ukraine's past debts and future payments to the Russians, include those pertaining to gas deliveries, ought to be considered unacceptable.

It is known that aggressors cannot be appeased (the classic example is the Munich Agreement of 1938). It is known that aggression must be resisted, because there is no other way of overcoming it (as evidenced by all of world history). It is known that "small, victorious wars" usually turn out to be big ones, not always victorious, and cost many human lives. If rulers and military leaders knew in advance how a war would actually end, not one war would be begun.

It is also known that it took a long time before the two most recent biggest wars in the history of mankind – those of 1914 and 1939 – began to be called "World Wars," and an even longer time before they received their consecutive numbers – First and Second. When in March 1938 Hitler occupied and annexed Austria, no one at the time thought that this in fact was the prologue to the Second World War. Nonetheless, a year and a half later, in September 1939, the war began, although no one except for Stalin wanted a major war, not even Hitler.

If it is evident that an aggressor cannot be appeased, it is even more evident that an occupied country must not pay tribute to an aggressor for the occupation. In ancient times, in exchange for tribute money, a conquered victim (a town, city, or even an entire state) would be left alone. Today, too, there are cases in which a tribute is paid: for example, Putin pays a tribute to

Ramzan Kadyrov, the President of the Chechen Republic.

In the twentieth century, the word "tribute" has not been used, as a rule, to describe relations between states. More modern words have appeared: "reparations" and "indemnity." But these sums were paid to the victor after the end of military actions and the signing of a truce.

During military action, such tribute is never paid, since who in their right mind would pay an aggressor money to continue the war before signing a truce? It would have seemed very strange indeed if, after the September 1938 annexation of the Sudetenland, the Czechoslovak government entered into negotiations with the German government, say, about repaying Germany its debt for previously purchased railway tracks, while Germany announced that it would now sell these railway tracks to Czechoslovakia only if it received payment in advance and at double the price. Or if Germany, after occupying northern France in 1940, demanded from unoccupied southern France payment for the French government's debts for metal shipped to France during the previous years. All of this would have seemed like utter nonsense. Not even Hitler would have imagined it.

What looked like nonsense in 1938-1940 and was inconceivable to Hitler, however, became a reality in 2014, because it was imagined by Putin. After occupying Crimea and part of eastern Ukraine, and while continuing to carry out military actions against Ukraine, Russia is at the same time demanding that Ukraine pay out billions of dollars for deliveries of gas (which Russia has long ceased to deliver).

At first, this seemed to be a propaganda ploy of the Russian government, an attempt to reduce the newly begun Russian-Ukrainian war to an economic conflict over gas. But astonishingly, on May 30, 2014, Ukraine unexpectedly paid Russia $786 million toward the settling of its debt. Gas deliveries to Ukraine, of course, did not resume after this payment. Ukraine's debt did not decrease by much, nor was there much point in discussing it, since Russia turned on a "meter" for Ukraine, and Ukraine could not pay this debt – it could only surrender.

After receiving $786 million, Russia continued concentrating troops on the border with Ukraine; it redeployed new equipment and additional special units of the GRU and the FSB to districts of eastern Ukraine under the control of pro-Russian "separatists"; shot down a dozen helicopters and airplanes of the Ukrainian armed forces; took a number of Ukrainian servicemen prisoner; shot down a Malaysian civilian airliner, which (alas for Russia!) did not have a single Ukrainian onboard... How many "useful" things were done for only $786 million of tribute paid! People were now dying by the hundreds.

On July 21, Ukraine's finance minister, Alexander Shlapak, announced that it cost one and a half billion hryvnias per month to fund the anti-terrorist operation (ATO) in the east, while "there [are] about 520 million hryvnias left in the reserve fund at present." On July 24, he further stated that there would be enough money only until August 1. On July 22, the Verkhovna Rada passed President Petro Poroshenko's bill endorsing a partial mobilization. On July 25, the government of Ukraine declared its intention to levy a war tax of 1.5 percent on incomes to finance the ATO until the year's end. This was announced by Ukrainian Deputy Finance Minister Vladimir Matviychuk: "In this way, we can obtain about 2.9 billion hryvnias that can be used toward balancing the budget."

We should note that in those days, at an exchange rate of 11.8 hryvnias to the dollar, one billion hryvnias constituted approximately $85 million, while the $786 million paid by Ukraine to Russia amounted to over nine billion hryvnias. In other words, the Ukrainian government might have just as well not levied the "war tax," which would fund the Ukrainian operation in the east of the country for only two months, and not paid Russia a tribute of $786 million, but instead used these nine billion hryvnias to fight against the aggressor in the east. Nine billion hryvnias at a cost of 1.5 billion per month would have lasted for half a year of resistance against aggression.

Instead of this, Ukraine paid Russia $786 million, deprived itself of money for its own defense, but what is still worse – it gave the Russian budget an additional $786 million to fund the war. So that the difference in Ukrainian-Russian war expenditures constituted $1.572 billion in Russia's favor. What money did Russia use to install the Buk missile system for the "separatists" so they could shoot down the Malaysian airliner? That's what the $786 million paid for.

On July 24, Ukraine's Energy and Coal Industry Minister Yuri Prodan, arriving in Brussels for a consultation with Günther Oettinger, the EU's Commissioner for Energy, announced that Ukraine was ready to renew talks with Russia and the European Commission concerning gas deliveries: "We are ready to resume these consultations and talks at any moment." Meanwhile, Russia insisted that Ukraine pay its debt for previously delivered gas. In the opinion of Gazprom head Alexey Miller, this sum constituted $5.296 billion. It is easy to calculate how this money might be used if it is not given back to Russia. A million dollars might be paid to the heirs of every passenger of shot down Malaysian airliner; and to the heirs of every killed Ukrainian soldier and civilian. This sum would be enough for 5000 victims. Or the money might be used to continue the "anti-terrorist operation", which costs one and a half billion hryvnias per month. In that case, this money would last for three years of struggle.

It should be noted that, in exacting tribute (payment) from his victim, Putin did not come up with anything new. This approach was used by Stalin at least twice. The first time was in Spain, when the Soviet government took the Spanish gold reserves out of Spain and never brought them back to Spain again, claiming that the gold had been confiscated to pay for the USSR's expenditures on the Spanish Civil War, in particular, for the deliveries of arms to Spain's Republican government. The second time Stalin forced his victims to pay for their occupation was in 1940, when the Red Army entered Bessarabia and northern Bukovina. After Romania had occupied Bessarabia in 1918, the Soviet government seized the Romanian gold reserves that were stored in Russia, 92 tons of gold transferred by Romania to Russia for safekeeping in 1916-1917. In 1940, Bessarabia (with northern Bukovina added on) were occupied by the Red Army and annexed to the USSR as part of the general agreement between Stalin and Hitler. But Stalin refused to return Romania's gold reserves, declaring that it had been confiscated as payment for the exploitation of Bessarabia during the period 1918-1940.

Will there be a Third World War?[211]

The leaders of the United States and Europe, of course, cannot mention the Third World War (all stock markets would crash), but they, too, knew from the experience of 1938-1939 that the distance from a triumphant blitzkrieg by an aggressor to a protracted war against the aggressor is short. Common sense told us that Russian aggression ought to be resisted already now, on the territory of Ukraine, with Ukraine as an ally, and not after Russia has conquered Ukraine and taken over the whole military-industrial complex of eastern Ukraine (for the sake of which Russia is now fighting on the pretext of protecting ethnic Russians).

It was also easier to resist Russia's aggression in Ukraine because Ukraine was not a member of NATO and there was no need formally to declare war on Russia. From a military point of view, it would be best to make preventive strikes against Russian troops (the troops of the enemy) concentrated along the Ukrainian border, but for that the people in charge would have to be Israelis, not Ukrainians.

Russia's open aggression in eastern Ukraine was in many ways the result of Ukraine surrendering Crimea without a fight. Had Ukraine defended Crimea by taking up arms, Crimea would have still gone over to Russia (the powers were too unequal), but the "uprisings" in eastern Ukraine would not have begun with the ease and speed with which eastern Ukraine became mired in them. Like Finland in 1940, like Georgia in 2008, Ukraine would have lost part of its territory, but it would have preserved its independence and peace on the continent. Like the payment of $786 million, there remains a questionable story to be told.

Redrawing territories in the twenty-first century might seem absurd – something old and long forgotten. Before 1945, borders in Europe were redrawn constantly. It is very important to emphasize that they were not redrawn because of states uniting or breaking up: they were redrawn between neighboring states in favor of one of the neighbors. We will not cite any of the numerous examples here. But both in 1918 and in 1938-1945, the map of Europe was transformed globally. From 1946 to 1991, however, no borders were changed between European countries. And even after 1991, until August of 2008 when Russia invaded Georgia, we witnessed the creation of new European and Asian states, but we never once witnessed annexations or invasions. It was precisely for this reason that German Chancellor Angela Merkel said about Putin after the annexation of Crimea that Putin lives in a different world, by which she did not mean that Putin was crazy, but that the world into which Putin is trying to push Europe back disappeared in 1945, that is, 70 years ago.

Was it worth disturbing the world order for the sake of Crimea? Naturally, no. And what about for the sake of Ukraine? Also, no. And what about for Transnistria and Belarus? Perhaps, yes, if these territories are viewed as the limit of ambitions. But that is not how dictators end up thinking. Putin does not think like a minimalist. A minimalist program, once realized, will no longer satisfy him. Indeed, at that point he will forget that there once was any idea of not going beyond Belarus. If his head started spinning from successes after Crimea, then one can imagine what will happen to Putin after annexation of Ukraine and Belarus and how great, clever and brilliant he will then seem to himself.

This will be the moment when the threat of a war between Russia and NATO will arise before us, and Putin will be convinced that NATO will not begin a war over the Baltic States, just as it will not risk a full-scale nuclear war. In exactly the same way, Hitler believed that France and Britain would not declare war on Germany over Poland, for Germany was supported at that time by Italy, Japan, and the USSR. He knew perfectly well that there was a British-French-Polish agreement providing for mutual assistance in the event of aggression against one of these countries. Putin also knows that among the members of NATO there is an agreement providing for mutual assistance. But, like Hitler, he will believe that the Western democracies will lose their nerve.

The democratic world, by contrast with dictatorships, is governed by political parties through their leaders. Its governance resembles an upside-down tree – all kinds of different people try and often do influence the leaders of political parties: wives, children, donors, friends, clerical workers, public opinion, the press. There are laws, lawyers, and supreme courts. There are parliaments and even kings and queens. There is an international community. There are alliances. There are international organizations.

In dictatorships, everything is much simpler. Russia, for example, is governed by a junta – the officers of the KGB-FSB: Putin, the Ivanovs, Sechin, Patrushev. It plans an operation and gives its apparatchiks the task of formulating objectives for those who will execute it; it orders the parliament to vote "for" or "against"; it gives instructions to Foreign Affairs Minister Lavrov and Russia's UN Representative Vitaly Churkin about what to say to the international community... Even the Russian elite, which emerged after 1991, no longer has any relation to the process of governing the state, precisely because the regime in Russia became a dictatorial one, and in a dictatorship the elite cannot govern the country.

In 1938, fascism almost won in Europe. The USSR had Stalin, Germany had Hitler, Italy had Mussolini, Spain had Franco. Austria had been conquered; Czechoslovakia dismembered. Hungary, Portugal, Romania, Bulgaria – dictators here, kings there… There was no place on the map left for democrats. And in democratic countries, too, Fascist and Communist parties had strong public support. Does this mean that today we are again entering into a dark period of fascism? Perhaps. Does it follow from this that European civilization, in the form in which it existed before 2014, will be destroyed by Putin? This now depends only on Ukraine and NATO.

War always means bloodshed. War always means ruined lives. It means millions of refugees, escaping from coming catastrophes. Will there be more killings in Ukraine? Yes. This is Putin's main objective – to unleash bloodshed there. It was for this reason that he went into Crimea – not to establish peace in Crimea, but to unleash war in Europe. It would be a big mistake to believe that the Ukrainian army is fighting the Russian army as well as "militants" and "separatists." These are propaganda terms used by the Russian government and hammered into people's heads by Russian television for their combatants. There are people with weapons who are fighting against Ukraine. Some of them have been sent from Russia. Others have been recruited locally. It will be possible to determine the numbers of the former and the latter only after a victory. It makes no difference whether they took up arms out of stupidity, for money, or because of convictions. They are fighting for the interests of Russia – a state that is hostile (in the context of today's armed conflict) to Ukraine. They have been lined up to kill for the sake of Putin's interests.

It is difficult to find mentally healthy people who will say: "I want blood to flow like water." For the most part, everyone always calls for peace. Hitler and Stalin also spoke of peace, calling Churchill a warmonger. There is a certain category of people whose words should be taken with caution, since they use speech to disseminate false information. Unfortunately, Putin is one of these people. He is not declaring war on Ukraine and Europe, just as Hitler did not declare war when he attacked his neighbors. In the end, war was declared on September 3, 1939 on Germany by Britain and France.

Russia, too, is waging its European war without a declaration, and this war is even being partially funded by Ukraine – through payments for Russian gas; and Russian television, which has complete control over the airwaves, ceaselessly revels in Ukrainian losses and mocks the helpless Ukrainians, who still are not ready to recognize that Russia's plan is to smash and to subjugate them, like the Poles in 1939-1941. To recognize this is indeed very difficult, almost impossible. Jews also could not understand why Hitler hated them and sought to destroy them. This lack of an understanding and a rational explanation for what was happening did not save the Jews. The overwhelming majority of them perished. In the case of Ukrainians today (as in the case of Poles and Jews during the Second World War), salvation cannot come through surrender, but only through resistance, through fighting for freedom.

The economic and military might of contemporary Russia is a bluff, a public relations project, successfully promoted by several Russian television channels. In the Soviet Union, the news program Vremya (Time) on central Soviet television constantly showed Soviet tractors harvesting grain, conveyors dumping grain into trucks, flour being baked into bread, and Soviet people living happy lives. Today we know that none of this existed. There was one film camera, one tractor, one working conveyor, one truck, and actors hired to play a happy Soviet family. In reality, grain was bought in the United States and Canada. The same is true now. No one actually knows and no one says how many working airplanes and tanks Russia owns. But it may turn out that the might of the Russian army is merely a bluff of Putin's, who even in this respect may resemble Hitler, a leader who constantly exaggerated the might of Germany and the German army.

Russia is poorer than the West. Russia is a big gas station and an enormous oil tank. When people buy Russian oil and gas, Russia has money. When people do not buy them, or buy them but not from Russia, or buy them at falling prices, Russia has no money. This is a simple truth. The whole history of the gas-related part of Russia's war against Ukraine proves this.

If Russia had money for war against Ukraine, it would not have threatened to cut off Ukraine's gas supply, but would have simply cut if off, on the very first day, already in March, when Crimea was annexed. One should not harbor any illusions and think that Russia is interested in the growth, wellbeing, and stability of an independent Ukraine. Russia – Putin's Russia, which the world is witnessing – is interested in the exact opposite.

Thus far, Russia has used Ukrainian money to embark on a venture to conquer Ukraine that pays for itself, and the Ukrainian government is helping Russia in this venture. Putin also has the possibility to use this same money to buy up politicians, particularly those who decide whether or not to pay for Ukraine's "gas debts." Using KGB-FSB agents and influence in European organizations, Putin can exert pressure on Ukraine to get Ukraine to agree to Russian prices for gas, to agree to repay its "debts," and to agree to pay for gas deliveries in advance.

We put the word "debts" in quotes because Ukraine no longer owes Russia anything. After the annexation of Crimea, after the start of a diversionary war in eastern Ukraine, by any international standards Ukraine owes Russia nothing. Moreover, the Ukrainian government should have instigated legal proceedings against Russia. If we calculate the damage sustained by Ukraine up to the present moment, it will be substantially larger in value than Ukraine's gas debt of several billion dollars (according to Gazprom's accounts).

For Putin, everything is timed to the day. No aggressor plans a long siege – only a blitzkrieg. Putin is no exception (he does not differ from Hitler in this respect, either). He rapidly conquered Crimea, held a referendum, and announced an annexation. An ordinary politician would have needed months of playing a delicate political game to accomplish the same purpose. But Putin has no money for a long siege. A blitzkrieg is all that he can afford. On the gas front, there is another blitzkrieg. It is telling that in all discussions about gas, the Russian side is always counting days: President Putin, Prime Minister Medvedev, and Gazprom head Miller demand that Ukraine repay its gas debts "by the end of the week", "by the end of the month". The possibility of postponing the payments for a year or two is not even mentioned – because Putin has no time for this. Russia's objective is to swallow up Ukraine. This can be done with tanks and airplanes, or it can be done with gas. The two approaches can also be combined. But tanks and airplanes cost money. Russia plans to obtain this money from Ukraine as a "gas debt."

In its whole history, Ukraine has never been at the center of the world's attention as it is now. In its resistance against Russia, it has won the sympathies of truly all of mankind (apart from its Russian part). Until now, Ukraine has resisted Russia in isolation. Of course, in a fight with such a strong adversary, Ukraine cannot win without NATO as an ally. Meanwhile, NATO is in no hurry to become an ally, fearing the risk of a major war. *then how does it end?*

Nonetheless, Putin can be stopped without a single shot being fired by a NATO soldier – through severe economic sanctions. To be sure, such sanctions will inevitably create economic problems for Europe, including interruptions in deliveries of Russian gas. But the European economic difficulties produced by the imposition of sanctions on Russia will be trifling by comparison with the problems that would ensue from a war with Russia. In that event, gas and oil prices, world stock market indices, and currency exchange rates, will no longer be of very much concern to anyone. It will be necessary to begin a major war. And if many now think that this is impossible, they are not alone: in 1938, this is exactly what the whole world thought, too.

CONCLUSIONS

We have witnessed how Ukraine has defended its independence. It has preserved it, for now… It received a respite, which it urgently needed in order to regroup its forces, to form a government, to create an army, and to revive its economy. Along with Ukraine, the rest of the world, too, received a respite for making sense of what had happened. This respite will not last long, because Putin's main objective is still to take over Ukraine. Putin's Ukrainian complex can now be compared only to Stalin's Polish complex and Hitler's Jewish complex.

Advancing into eastern Ukraine after the blitzkrieg in Crimea, Putin, of course, hoped for a similarly easy victory. Because everyone always hopes. And at first it appeared, especially judging by Russian television, that everything was moving along swiftly and without problems. Then something stalled: Ukraine let it be understood that it had no intention of surrendering. Meanwhile, the plans for a blitzkrieg in continental Ukraine were based on the assumption that Ukraine would surrender even before the Presidential Election. But Ukraine began to resist: as best it could, without an army (which it didn't have), without technology (which had long ago become rusty), without a creed (what kind of creed could Ukraine have to wage war with Russia?). Imagine the Czech Republic, after voluntarily separating from Slovakia, suddenly raising an army and going to war with Slovakia to correct a "historical mistake." It would be sheer lunacy.

This is the kind of lunacy that we have ended up with, thanks to Putin. And the reality of this lunacy consists in the fact that no one would offer Ukraine any aid until, first, Russia launched a full-scale war; second,

Ukrainians started dying by the thousands; and third, Russian troops started dying by the hundreds and thousands. Only after this was Ukraine given aid. Ukraine will see no NATO presence – no air force presence, no naval presence, and certainly no on-the-ground presence.

Looking at the situation dispassionately, it is clear that the longer the opposition of Russia's aggression in Ukraine lasts – the longer Ukraine sustains the blow – the more time NATO will have to gather its forces and to rethink that new world. Because the history of the twenty-first century will now be divided into a period "before" and a period "after" the Third World War; or into "before" and "after" March 2014, or "before" and "after" February 2022.

It should be pointed out that, as a matter of history, the West is not to blame for all that is taking place. Not yet. Thus far, only Ukraine is to blame for everything that has happened. It is to blame for not having used the period since 1991 in order to create a truly independent government, which is not constantly turning around and looking at Russia; it is to blame for failing to create a stable political system, because a situation in which the President is elected each time by a one-vote majority and half the country believes that the election is unfair is ruinous for the government. The political ambitions of leaders are a natural thing and are to be expected in a competitive struggle. But they must coexist with a governing wisdom, and none of Ukraine's political leaders ever possessed this.

One of the authors of this book, Yuri Felshtinsky, asked Yulia Tymoshenko: "Tell me, is Yushchenko your ally?" "More of a rival," Tymoshenko replied. This was in 2004, even before the electoral campaign, at the end of which Yushchenko ultimately won. This was an honest answer, and these words shed light on the entire subsequent history of Ukraine: that Yushchenko would win the election thanks to Tymoshenko's support; that in return, he would appoint her Prime Minister; that somewhat later, he would dismiss her from her post, because she is his rival; and that in the next Presidential Election, Tymoshenko would try to become President and lose, since she would be too sure of her victory.

Nor was the West to blame for the fact that Yanukovych won the election. Ukraine was to blame. The West was not to blame for Ukraine's corruption and the clan system that controlled the country. Ukraine was to blame for this too. The West was not to blame for the fact that Lenin monuments and "Lenin Streets" remained standing everywhere and were not renamed, and that they were gathering places for those who supported Ukraine's entry into the USSR (precisely the USSR, and not Russia, because the people who fought for an "Anschluss" with Russia believed that they were returning to the old USSR).

The West was to blame only for not foreseeing March 2014 and for refusing to believe that Putin remained a KGB officer who had come to power on an assignment from the KGB, in order to implement the KGB's foreign and domestic political plans. But this, frankly speaking, was something that almost no one saw.

Putin today remains absolutely convinced that the United States is weak, that Europe is barely breathing, and that in Russia everything is decided by the FSB and the President's administration (which is controlled by the FSB, since FSB General Sergei Ivanov is in charge of the President's administration). Putin knows that, having grown hungry for medals, promotions, and bonuses, the army generals – on orders from General Sergey Shoigu – will move their tanks wherever the Defense Minister tells them to move them. In such a state of euphoria, can Putin believe that Ukraine, which has almost never even existed on the map as an independent state, will become an obstacle in the realization of his great plans to conquer mankind? He cannot believe it. He believes that Ukraine will be swept away before the fall of 2015, however many Russian and Ukrainian lives it takes to do so. After all, tens of thousands died during the First and Second Chechen Wars, yet Chechnya was kept a part of Russia.

Government tyrannies endure because they use the instruments at their disposal (for example, authority or propaganda) to arouse, develop, and sustain in their subject exclusively bad tendencies, while the good ones gradually recede into the background and eventually disappear. The objective of any dictator is to pit one part of the population against the other. Lenin used the class theory for this purpose (the rich against the poor, city dwellers against rural populations, the illiterate against the educated, the Bolsheviks against the Mensheviks). The most important thing is to find the line for a split. Lenin always found it, as did Stalin after him. Hitler split people along national lines: Germans against Jews; Germans against Poles; Germans against the French; Germans against all. In this respect, Putin has not come up with anything new and is trying to combine the methods employed by Lenin, Stalin, and Hitler. In Chechnya, he fought the Chechens; in Ukraine, the Ukrainians. But when it comes to a conflict with the United States, the first thing that comes to Putin's mind is the Soviet experience, at the root of which lies the Stalinism of 1923-1953. Can one, by crossing the worst dictators of the twentieth century, Hitler and Stalin, become a super-dictator in the twenty-first century? Probably not. To prove that this is impossible is difficult. But it is likewise difficult to imagine Putin as the President of a state which encompasses, say, Russia, Ukraine, Moldavia, Belarus, the Baltic States, Georgia, Armenia, and Kazakhstan. Because the only talent that Putin has is KGB-style duplicity and familiarity with killing. There are no other tricks up his sleeve.

Putin's initial plan consisted of an attempt to annex Belarus (the former Belorus, an inseparable part of the Soviet Union) first. This objective, as the Kremlin saw it, would be very simple. Belarus had never been an independent state, and this was supposed to be the main argument of the Kremlin's propagandists during the Belarusian Anschluss. Strategically, Belarus gave Russia access to eastern European borders that were very important to it: Lithuania, western Ukraine, and Poland. To organize unrest in Minsk was even easier than to do so in eastern Ukraine. President Alexander Lukashenko was not popular either in his own country or abroad. He could not ask anyone for protection. In the eyes of Europe and the United States, Lukashenko was simply a dictator. No one has and no one had any sympathy for him. This does not mean, of course, that the world would have recognized an annexation of Belarus by Russia. But Belarus could not resist Russia on its own, and it could not count on help from NATO countries.

At the same time, Belarus is an extremely important launching ground for a Russian attack on Ukraine and eastern Europe, and a full-scale war with Ukraine is impossible without the violation of Belarus's sovereignty by Russia. In the run-up to such an attack, the Russian government will need either to annex Belarus, making it part of the Russian Federation, as was done with Crimea, or to obtain permission from Lukashenko for the Russian army to pass through Belarusian territory for an attack on Ukraine. Lastly,

Russia might demand that Belarus participate in military operations against Ukraine as an ally. In all of these cases, Russia acquires the possibility of entering western Ukraine through Belarus and of sending its tanks not through pro-Russian eastern Ukraine, but through anti-Russian western Ukraine.

But why in this case did Putin make the decision to start in spring 2014 with the occupation of Crimea, and not of Minsk?

Possibly, after witnessing the EuroMaidan in Kyiv, Putin and his team became concerned. In their hearts, all of these individuals despised the Ukrainians, believing them to be an easily controlled rabble. Ukraine was Russia's closest foreign neighbor, and Russia was methodically taking steps to bring under its control both the Ukrainian government and Ukrainian politics. All this suddenly collapsed before the Kremlin's eyes: Ukraine turned in the direction of the European Union. Students in the streets, the EuroMaidan uprising, the flight of Yanukovych... To say that Moscow was not expecting any of this is to say nothing. Then the Kremlin tried to seize the initiative by taking over Crimea.

In spring 2014, Europe and the United States, in Putin's understanding, were weak and could not check Russian aggression. Germany was dependent on Russia's gas, Britain on Russia's capital. France wanted to sell Mistrals; Switzerland kept Russia's money. The United States was involved in wars with Islamic extremism, and Barack Obama – winner of the Nobel Peace Prize – was seen by Putin as a pacifist, nor ready for a conflict with Russia.

Putin expected the history of 2008 to repeat itself in 2014. In 2008, Russia invaded Georgia, and the West ignored the first Russian aggression since the Soviet invasion of Afghanistan in January 1980. Of course, in 2008 the West had made a mistake, first, by not defending the small democratic state; and second, by giving Putin the wrong signal. Putin understood the West's silence as permission for Russian troops to enter the boundaries of former Soviet republics. Entering Crimea in 2014, Putin expected and got the same reaction from the West that he had been counting on: inaction.

However, over several months of Russian aggression, Europe and the United States went from total incomprehension of what was going on to a clear recognition of the fact that Putin is starting a Third World War. Some call it the Fourth World War (reckoning the Cold War as the Third); some call it the Second Cold War; some write about a European war; some about a Russian-Ukrainian war. Nonetheless, everyone is writing and thinking about war, and General Martin Dempsey, head of the United States Armed Forces, compares Putin with Stalin, and Russia's actions with the Soviet invasion of Poland in September 1939.

The point of view of the American military is undoubtedly an important component of the world's general sense and understanding of the global problem created by Putin. As Dempsey has noted, You've got a Russian government that has made a conscious decision to use its military force inside another sovereign nation to achieve its objectives. It's the first time since 1939 or so that that's been the case…. They clearly are on a path to assert themselves differently not just in eastern Europe, but Europe in the main, and towards the United States…. This is very clearly Putin, the man himself… what he considers to be an effort to redress grievances that we burdened upon Russia after the fall of the Soviet Union and also to appeal to ethnic Russian enclaves across eastern Europe…. He's very aggressive about it, he's got a playbook he's been successful with two or three times, and he will continue" to act in the same manner.

In Dempsey's view, Putin shows no indication of readiness to pull back under pressure:

At a time when some folks could convince themselves that Putin would be looking for a reason to de-escalate, he's actually taken a decision to escalate. Joseph Stalin used similar rhetoric and justifications when he invaded Poland in September 1939…. "The Soviet Government cannot regard with indifference the fact that the kindred Ukrainian and White Russian people, who live on Polish territory and who are at the mercy of fate, are now left defenseless…. In these circumstances, the Soviet Government has directed the high command of the Red Army to order the troops to cross the frontier and to take under their protection the life and property of the population of western Ukraine and western White Russia".

Dempsey quoted the note sent by the USSR Ministry of Foreign Affairs on

September 17, 1939 to the Polish ambassador in Moscow.

Putin's actions have preoccupied or outraged European politicians, American senators and congressmen, State Department officials and experts, not to mention the many-voiced Russian opposition, which is everywhere on the internet.

There is only one problem: while there is an understanding of what is going on, there is no possibility of influencing Putin. The democratic world encountered an analogous difficulty in 1938-1939. It was clear that Germany was ruled by evildoers. But it was not clear what should be done: there were no civilized instruments for exerting pressure on Hitler, while it was not evident that there were sufficient resources for a military intervention. Today, by contrast with 1938-1939, the democratic world has the military potential, but lacks the political will to use even peaceful instruments of pressure (for example, sanctions). The stable comfort that Europe is used to remains more valuable to it than the risks associated with sanctions, at least so far.

Europe and the United States believed that the Crimean problem would resolve itself. A few months later, inaction had to be paid for with the lives of almost 300 air passengers: on July 17, a Malaysian airliner was shot down. The Russian saboteurs made a mistake: there was not a single Ukrainian onboard the airplane. If a Ukrainian passenger plane had been shot down, the "separatists' rejoicing would have known no end. But the plane turned out to be foreign. And Putin was forced to tell Obama about the "mistake" (because the Russian army had shot down the Malaysian airliner), while Russia's cabinet of ministers (including Defense Minister Shoigu) had to stand up to honor the memory of the killed foreigners with a minute of silence, because it was they who had sanctioned it.

During this minute of silence, that which had been skillfully concealed was explicitly demonstrated on television, to the whole world: Ukraine had no pro-Russian "militias" and "separatists." There was a war going on in the east of Ukraine, unleashed by Russia. This Russian-Ukrainian war already a world war, since several hundred innocent foreigners had died in it. As Putin cynically remarked, if there had been no fighting in eastern Ukraine, the airplane would not have been shot down. Hopefully, we won't need to add if Putin's aggression had been stopped in 2008, 2014, 2022...

The problem of restoring peace in Europe is exacerbated by the fact that only thing we can rely on is that Putin cannot be relied on, that it is impossible to form agreements with him. After promising and signing any accord, he will still lie at the first possible opportunity and do what he wants. Like the Terminator in the film with Arnold Schwarzenegger, Putin will not retreat, will not stop, and will not rest, until time sweeps him away.

The diplomatic war outside Russia is in the hands of the Foreign Affairs Minister Sergey Lavrov and Russia's UN Representative Vitaly Churkin. The ideological foundation within Russia is being built by Vyacheslav Surkov and Dmitry Rogozin. They are supported by fascists and communists. The latter forgave Putin all of his sins – his corruption, the thievery promoted by the government at all levels, and his largely anti-populist policies – for the chance to revive the empire and to wage a war against the world. Having begun an anti-Western and anti-Ukrainian campaign, Putin has found support in many strata of Russian society, a part of which still feels nostalgic about the USSR, while another part dreams of the lost empire. The desire to be not the Russian Federation, but the Russian empire, is embraced by those who for many years have considered themselves to be the political opposition in Russia.

Even Mikhail Khodorkovsky, the former head of Yukos, who spent ten years in Putin's prison, and Alexei Navalny, Putin's main political opponent in Russia, for all their criticism of Putin, point out that Crimea was annexed fairly and must belong to Russia.

In different versions, from top officials, including Putin himself, we hear about a "new order" that must be established in the world. The last time there was talk of a "new order" in Europe, it came from Hitler and his party comrades. Not by chance did even the courteous Prince Charles, who usually stays out of politics, compare Putin with Hitler. There is no one else to compare Putin with. This is how he will enter history – as a Russian Hitler. It should be noted that during the Nuremberg Trials, both the Anschluss of Austria and the annexation of the Sudetenland were regarded as war crimes with which Nazi leaders were charged, although both annexations had been carried out on the whole without casualties and with the consent of the majority of the population of the annexed territories.

After the catastrophe that befell Europe – the Second World War –

Europeans were afraid of two things: war, and government falling into the hands of fascists. The latter was more dangerous than the former, since fascism leads inevitably not simply to war, but to large-scale war. The regime of Slobodan Milosevic was destroyed precisely because Europe saw in him a new dictator, a new Hitler, carrying out another genocide. After the Second World War, Europeans could not allow this.

Actions against an aggressor should be taken at the earliest stage of the aggression. In terms of Putin and Russia, this initial stage ended in August 2008, when Russian troops entered Georgia. Six years later Putin set his sights on Ukraine. It is clear that Russia is not Yugoslavia, and that a problem arising out of Russia's expansion cannot be solved by bombing, as in Belgrade. But in 2014 and 2022, everyone understood that it must be solved. And this is Putin's global miscalculation: he does not understand the level of the conflict with the West. The same was the case with Hitler, who attacked Poland and believed that France and Britain, weak and indecisive, would let it go, just as they had earlier accepted the occupation of Czechoslovakia. Hitler's lack of understanding of the essence of European democracy led him and Europe into a large-scale war. Putin now finds himself on the path to a large-scale war for the same reason.

Putin has been preparing for this large-scale war. Russia is conducting military exercises along all of its borders, from the Kuril Islands to the Kaliningrad Oblast, from the Black Sea to the Baltic. Intricate bilateral military agreements are being unilaterally torn up, and no one is even paying attention to this. For example, against the din of unrest in eastern Ukraine, the Russian government unilaterally terminated an agreement with Lithuania, signed in 2001, regarding additional measures for reinforcing trust and security. According to this agreement, Russia was to exchange information with Lithuania concerning its military capabilities in the Kaliningrad region, and jointly with the Lithuanian side to carry out military inspections of these capabilities. Lithuania adhered to all of the conditions of this agreement and gave no cause for its termination. "This step by Russia demonstrates its unwillingness to support mutual trust and can be considered as yet another step toward the destruction of mutual trust and the security system in Europe," the Lithuanian defense ministry declared in its official response to this action.

It should be noted that the territory concerned was Kaliningrad, the farthest, westernmost point in Russia. Add to this Putin's rhetoric concerning the creation of a powerful military base in Crimea, the concentration of Russian troops on the border with Ukraine, the presence of a powerful military force posing as "peacekeepers" in Transnistria, numerous violations by the Russian navy of the maritime boundaries of neighboring states, joint military exercises with Belarus, the call-up of reserves for summer training, changes in the law governing how often reservists may be called up and how long they must serve, constantly increasing spending on arms, boorish provocative rhetoric from Duma deputies such as Vladimir Zhirinovsky, head of the Liberal Democratic Party of Russia (LDPR) and a close ally of the Kremlin and Putin, and even the policies of Russia's Central Bank, which is buying up gold – and it becomes clear that Russia is building a war machine.

The Kremlin's "retaliatory" sanctions against Europe and the United States also indicate that Russia is preparing for isolation. Russia knows that after the start of full-scale military actions, it will find itself absolutely isolated, and it has been actively preparing for this isolation and split with the civilized world. It has stopped supplying gas on credit; the importation of foreign food products has been prohibited, so that Russia might gradually reform itself in a timely manner and begin to feed itself. Organizations close to the Kremlin, such as Lukoil, are selling their foreign holdings. This is even more the case for "private citizens" who are close to the Kremlin: they have been preparing for this war for a long time and have been selling assets abroad. And all of this is taking place even as Russian strategic bombers have again started to violate the airspace of NATO countries, while Russian fighter planes have started to chase NATO airplanes. This is something that has not been seen since the time of Brezhnev. Ukraine simply happened to be first front in this war.

The weakest link in Putin's policies is his absence of allies. Hitler's allies were Italy and Japan, and sympathies for the Führer and for the fascist movement were strong in many other European countries. Putin has no such support on his side. Stalin's Soviet Union won the Second World War, of course, when together with Britain and the United States it fought against Germany and Italy. But this is not the same thing as fighting in complete isolation, using Russian forces alone, against the United States, Britain, Germany, Italy, and the rest of Europe, especially since Putin's Russia is not Stalin's Soviet Union, but a far weaker state.

The Kremlin, naturally, waves the Chinese flag as a lifeline. However, it is only due to our European ignorance that China might appear to be a monolithic state. China was created – in the form in which it exists today – in 1928. So, while its civilization is ancient, as a state it is very young, with its own serious problems. And the fact that China's government-controlled media do not report all of the country's problems does not make these problems go away. China is the last country interested in breaking up the world order and world stability, and in seeing war in Europe, let alone in the world, since the Chinese economy is interested above all in stability. Any large-scale war will undermine that stability. Getting involved in an international conflict on the side of Russia is something that China obviously will not do.

At the same time, China will not take action against Russia and will not use Russia's involvement in war in Europe either to strengthen its positions in Russia, or to expand territorially at Russia's expense. China patiently waited one hundred years until Britain's lease of Hong Kong came to an end. China still has not taken any military steps to annex Taiwan, although Taiwan, in Putin's classification, is another "historic mistake" that should be "corrected" since Taiwan is "primordial Chinese land." Chinese politicians think in terms of centuries, not "Presidential terms." For the Chinese, Putin's Ukrainian leap is the gamble of a short-sighted European tribal leader, who is unable to think in the long term, for generations ahead, with the wisdom befitting a head of state. China will get out of Putin's European war advantageous oil and gas contracts. And what will be advantageous for China will become unprofitable for Russia. In trade, zero price gives rise to infinite demand. But Russia will never again see high European prices for its oil and gas. As a buyer, China will never replace Europe for Russia.

Do people in Russia understand this? Yes, of course. However, what has been happening to Russia is no longer about money. In general, everything that Putin has been doing is not about money. It is about glory, as Putin understands it; it is about empire, as he sees it; it is about history and geopolitics, as he perceives them. The period of making money is over for everyone, first and foremost for Russia. The period of spending accumulated capital and resources has begun. Russia has paid a high price for the territories it gained in Ukraine and Georgia. It lost whatever respect it had and the value of the ruble halved. So, it was expensive. But Putin and his comrades don't really care about Russia and its prosperity. They don't even care about lives. Like Stalin, Putin doesn't count the Russian deaths his policies cost. Russians are cannon fodder in this game.

Putin spent decades building a political system in which the government could exist in absolute suspension from the people, and the people had no means of influencing the government. In reality, this is the old Soviet system, in which the entire Soviet Union lived for decades, in which Putin himself lived and worked in the KGB. He knows this system well, loves it, and personally finds it on the whole satisfactory. Someone will die, someone will be ruined financially, someone will leave, someone will get rich. As always happens with any change of scene or regime change, new possibilities will open up. The old "elite" will disappear, a new one will emerge. The new elite will differ from the old elite exactly as Hitler's elite of the Third Reich differed from the elite of the Weimar Republic. There will be nothing enlightened about this new elite.

Putin has built the country he wanted. Stalin, after Hitler's defeat, raised a toast at a banquet to the patience of the Russian people. Putin today would do well to raise a toast to the submissiveness of the people of Russia, for they have allowed dictatorship to be reborn in their country. Russian reporters write what they are told to write; Russian television reports what it is allowed to report; Russian officials serve as they know how. Not one reporter slammed the door; not one minister left the government; not one member of parliament spoke out against the Kremlin; there was not a single resignation caused by Russia's invasion of Ukraine. And yet how bold, proud, and principled everyone was during the wild Yeltsin decade! Today's Russia is Putin's image.

Only force can stop an aggressor. There are no other examples, no other methods. Force can assume different forms: military, diplomatic, economic. Spiritual force is also force, naturally, but it does not usually stop an aggressor. Unfortunately for us all, money is the main Russian weapon. The oligarchs who surround Putin's inner circle of power support him because the conquests bring in spoils to be taken from Ukrainian oligarchs – in east Ukraine and Crimea, mining, oil and gas and vacation resorts; dividends they spread outside the Russian Federation through conspicuous consumption and by buying influence. Putin's Russia leaves a trail of money and corruption, and now war.

History very rarely teaches us lessons on the basis of which we can learn anything. Today, we are dealing with a classic repetition of the prewar situation in Europe in 1938-1939. It is remarkable how similar everything is. Everyone is making mistakes. Putin is also making mistakes and will make many more. Putin's objective is to realize himself, drawing the world into a Third World War. We know how the two previous world wars ended for Europe: with complete ruin and destruction. For the defeated as well as the victors. Even Britain suffered, and not only in terms of lives lost. After the First World War, the continental empires broke up. After the Second World War, Germany and Europe were divided into East and West. In discussing the dangers associated with the Third World War, it is impossible not to mention the probability that it will become a nuclear conflict. Is Putin a type of person who would risk such a war? In order to answer this question correctly, let us formulate it another way: could Adolf Hitler have used nuclear weapons against his enemies? The answer to this question is one that we, undoubtedly, know, although Germany did not have nuclear weapons. Modern Russia does have nuclear weapons at its disposal. And this is Russia's only ally in the poker bluff that has been undertaken by Vladimir Putin.

APPENDIX

"On the Historical Unity of Russians and Ukrainians"
By Vladimir Putin, July 12, 2021
en.kremlin.ru/events/President/news/66181

This essay, one of several to which Vladimir Putin put his name, shows the pedigree of "Substitution of Ideas": Russia's highest official, the President himself, hands it down. Like the others, it illustrates the Kremlin's way of using isolated historical facts to create a narrative that make its actions in the present appear as logical consequences. It is akin to the principle of history "control" in George Orwell's *1984* and Putin deploys all methods he identified. An example of Putin using double-speak is: "I am confident that true sovereignty of Ukraine is possible only in partnership with Russia". The piece is meant to create a state of bewilderment about the truth rather than convince.

While names and dates in Putin's essay are accurate, every connection that is made between them is historical nonsense. Russians have been subjected to this tsunami of propaganda since 2014. They are not the only ones taken in by what comes from the Kremlin and other Russian officials. Western media, while they may not believe a word of what is said, still faithfully report the fictions produced by Russian officials and, where they do, enable these empty fabrications by spreading them to a new audience through replication.

During the recent Direct Line [Putin's annual TV program with Q&As "from the Russian public"], when I was asked about Russian-Ukrainian relations, I said that Russians and Ukrainians were one people – a single whole. These words were not driven by some short-term considerations or prompted by the current political context. It is what I have said on numerous occasions and what I firmly believe. I therefore feel it necessary to explain my position in detail and share my assessments of today's situation.

First of all, I would like to emphasize that the wall that has emerged in recent years between Russia and Ukraine, between the parts of what is essentially the same historical and spiritual space, to my mind is our great common misfortune and tragedy. These are, first and foremost, the consequences of our own mistakes made at different periods of time. But these are also the result of deliberate efforts by those forces that have always sought to undermine our unity. The formula they apply has been known from time immemorial – divide and rule. There is nothing new here. Hence the attempts to play on the "national question" and sow discord among people, the overarching goal being to divide and then to pit the parts of a single people against one another.

To have a better understanding of the present and look into the future, we need to turn to history. Certainly, it is impossible to cover in this article all the developments that have taken place over more than a thousand years. But I will focus on the key, pivotal moments that are important for us to remember, both in Russia and Ukraine.

Russians, Ukrainians, and Belarusians are all descendants of Ancient Rus, which was the largest state in Europe. Slavic and other tribes across the vast territory – from Ladoga, Novgorod, and Pskov to Kyiv and Chernihiv – were bound together by one language (which we now refer to as Old Russian), economic ties, the rule of the princes of the Rurik dynasty, and – after the baptism of Rus – the Orthodox faith. The spiritual choice made by St. Vladimir, who was both Prince of Novgorod and Grand Prince of Kyiv, still largely determines our affinity today.

The throne of Kyiv held a dominant position in Ancient Rus. This had been the custom since the late 9th century. The Tale of Bygone Years captured for posterity the words of Oleg the Prophet about Kyiv, "Let it be the mother of all Russian cities."

Later, like other European states of that time, Ancient Rus faced a decline of central rule and fragmentation. At the same time, both the nobility and the common people perceived Rus as a common territory, as their homeland.

The fragmentation intensified after Batu Khan's devastating invasion, which ravaged many cities, including Kyiv. The northeastern part of Rus fell under the control of the Golden Horde but retained limited sovereignty. The southern and western Russian lands largely became part of the Grand Duchy of Lithuania, which – most significantly – was referred to in historical records as the Grand Duchy of Lithuania and Russia.

Members of the princely and "boyar" clans would change service from one prince to another, feuding with each other but also making friendships and alliances. Voivode Bobrok of Volyn and the sons of Grand Duke of Lithuania Algirdas – Andrey of Polotsk and Dmitry of Bryansk – fought next to Grand Duke Dmitry Ivanovich of Moscow on the Kulikovo field. At the same time, Grand Duke of Lithuania Jogaila – son of the Princess of Tver – led his troops to join with Mamai. These are all pages of our shared history, reflecting its complex and multi-dimensional nature.

Most importantly, people both in the western and eastern Russian lands spoke the same language. Their faith was Orthodox. Up to the middle of the 15th century, the unified church government remained in place.

At a new stage of historical development, both Lithuanian Rus and Moscow Rus could have become the points of attraction and consolidation of the territories of Ancient Rus. It so happened that Moscow became the center of reunification, continuing the tradition of ancient Russian statehood. Moscow princes – the descendants of Prince Alexander Nevsky – cast off the foreign yoke and began gathering the Russian lands.

In the Grand Duchy of Lithuania, other processes were unfolding. In the 14th century, Lithuania's ruling elite converted to Catholicism. In the 16th century, it signed the Union of Lublin with the Kingdom of Poland to form the Polish–Lithuanian Commonwealth. The Polish Catholic nobility received considerable land holdings and privileges in the territory of

Rus. In accordance with the 1596 Union of Brest, part of the western Russian Orthodox clergy submitted to the authority of the Pope. The process of Polonization and Latinization began, ousting Orthodoxy.

As a consequence, in the 16-17th centuries, the liberation movement of the Orthodox population was gaining strength in the Dnieper region. The events during the times of Hetman Bohdan Khmelnytsky became a turning point. His supporters struggled for autonomy from the Polish-Lithuanian Commonwealth.

In its 1649 appeal to the king of the Polish–Lithuanian Commonwealth, the Zaporizhzhian Host demanded that the rights of the Russian Orthodox population be respected, that the voivode of Kiev be Russian and of Greek faith, and that the persecution of the churches of God be stopped. But the Cossacks were not heard.

Bohdan Khmelnytsky then made appeals to Moscow, which were considered by the Zemsky Sobor. On 1 October 1653, members of the supreme representative body of the Russian state decided to support their brothers in faith and take them under patronage. In January 1654, the Pereyaslav Council confirmed that decision. Subsequently, the ambassadors of Bohdan Khmelnytsky and Moscow visited dozens of cities, including Kyiv, whose populations swore allegiance to the Russian tsar. Incidentally, nothing of the kind happened at the conclusion of the Union of Lublin.

In a letter to Moscow in 1654, Bohdan Khmelnytsky thanked Tsar Aleksey Mikhaylovich for taking "the whole Zaporizhzhian Host and the whole Russian Orthodox world under the strong and high hand of the Tsar". It means that, in their appeals to both the Polish king and the Russian tsar, the Cossacks referred to and defined themselves as Russian Orthodox people.

Over the course of the protracted war between the Russian state and the Polish–Lithuanian Commonwealth, some of the hetmans, successors of Bohdan Khmelnytsky, would "detach themselves" from Moscow or seek support from Sweden, Poland, or Turkey. But, again, for the people, that was a war of liberation. It ended with the Truce of Andrusovo in 1667. The final outcome was sealed by the Treaty of Perpetual Peace in 1686. The Russian state incorporated the city of Kyiv and the lands on the left bank of the Dnieper River, including Poltava region, Chernihiv region, and Zaporizhzhia. Their inhabitants were reunited with the main part of the Russian Orthodox people. These territories were referred to as "Malorossiya" (Little Russia).

The name "Ukraine" was used more often in the meaning of the Old Russian word "okraina" (periphery), which is found in written sources from the 12th century, referring to various border territories. And the word "Ukrainian", judging by archival documents, originally referred to frontier guards who protected the external borders.

On the right bank, which remained under the Polish–Lithuanian Commonwealth, the old orders were restored, and social and religious oppression intensified. On the contrary, the lands on the left bank, taken under the protection of the unified state, saw rapid development. People from the other bank of the Dnieper moved here en masse. They sought support from people who spoke the same language and had the same faith.

During the Great northern War with Sweden, the people in Malorossiya were not faced with a choice of whom to side with. Only a small portion of the Cossacks supported Mazepa's rebellion. People of all orders and degrees considered themselves Russian and Orthodox.

Cossack senior officers belonging to the nobility would reach the heights of political, diplomatic, and military careers in Russia. Graduates of Kyiv-Mohyla Academy played a leading role in church life. This was also the case during the Hetmanate – an essentially autonomous state formation with a special internal structure – and later in the Russian Empire. Malorussians in many ways helped build a big common country – its statehood, culture, and science. They participated in the exploration and development of the Urals, Siberia, the Caucasus, and the Far East. Incidentally, during the Soviet period, natives of Ukraine held major, including the highest, posts in the leadership of the unified state. Suffice it to say that Nikita Khrushchev and Leonid Brezhnev, whose party biography was most closely associated with Ukraine, led the Communist Party of the Soviet Union (CPSU) for almost 30 years.

In the second half of the 18th century, following the wars with the Ottoman Empire, Russia incorporated Crimea and the lands of the Black Sea region, which became known as Novorossiya. They were populated by people from all of the Russian provinces. After the partitions of the Polish-Lithuanian Commonwealth, the Russian Empire regained the western Old Russian lands, with the exception of Galicia and Transcarpathia, which became part of the Austrian – and later Austro-Hungarian – Empire.

The incorporation of the western Russian lands into the single state was not merely the result of political and diplomatic decisions. It was underlain by the common faith, shared cultural traditions, and – I would like to emphasize it once again – language similarity. Thus, as early as the beginning of the 17th century, one of the hierarchs of the Uniate Church, Joseph Rutsky, communicated to Rome that people in Moscovia called Russians from the Polish-Lithuanian Commonwealth their brothers, that their written language was absolutely identical, and differences in the vernacular were insignificant. He drew an analogy with the residents of Rome and Bergamo. These are, as we know, the center and the north of modern Italy.

Many centuries of fragmentation and living within different states naturally brought about regional language peculiarities, resulting in the emergence of dialects. The vernacular enriched the literary language. Ivan Kotlyarevsky, Grigory Skovoroda, and Taras Shevchenko played a huge role here. Their works are our common literary and cultural heritage. Taras Shevchenko wrote poetry in the Ukrainian language, and prose mainly in Russian. The books of Nikolay Gogol, a Russian patriot and native of Poltavshchyna, are written in Russian, bristling with Malorussian folk sayings and motifs. How can this heritage be divided between Russia and Ukraine? And why do it?

The south-western lands of the Russian Empire, Malorussia and Novorossiya, and the Crimea developed as ethnically and religiously diverse entities. Crimean Tatars, Armenians, Greeks, Jews, Karaites, Krymchaks, Bulgarians, Poles, Serbs, Germans, and other peoples lived here. They all preserved their faith, traditions, and customs.

I am not going to idealise anything. We do know there were the Valuev Circular of 1863 an then the Ems Ukaz of 1876, which restricted the publication and importation of religious and socio-political literature in the Ukrainian language. But it is important to be mindful of the historical context. These decisions were taken against the backdrop of dramatic events in Poland and the desire of the leaders of the Polish national movement to exploit the "Ukrainian issue" to their own advantage. I should add that works of fiction, books of Ukrainian poetry and folk songs continued to be published. There is objective evidence that the Russian Empire was witnessing an active process of development of the Malorussian cultural identity within the greater Russian nation, which united the Velikorussians, the Malorussians and the Belarusians.through

At the same time, the idea of Ukrainian people as a nation separate from the Russians started to form and gain ground among the Polish elite and a part of the Malorussian intelligentsia. Since there was no historical basis – and could not have been any, conclusions were substantiated by all sorts of concoctions, which went as far as to claim that the Ukrainians are the true Slavs and the Russians, the Muscovites, are not. Such "hypotheses" became increasingly used for political purposes as a tool of rivalry between European states.

Since the late 19th century, the Austro-Hungarian authorities had latched onto this narrative, using it as a counterbalance to the Polish national movement and pro-Muscovite sentiments in Galicia. During World War I, Vienna played a role in the formation of the so-called Legion of Ukrainian Sich Riflemen. Galicians suspected of sympathies with Orthodox Christianity and Russia were subjected to brutal repression and thrown into the concentration camps of Thalerhof and Terezin.

Further developments had to do with the collapse of European empires, the fierce civil war that broke out across the vast territory of the former Russian Empire, and foreign intervention.

After the February Revolution, in March 1917, the Verkhovna Rada was established in Kyiv, intended to become the organ of supreme power. In November 1917, in its Third Universal, it declared the creation of the Ukrainian People's Republic (UPR) as part of Russia.

In December 1917, UPR representatives arrived in Brest-Litovsk, where Soviet Russia was negotiating with Germany and its allies. At a meeting on 10 January 1918, the head of the Ukrainian delegation read out a note proclaiming the independence of Ukraine. Subsequently, the Verkhovna Rada proclaimed Ukraine independent in its Fourth Universal.

The declared sovereignty did not last long. Just a few weeks later, Rada delegates signed a separate treaty with the German bloc countries. Germany and Austria-Hungary were at the time in a dire situation and needed Ukrainian bread and raw materials. In order to secure large-scale supplies, they obtained consent for sending their troops and technical staff to the UPR. In fact, this was used as a pretext for occupation.

For those who have today given up the full control of Ukraine to external forces, it would be instructive to remember that, back in 1918, such a decision proved fatal for the ruling regime in Kyiv. With the direct involvement of the occupying forces, the Verkhovna Rada was overthrown and Hetman Pavlo Skoropadskyi was brought to power, proclaiming instead of the UPR the Ukrainian State, which was essentially under German protectorate.

In November 1918 – following the revolutionary events in Germany and Austria-Hungary – Pavlo Skoropadskyi, who had lost the support of German bayonets, took a different course, declaring that "Ukraine is to take the lead in the formation of an All-Russian Federation". However, the regime was soon changed again. It was now the time of the so-called Directorate.

In autumn 1918, Ukrainian nationalists proclaimed the West Ukrainian People's Republic (WUPR) and, in January 1919, announced its unification with the Ukrainian People's Republic. In July 1919, Ukrainian forces were crushed by Polish troops, and the territory of the former WUPR came under the Polish rule.

In April 1920, Symon Petliura (portrayed as one of the "heroes" in today's Ukraine) concluded secret conventions on behalf of the UPR Directorate, giving up – in exchange for military support – Galicia and western Volhynia lands to Poland. In May 1920, Petliurites entered Kyiv in a convoy of Polish military units. But not for long. As early as November 1920, following a truce between Poland and Soviet Russia, the remnants of Petliura's forces surrendered to those same Poles.

The example of the UPR shows that different kinds of quasi-state formations that emerged across the former Russian Empire at the time of the Civil War and turbulence were inherently unstable. Nationalists sought to create their own independent states, while leaders of the White movement advocated indivisible Russia. Many of the republics established by the Bolsheviks' supporters did not see themselves outside Russia either. Nevertheless, Bolshevik Party leaders sometimes basically drove them out of Soviet Russia for various reasons.

Thus, in early 1918, the Donetsk-Krivoy Rog Soviet Republic was proclaimed and asked Moscow to incorporate it into Soviet Russia. This was met with a refusal. During a meeting with the republic's leaders, Vladimir Lenin insisted that they act as part of Soviet Ukraine. On 15 March 1918, the Central Committee of the Russian Communist Party (Bolsheviks) directly ordered that delegates be sent to the Ukrainian Congress of Soviets, including from the Donetsk Basin, and that "one government for all of Ukraine" be created at the congress. The territories of the Donetsk-Krivoy Rog Soviet Republic later formed most of the regions of south-eastern Ukraine.

Under the 1921 Treaty of Riga, concluded between the Russian SFSR, the Ukrainian SSR and Poland, the western lands of the former Russian Empire were ceded to Poland. In the interwar period, the Polish government pursued an active resettlement policy, seeking to change the ethnic composition of the eastern Borderlands – the Polish name for what is now western Ukraine, western Belarus and parts of Lithuania. The areas were subjected to harsh Polonization, local culture and traditions suppressed. Later, during World War II, radical groups of Ukrainian nationalists used this as a pretext for terror not only against Polish, but also against Jewish and Russian populations.

In 1922, when the USSR was created, with the Ukrainian Soviet Socialist Republic becoming one of its founders, a rather fierce debate among the Bolshevik leaders resulted in the implementation of Lenin's plan to form a union state as a federation of equal republics. The right for the republics to freely secede from the Union was included in the text of the Declaration on the Creation of the Union of Soviet Socialist Republics and, subsequently, in the 1924 USSR Constitution. By doing so, the authors planted in the foundation of our statehood the most dangerous time bomb, which exploded the moment the safety mechanism provided by the leading role of the CPSU was gone, the party itself collapsing from within. A "parade of sovereignties" followed. On 8 December 1991, the so-called Belovezh Agreement on the Creation of the Commonwealth of Independent States was signed, stating that "the USSR as a subject of international law and a geopolitical reality no longer existed." By the way, Ukraine never signed or ratified the CIS Charter adopted back in 1993.

In the 1920's-1930's, the Bolsheviks actively promoted the "localization policy", which took the form of Ukrainization in the Ukrainian SSR. Symbolically, as part of this policy and with consent of the Soviet authorities, Mykhailo Grushevskiy, former chairman of Verkhovna Rada, one of the ideologists of Ukrainian nationalism, who at a certain period of time had been supported by Austria-Hungary, was returned to the USSR and was elected member of the Academy of Sciences.

The localization policy undoubtedly played a major role in the development and consolidation of the Ukrainian culture, language and identity. At the same time, under the guise of combating the so-called Russian great-power chauvinism, Ukrainization was often imposed on those who did not see themselves as Ukrainians. This Soviet national policy secured at the state level the provision on three separate Slavic peoples: Russian, Ukrainian and Belarusian, instead of the large Russian nation, a triune people comprising Velikorussians, Malorussians and Belarusians.

In 1939, the USSR regained the lands earlier seized by Poland. A major portion of these became part of the Soviet Ukraine. In 1940, the Ukrainian SSR incorporated part of

Bessarabia, which had been occupied by Romania since 1918, as well as northern Bukovina. In 1948, Zmeyiniy Island (Snake Island) in the Black Sea became part of Ukraine. In 1954, the Crimean Region of the RSFSR was given to the Ukrainian SSR, in gross violation of legal norms that were in force at the time.

I would like to dwell on the destiny of Carpathian Ruthenia, which became part of Czechoslovakia following the breakup of Austria-Hungary. Rusins made up a considerable share of local population. While this is hardly mentioned any longer, after the liberation of Transcarpathia by Soviet troops the congress of the Orthodox population of the region voted for the inclusion of Carpathian Ruthenia in the RSFSR or, as a separate Carpathian republic, in the USSR proper. Yet the choice of people was ignored. In summer 1945, the historical act of the reunification of Carpathian Ukraine "with its ancient motherland, Ukraine" – as The Pravda newspaper put it – was announced.

Therefore, modern Ukraine is entirely the product of the Soviet era. We know and remember well that it was shaped – for a significant part – on the lands of historical Russia. To make sure of that, it is enough to look at the boundaries of the lands reunited with the Russian state in the 17th century and the territory of the Ukrainian SSR when it left the Soviet Union.

The Bolsheviks treated the Russian people as inexhaustible material for their social experiments. They dreamt of a world revolution that would wipe out national states. That is why they were so generous in drawing borders and bestowing territorial gifts. It is no longer important what exactly the idea of the Bolshevik leaders who were chopping the country into pieces was. We can disagree about minor details, background and logics behind certain decisions. One fact is crystal clear: Russia was robbed, indeed.

When working on this article, I relied on open-source documents that contain well-known facts rather than on some secret records. The leaders of modern Ukraine and their external "patrons" prefer to overlook these facts. They do not miss a chance, however, both inside the country and abroad, to condemn "the crimes of the Soviet regime," listing among them events with which neither the CPSU, nor the USSR, let alone modern Russia, have anything to do. At the same time, the Bolsheviks' efforts to detach from Russia its historical territories are not considered a crime. And we know why: if they brought about the weakening of Russia, our ill-wishes are happy with that.

Of course, inside the USSR, borders between republics were never seen as state borders; they were nominal within a single country, which, while featuring all the attributes of a federation, was highly centralized – this, again, was secured by the CPSU's leading role. But in 1991, all those territories, and, which is more important, people, found themselves abroad overnight, taken away, this time indeed, from their historical motherland.

What can be said to this? Things change: countries and communities are no exception. Of course, some part of a people in the process of its development, influenced by a number of reasons and historical circumstances, can become aware of itself as a separate nation at a certain moment. How should we treat that? There is only one answer: with respect!

You want to establish a state of your own: you are welcome! But what are the terms? I will recall the assessment given by one of the most prominent political figures of new Russia, first mayor of Saint Petersburg Anatoly Sobchak. As a legal expert who believed that every decision must be legitimate, in 1992, he shared the following opinion: the republics that were founders of the Union, having denounced the 1922 Union Treaty, must return to the boundaries they had had before joining the Soviet Union. All other territorial acquisitions are subject to discussion, negotiations, given that the ground has been revoked.

In other words, when you leave, take what you brought with you. This logic is hard to refute. I will just say that the Bolsheviks had embarked on reshaping boundaries even before the Soviet Union, manipulating with territories to their liking, in disregard of people's views.

The Russian Federation recognized the new geopolitical realities: and not only recognized, but, indeed, did a lot for Ukraine to establish itself as an independent country. Throughout the difficult 1990's and in the new millennium, we have provided considerable support to Ukraine. Whatever "political arithmetic" of its own Kyiv may wish to apply, in 1991–2013, Ukraine's budget savings amounted to more than USD 82 billion, while today, it holds on to the mere USD 1.5 billion of Russian payments for gas transit to Europe. If economic ties between our countries had been retained, Ukraine would enjoy the benefit of tens of billions of dollars.

Ukraine and Russia have developed as a single economic system over decades and centuries. The profound cooperation we had 30 years ago is an example for the European Union to look up to. We are natural complementary economic partners. Such a close relationship can strengthen competitive advantages, increasing the potential of both countries.

Ukraine used to possess great potential, which included powerful infrastructure, gas transportation system, advanced shipbuilding, aviation, rocket and instrument engineering industries, as well as world-class scientific, design and engineering schools. Taking over this legacy and declaring independence, Ukrainian leaders promised that the Ukrainian economy would be one of the leading ones and the standard of living would be among the best in Europe.

Today, high-tech industrial giants that were once the pride of Ukraine and the entire Union, are sinking. Engineering output has dropped by 42 per cent over ten years. The scale of deindustrialization and overall economic degradation is visible in Ukraine's electricity production, which has seen a nearly two-time decrease in 30 years. Finally, according to IMF reports, in 2019, before the coronavirus pandemic broke out, Ukraine's GDP per capita had been below USD 4 thousand. This is less than in the Republic of Albania, the Republic of Moldova, or unrecognized Kosovo. Nowadays, Ukraine is Europe's poorest country.

Who is to blame for this? Is it the people of Ukraine's fault? Certainly not. It was the Ukrainian authorities who waisted and frittered away the achievements of many generations. We know how hardworking and talented the people of Ukraine are. They can achieve success and outstanding results with perseverance and determination. And these qualities, as well as their openness, innate optimism and hospitality have not gone. The feelings of millions of people who treat Russia not just well but with great affection, just as we feel about Ukraine, remain the same.

Until 2014, hundreds of agreements and joint projects were aimed at developing our economies, business and cultural ties, strengthening security, and solving common social and environmental problems. They brought tangible benefits to people – both in Russia and Ukraine. This is what we believed to be most important. And that is why we had a fruitful interaction with all, I emphasize, with all the leaders of Ukraine.

Even after the events in Kyiv of 2014, I charged the Russian government to elaborate options for preserving and maintaining our economic ties within relevant ministries and agencies. However, there was and is still no mutual will to do the same. Nevertheless, Russia is still one of Ukraine's top three trading partners, and hundreds of thousands of Ukrainians are coming to us to work, and they find a welcome reception and support. So that what the "aggressor state" is.

When the USSR collapsed, many people in Russia and Ukraine sincerely believed and assumed that our close cultural, spiritual and economic ties would certainly last, as would the commonality of our people, who had always had a sense of unity at their core. However, events – at first gradually, and then more rapidly – started to move in a different direction.

In essence, Ukraine's ruling circles decided to justify their country's independence through the denial of its past, however, except for border issues. They began to mythologize and rewrite history, edit out everything that united us, and refer to the period when Ukraine was part of the Russian Empire and the Soviet Union as an occupation. The common tragedy of collectivization and famine of the early 1930s was portrayed as the genocide of the Ukrainian people.

Radicals and neo-Nazis were open and more and more insolent about their ambitions. They were indulged by both the official authorities and local oligarchs, who robbed the people of Ukraine and kept their stolen money in Western banks, ready to sell their motherland for the sake of preserving their capital. To this should be added the persistent weakness of state institutions and the position of a willing hostage to someone else's geopolitical will.

I recall that long ago, well before 2014, the US and EU countries systematically and consistently pushed Ukraine to curtail and limit economic cooperation with Russia. We, as the largest trade and economic partner of Ukraine, suggested discussing the emerging problems in the Ukraine-Russia-EU format. But every time we were told that Russia had nothing to do with it and that the issue concerned only the EU and Ukraine. De facto Western countries rejected Russia's repeated calls for dialogue.

Step by step, Ukraine was dragged into a dangerous geopolitical game aimed at turning Ukraine into a barrier between Europe and Russia, a springboard against Russia. Inevitably, there came a time when the concept of "Ukraine is not Russia" was no longer an option. There was a need for the "anti-Russia" concept which we will never accept.

The owners of this project took as a basis the old groundwork of the Polish-Austrian ideologists to create an "anti-Moscow Russia". And there is no need to deceive anyone that this is being done in the interests of the people of Ukraine. The Polish-Lithuanian Commonwealth never needed Ukrainian culture, much less Cossack autonomy. In Austria-Hungary, historical Russian lands were mercilessly exploited and remained the poorest. The Nazis, abetted by collaborators from the OUN-UPA, did not need Ukraine, but a living space and slaves for Aryan overlords.

Nor were the interests of the Ukrainian people thought of in February 2014. The legitimate public discontent, caused by acute socio-economic problems, mistakes, and inconsistent actions of the authorities of the time, was simply cynically exploited. Western countries directly interfered in Ukraine's internal affairs and supported the coup. Radical nationalist groups served as its battering ram. Their slogans, ideology, and blatant aggressive Russophobia have to a large extent become defining elements of state policy in Ukraine.

All the things that united us and bring us together so far came under attack. First and foremost, the Russian language. Let me remind you that the new "Maidan" authorities first tried to repeal the law on state language policy. Then there was the law on the "purification of power", the law on education that virtually cut the Russian language out of the educational process.

Lastly, as early as May of this year, the current President [Zelensky] introduced a bill on "indigenous peoples" to the Rada. Only those who constitute an ethnic minority and do not have their own state entity outside Ukraine are recognized as indigenous. The law has been passed. New seeds of discord have been sown. And this is happening in a country, as I have already noted, that is very complex in terms of its territorial, national and linguistic composition, and its history of formation.

There may be an argument: if you are talking about a single large nation, a triune nation, then what difference does it make who people consider themselves to be – Russians, Ukrainians, or Belarusians. I completely agree with this. Especially since the determination of nationality, particularly in mixed families, is the right of every individual, free to make his or her own choice.

But the fact is that the situation in Ukraine today is completely different because it involves a forced change of identity. And the most despicable thing is that the Russians in Ukraine are being forced not only to deny their roots, generations of their ancestors but also to believe that Russia is their enemy. It would not be an exaggeration to say that the path of forced assimilation, the formation of an ethnically pure Ukrainian state, aggressive towards Russia, is comparable in its consequences to the use of weapons of mass destruction against us. As a result of such a harsh and artificial division of Russians and Ukrainians, the Russian people in all may decrease by hundreds of thousands or even millions.

Our spiritual unity has also been attacked. As in the days of the Grand Duchy of Lithuania, a new ecclesiastical has been initiated. The secular authorities, making no secret of their political aims, have blatantly interfered in church life and brought things to a split, to the seizure of churches, the beating of priests and monks. Even extensive autonomy of the Ukrainian Orthodox Church while maintaining spiritual unity with the Moscow Patriarchate strongly displeases them. They have to destroy this prominent and centuries-old symbol of our kinship at all costs.

I think it is also natural that the representatives of Ukraine over and over again vote against the UN General Assembly resolution condemning the glorification of Nazism. Marches and torchlit processions in honor of remaining war criminals from the SS units take place under the protection of the official authorities. Mazepa, who betrayed everyone, Petliura, who paid for Polish patronage with Ukrainian lands, and Bandera, who collaborated with the Nazis, are ranked as national heroes. Everything is being done to erase from the memory of young generations the names of genuine patriots and victors, who have always been the pride of Ukraine.

For the Ukrainians who fought in the Red Army, in partisan units, the Great Patriotic War was indeed a patriotic war because they were defending their home, their great common Motherland. Over two thousand soldiers became Heroes of the Soviet Union. Among them are legendary pilot Ivan Kozhedub, fearless sniper, defender of Odessa and Sevastopol Lyudmila Pavlichenko, valiant guerrilla commander Sidor Kovpak. This indomitable generation fought, those people gave their lives for our future, for us. To forget their feat is to betray our grandfathers, mothers and fathers.

The anti-Russia project has been rejected by millions of Ukrainians. The people of Crimea and residents of Sevastopol made their historic choice. And people in the southeast peacefully tried to defend their stance. Yet, all of them, including children, were labeled as separatists and terrorists. They were threatened with ethnic cleansing and the use of military force. And the residents of Donetsk and Luhansk took up arms to defend their home, their language and their lives. Were they left any other choice after the riots that swept through the cities of Ukraine, after the horror and tragedy of 2 May 2014 in Odessa where Ukrainian neo-Nazis burned people alive making a new Khatyn out of it? The same massacre was ready to be carried out by the followers of Bandera in Crimea, Sevastopol, Donetsk and Luhansk. Even now they do not abandon such plans. They are biding their time. But their time will not come.

The coup d'état and the subsequent actions of the Kyiv authorities inevitably provoked confrontation and civil war. The UN High Commissioner for Human Rights estimates that the total number of victims in the conflict in Donbas has exceeded 13,000. Among them are the elderly and children. These are terrible, irreparable losses.

Russia has done everything to stop fratricide. The Minsk agreements aimed at a peaceful settlement of the conflict in Donbas have been concluded. I am convinced that they still have no alternative. In any case, no one has withdrawn their signatures from the Minsk Package of Measures or from the relevant statements by the leaders of the Normandy format countries. No one has initiated a review of the United Nations Security Council resolution of 17 February 2015.

During official negotiations, especially after being reined in by Western partners, Ukraine's representatives regularly declare their "full adherence" to the Minsk agreements, but are in fact guided by a position of "unacceptability". They do not intend to seriously discuss either the special status of Donbas or safeguards for the people living there. They prefer to exploit the image of the "victim of external aggression" and peddle Russophobia. They arrange bloody provocations in Donbas. In short, they attract the attention of external patrons and masters by all means.

Apparently, and I am becoming more and more convinced of this: Kyiv simply does not need Donbas. Why? Because, firstly, the inhabitants of these regions will never accept the order that they have tried and are trying to impose by force, blockade and threats. And secondly, the outcome of both Minsk-1 and Minsk-2 which give a real chance to peacefully restore the territorial integrity of Ukraine by coming to an agreement directly with the DPR and LPR with Russia, Germany and France as mediators, contradicts the entire logic of the anti-Russia project. And it can only be sustained by the constant cultivation of the image of an internal and external enemy. And I would add – under the protection and control of the Western powers.

This is what is actually happening. First of all, we are facing the creation of a climate of fear in Ukrainian society, aggressive rhetoric, indulging neo-Nazis and militarising the country. Along with that we are witnessing not just complete dependence but direct external control, including the supervision of the Ukrainian authorities, security services and armed forces by foreign advisers, military "development" of the territory of Ukraine and deployment of NATO infrastructure. It is no coincidence that the aforementioned flagrant law on 'indigenous peoples" was adopted under the cover of large-scale NATO exercises in Ukraine.

This is also a disguise for the takeover of the rest of the Ukrainian economy and the exploitation of its natural resources. The sale of agricultural land is not far off, and it is obvious who will buy it up. From time to time, Ukraine is indeed given financial resources and loans, but under their own conditions and pursuing their own interests, with preferences and benefits for Western companies. By the way, who will pay these debts back? Apparently, it is assumed that this will have to be done not only by today's generation of Ukrainians but also by their children, grandchildren and probably great-grandchildren.

The Western authors of the anti-Russia project set up the Ukrainian political system in such a way that Presidents, members of parliament and ministers would change but the attitude of separation from and enmity with Russia would remain. Reaching peace was the main election slogan of the incumbent President. He came to power with this. The promises turned out to be lies. Nothing has changed. And in some ways the situation in Ukraine and around Donbas has even degenerated.

In the anti-Russia project, there is no place either for a sovereign Ukraine or for the political forces that are trying to defend its real independence. Those who talk about reconciliation in Ukrainian society, about dialogue, about finding a way out of the current impasse are labelled as "pro-Russian" agents.

Again, for many people in Ukraine, the anti-Russia project is simply unacceptable. And there are millions of such people. But they are not allowed to raise their heads. They have had their legal opportunity to defend their point of view in fact taken away from them. They are intimidated, driven underground. Not only are they persecuted for their convictions, for the spoken word, for the open expression of their position, but they are also killed. Murderers, as a rule, go unpunished.

Today, the "right" patriot of Ukraine is only the one who hates Russia. Moreover, the entire Ukrainian statehood, as we understand it, is proposed to be further built exclusively on this idea. Hate and anger, as world history has repeatedly proved this, are a very shaky foundation for sovereignty, fraught with many serious risks and dire consequences.

All the subterfuges associated with the anti-Russia project are clear to us. And we will never allow our historical territories and people close to us living there to be used against Russia. And to those who will undertake such an attempt, I would like to say that this way they will destroy their own country.

The incumbent authorities in Ukraine like to refer to Western experience, seeing it as a model to follow. Just have a look at how Austria and Germany, the US and Canada live next to each other. Close in ethnic composition, culture, in fact sharing one language, they remain sovereign states with their own interests, with their own foreign policy. But this does not prevent them from the closest integration or allied relations. They have very conditional, transparent borders. And when crossing them the citizens feel at home. They create families, study, work, do business. Incidentally, so do millions of those born in Ukraine who now live in Russia. We see them as our own close people.

Russia is open to dialogue with Ukraine and ready to discuss the most complex issues. But it is important for us to understand that our partner is defending its national interests but not serving someone else's, and is not a tool in someone else's hands to fight against us.

We respect the Ukrainian language and traditions. We respect Ukrainians' desire to see their country free, safe and prosperous.

I am confident that true sovereignty of Ukraine is possible only in partnership with Russia. Our spiritual, human and civilizational ties formed for centuries and have their origins in the same sources, they have been hardened by common trials, achievements and victories. Our kinship has been transmitted from generation to generation. It is in the hearts and the memory of people living in modern Russia and Ukraine, in the blood ties that unite millions of our families. Together we have always been and will be many times stronger and more successful. For we are one people.

Today, these words may be perceived by some people with hostility. They can be interpreted in many possible ways. Yet, many people will hear me. And I will say one thing – Russia has never been and will never be "anti-Ukraine". And what Ukraine will be – it is up to its citizens to decide.

END NOTES

1 Also published under the title *The Corporation* (USA) *The Putin Corporation* (UK) and *The Corporation of Assassins* (Poland), *A Era Dos Assassinos* (Brazil), *De Onderneming* (Netherlands).

2 They belong to the Ukrainian Orthodox Church (Moscow Patriarchate), the Ukrainian Orthodox Church (Kyiv Patriarchate), and the Ukrainian Autocephalous Orthodox Church (mostly the Ukrainian diaspora abroad). Only the Ukrainian Orthodox Church (Moscow Patriarchate) has canonical status (recognition by the autocephalous local Orthodox Churches).

3 Where the trial of the main Nazi criminals was held after World War II.

4 It was, in fact, the second referendum on this subject. The first one was held in March 1991, before the putsch. At that time, citizens throughout the Soviet Union who voted had to answer two questions: "on the need to preserve the USSR as a renewed federation of equal sovereign republics" and on the desire of each particular republic "to remain within the Union of Soviet Sovereign States". In Ukraine, 70.2% voted in favor of the first question and 80.2% voted in favor of the second question. After that March result, a long process began for the preparation and signing of the new Union Treaty. The signing was scheduled for August 20, but it did not take place because of the coup d'etat in Moscow on August 19. It is possible that conspirators in Moscow were in a hurry in order to prevent the legal reform of the USSR.

5 From 1988 he was head of the ideological department and secretary of the Communist Party; from 1989 candidate to the Politburo; from 1990 member of the Politburo, Second Secretary of the Central Committee, member of the CPSU Central Committee, Chairman of the Supreme Soviet of the Ukraine SSR.

6 With funds transferred abroad before August 1991, under the direction and control of the KGB through foreign agents of the Soviet security services, firms and banks were established abroad. These invested Soviet "party money" (i.e., budget money of the Soviet state), then purchased goods abroad and, using demand created by the Soviet government and the absence of competition and market system, sold them the imported goods, bypassing all customs and taxes and benefiting their own firms.

7 Usually parliamentary and presidential elections would have been held in March 1995 and late 1996, respectively.

8 In response, the U.S., U.K. and Russia promised Ukraine to:
    - Respect Ukraine's independence, sovereignty, and existing borders;
    - to refrain from the threat or use of force against the territorial integrity or political inde-pendence of Ukraine;
    - Refrain from economic coercion aimed at subordinating to their own interests the exercise by Ukraine of the rights inherent in its sovereignty and thereby securing for itself advantages of any kind;
    - To seek immediate action by the UN Security Council to assist Ukraine as a non-nuclear-weapon State Party to the Treaty on the Non-Proliferation of Nuclear Weapons, in the event that Ukraine becomes a victim of an act of aggression or is threatened with aggression involving nuclear weapons;
    - Not to use nuclear weapons against any non-nuclear-weapon State party to the Treaty on the Non-Proliferation of Nuclear Weapons;
    - The Russian Federation, the United Kingdom of Great Britain and Northern Ireland, the United States of America, and Ukraine will consult in the event of a situation that raises an issue regarding these commitments.

9 Wishing to have the maximum range of opportunities, the groups were formed through

informal relationships. This fact explains the non-transparent ownership structure of those groups that were created during the period of this decree (it was abolished in 1999). Examples of such groups are the FIG "Finance and Credit", FIG "Privat-Invest", FIG "UkrSibbank". Unlike these groups, the FIG "Industrial Union of Donbass", which underwent restructuring in 2000, has a rather transparent ownership structure. In any case the activity of FIG is a reflection of the real economic situation in Ukraine in the early 90s.

One of the leading financial and industrial groups in Ukraine is System Capital Management (SCM), established in 2000 for asset management in the mining, metallurgy and energy industries and headed by one of Ukraine's richest men, Rinat Akhmetov. During the subsequent years new business areas emerged within SCM Group and corporate restructuring was carried out, during which assets of SCM JSC within individual industries were merged into specialized holdings. Subsidiaries were also established abroad, particularly in London. The group included over 100 enterprises employing over three hundred thousand people.

SCM is present in Ukraine, Russia, the USA, Italy, Great Britain, Switzerland and Bulgaria. In 2011 it was decided to separate the ownership and strategic business management functions. As a result of these transformations SCM JSC (the group's management company) concentrated on strategic business management, while the corporate rights ownership function of all assets (both Ukrainian and foreign) was transferred to SCM Holdings Limited. At the same time, the shares of both SCM JSC and SCM Holdings Limited became directly owned by Rinat Akhmetov (previously Rinat Akhmetov owned SCM Holdings Limited indirectly through SCM JSC).

10 After graduation, he became an operations officer in the regional department of the KGB, then a senior operations officer, deputy head of department, head of department, deputy head of department, and head of inspection of the KGB of the Ukrainian SSR. He also worked in the Fifth Directorate of the KGB (combating dissent) and headed the Fifth Directorate of the KGB of the Ukrainian SSR.

11 Major Mykola Melnychenko.

12 The perpetrators were eventually killed or detained. But those who ordered these murders have not been identified or found.

13 Allegedly belonging to the Solntsevsky Organized Crime Group.

14 In 2003, Bolotskikh was convicted of murder. He stated that he was not paid for the murder, but carried out the assassination at the request of his "friends." The murder was prepared in Moscow and carried out by Muscovites; Shcherban was returning that day from Moscow from KGB-FSB agent Kobzon. Bolotskikh was considered a specialist in sabotage activities, having done anti-terrorist training, was serving in the army He then surfaced as a leading specialist in sabotage working for man named Sinyakin – a Moscovite engaged in trafficking weapons under the hood of the Russian special services.

15 He served as Prime Minister twice - during the Ukrainian SSR in 1987-1990 and during the first years of independence in 1994-1995.

16 "I knew Shcherban. He came to me when I was the Prime Minister. He asked to be my freelance counselor. I even gave him a pass. I liked him for his healthy ideas. And here Shcherban is killed. The director of the mine Ampilov, whom I built three houses for, told me how they did it,"Masol remembered.

17 On February 20, 1999, Lazarenko was detained at the New York airport for visa violations and on suspicion of attempting to enter the United States illegally. In response, Lazarenko sought political asylum in the United States, but instead of asylum, he was charged with extortion, money laundering, and fraud in 2000. According to various reports, by the time of his arrest, Lazarenko had between $114 million and $477 million in U.S. bank accounts. Of these funds, between $200 (according to the UN) and $320 million (according to the Office of the Prosecutor General of

Ukraine) was stolen. As a result, Lazarenko was convicted in the US and sentenced to long-term imprisonment and a multi-million dollar fine. Ukrainian authorities repeatedly asked the US to extradite Lazarenko, but the US side refused, citing the absence of an extradition treaty.

18 Melnichenko, repeatedly claimed later that he had started recording Kuchma on his own initiative back in 1998. He said about the idea to wiretap Kuchma's office, "The idea was what? To collect evidence indicating that Kuchma was indeed a criminal, and that such a person could not be in office as President of Ukraine. And these tapes were the physical evidence of all this. ...I already had quite a good collection of tapes and had information confirming that Kuchma violated the Constitution and the Criminal Code. I had a meeting with Marchuk in early spring of 1999. I introduced myself to him and showed him my ID. I had already reached the rank of captain and my post was that of senior security officer of the State Guard Department of Ukraine. I introduced myself to him, I told him: So-and-so, I am so-and-so, and I have evidence that Kuchma is a criminal. I recorded Kuchma and I wish Kuchma would not be President, because he is a criminal. And I asked Marchuk for advice. We had a face-to-face conversation. ...I couldn't talk to Marchuk on the phone because his phones were tapped. Both the city phones and the government phones were tapped. Because he was Kuchma's rival in the presidential election. ...Marchuk was much closer to me in spirit, as he was from the secret service after all." Melnichenko did not produce these recordings.

19 "He asked me: what about money? I said: it was very hard with money... For some support, he gave me... a thousand marks in one bill... to buy batteries, for one day, for one day, the batteries cost... there are specific batteries that go into this SSU recorder... about $1.50 one battery. ...You needed six batteries then. That is, $10 just for one day for the batteries alone. For cassettes, for these ones, the ones that go in this recorder, it's $100 a day. To ... to buy these tapes, it's $100 a tape..."

20 "Then we set up the next meeting," Melnichenko continues to tell – "He drew me a picture of where we were to meet. He drew it on... on the Constitution of Ukraine. By the way, I still have his drawing - where and how we should meet. Well, Marchuk says that evil must be removed, and we will remove it. Well, then my wings grew, and it was agreed that at the most after the first round of presidential elections Kuchma should not be, well, with the help and these notes, Kuchma should not be... I met Marchuk - I can't tell you how many times: I met him about ten times or so. In different places. Well, this is the place where he drew. We exchanged information on how we could find each other. It was pagers, and code signs, and cell phones. He gave me his secret cell phone that he only had for communicating with me. That was all... in the early spring of 1999... I started working more actively and recording Kuchma. We were sure that Kuchma as President was already serving out his last months, October-November 1999 at the most... We had very interesting ways to meet. Marchuk had a driver, Tolya, I think, at the time. And I was waiting at the place we had agreed. That day Marchuk's jeep arrived, but Marchuk wasn't there himself. The doors opened and I saw that driver. I got in, and we drove away. We made appointments very late, either at twelve o'clock or one o'clock or two o'clock in the morning - when it was obvious that there were no cars and no tail. I do not remember. [...] I was waiting there, a jeep stopped, I quickly got in, and they drove us, the jeep took us to a meeting with Marchuk. I gave him all my information; he was very grateful. We agreed that we would meet next time in a different place - it was near the Verkhovna Rada Commission, not far from our office. And we agreed about the time, that it would be somewhere after two in the morning."

21 One of those pieces of information that... was transmitted... when I was recording, it was, I think, the month of May... Ryabets - this is the head of the Central Election Commission Mikhail Ryabets - came to Kuchma. He was reporting to Kuchma how Ryabets and the Central Electoral Commission, would not allow Marchuk to participate in the presidential campaign. I listened to it all, I was shocked that they were going to deregister Marchuk, or rather not to deregister him, but

not to allow him to register as a presidential candidate. I contacted Marchuk and we had an urgent meeting. I gave him the tape. Let's put it this way, at that time still through my channels, through my people, through whom I contacted Marchuk urgently in the place he had drawn, I handed him the tape, told him the scheme. Marchuk was very grateful. And... he said: that's it, we'll be in contact. We agreed - where we would meet next time. That is, we changed our meeting places every time... For example, today we met at Sevastopol Square, tomorrow we met near the Lesya Ukrainka Theater."

22 "Sometime near lunchtime, Aleksandr Mikhailovich Volkov, a well-known oligarch, comes in to see Kuchma and says: Leonid Danilovich, we have two pieces of news. One of the news is very unpleasant. He says: Marchuk knows everything about what you agreed with Ryabtz yesterday, how to take him off the register - he knows all about it. Today he called Ryabets and told me word for word the mechanism of how the Central Electoral Commission will not allow Marchuk to participate in the presidential campaign... Ryabets called me by phone and said so and so. And Ryabets swears that he didn't tell anyone. ...And you talked about it yesterday, and only you knew. ...Either Ryabets told, or you were overheard. And Kuchma immediately dialed Derkach and gave him a command to conduct an urgent check."

"...I got a phone call from Alexander Nikolayevich Garanin, deputy head of the Operative-Technical Department. He said: Kolya, what kind of inspection do you have there? I said: what kind of inspection?

- Well, in Kuchma's office, what kind of inspection?

I said: I don't know anything. I said: let me find out.

I went to Boris Ivanovich Movchan, the head of the President's security. I said: So-and-so, I have such information...

Then he went to Kuchma. Kuchma said: yes. In two hours, I got an inspection in my office. Well, the chief of security told me: yes, Kolya, in two hours there will be an inspection, 15 people from the SBU are here, but you must control everything, make sure everything is under control, that no one does what he should not do. I say: yes.

...That is, I was instructed to control it all. As soon as Kuchma came out of his office, I immediately went in... instantly pulled out the recorder and hid it. This was all done in a matter of seconds...

I took this tape that he... planned to take out Marchuk. To keep him out of the presidential campaign. Gave it to Marchuk. And the next day, this command to make an urgent inspection of Kuchma's office. And the Security Service of Ukraine came, and I did not understand how it could happen, how it could happen that Kuchma interrupts his working day, leaves, and 15 SBU officers with cars, with equipment coming to check the cabinet. I could not understand it. And the only thing that saved my life, as I say, was the fact that I was able to do it in a purely organizational way so that I could control it. And I was in the Presidential Administration every day in the morning, from 7 o'clock till 11 o'clock, till 12 o'clock, till 1 o'clock in the morning - and I was controlling that nobody could do something like that. And I tell you, it saved my life...Then I called Marchuk and said: "What are you doing, I said, you bastard? I mean, he just set me up, just set me up. As I understood it, in this case a human life is worthless for him. How could he do that? He said: Well, it happened. The topic was hushed up.

23 And CEO of the Center of European Creative Association.

24 Any objective reader, after listening to these discursive texts, should have concluded that the President of Ukraine could have been directly involved in organizing the kidnapping or even murder of journalist Georgiy Gongadze. But another thing is just as obvious: in no impartial court could the recordings of conversations from the president's office be considered sufficient evidence to convict Kuchma for a number of reasons. While the recordings were certainly authentic, it was impossible to prove in court that they had not been edited or that there had been

no outside interference; the quality of the recordings was poor, and the transcripts lent themselves to double, not always obvious interpretations; the conversations showed that President Kuchma had an extremely negative attitude toward Gongadze and even suggested that he be deported to Georgia, or that he be kidnapped by "Chechens." Nevertheless, in none of the numerous conversations was there an unambiguous instruction (order) to kill Gongadze, although such an order could have been given clearly and concisely, briefly, once, without going back to the subject of Gongadze. Furthermore, legally, as President Kuchma had immunity from prosecution.

25 And this serves as indirect evidence that Kuchma was not obviously involved in organizing Gongadze's murder. Perhaps it was for this reason that General Marchuk ordered Melnichenko to stop wiretapping conversations in the presidential office: after September 16, the absence of conversations proving President Kuchma's involvement in the murder became an unprofitable indication for Marchuk that Kuchma had not given the order to kill Gongadze. "Melnichenko did not make public any recordings of conversations between the President and Minister [Kravchenko] that must have taken place after the journalist's disappearance," writes Yaroslav Kosiv, author of a book about Gongadze's murder.

26 It included the Socialist Party of Ukraine, the Ukrainian Republican Party, the Reforms and Order party, the Ukrainian National Assembly-Ukrainian People's Self-Defense (UNA-UNSO), a number of leftist parties, including the Ukrainian Communist Youth Union.

27 "There is no convincing reason to believe that President Kuchma "ordered" the murder of journalist Gongadze or that [he] was in any way involved in it. There are also no witnesses to Gongadze's disappearance and actual murder. Therefore, the charges must be based on existing evidence and recordings of conversations concerning the journalist, if these recordings are reliable. However, neither the circumstances of his disappearance nor the state of the integrity of the recordings available to us prove the president's involvement." the experts said.

28 Mostly members of the UNA-UNSO.

29 , in particular his son-in-law V. Pinchuk, the head of the Security Service of Ukraine (SBU). Pinchuk, his son-in-law, and L. Derkach, head of the SBU, representing Kuchma's family clan.

30 The previous seven had been privatized by the Surkis brothers for next to nothing).

31 The main figure was Colonel General Georgy Oleinik, head of the main financial administration of the Russian Army. The general was accused of exceeding his authority and transferring to Ukraine UESU accounts 450 million dollars for the supply of material and technical resources for the Russian military department. However, Oleinik was soon acquitted "due to the absence of corpus delicti."

32 Other scandals related to illegal arms trade also gained publicity. Firstly, Ukraine got in trouble with the US and the UN for supplying heavy artillery to the Macedonians who were fighting the Albanians. The latter, supported by the Kosovo Liberation Army and the Americans, undertook a series of successful military operations in Macedonia, jeopardizing the preservation of peace inside the country. President Kuchma developed quite close and friendly relations with the young and energetic President of the Republic of Macedonia, Boris Trajkovski. Macedonian diplomats, military and businessmen began to negotiate intensively with the Ukrainian side on arms deliveries for the Macedonian army. There was no direct international ban on this type of supplies. Nevertheless, the Ukrainian military tried to act cautiously, because during the meeting with Kuchma the U.S. Secretary of State, Condoleezza Rice, urged the Ukrainian side not to supply weapons to the Macedonians. The UN Arms Control Commission also launched a vigorous attack on Ukrainian diplomatic representatives abroad in order to influence Ukraine on this issue. Although in the end the Ukrainians promised to suspend arms deliveries to third countries, weapons were delivered to Macedonia, China and Iran. T-72 tanks and helicopters were sent to Macedonia; six long-range X-55 cruise missiles capable of carrying nuclear warheads were sent to

China and Iran. Ukraine's credibility as a partner in international negotiations was finally undermined.

33 His government had done so without relying on international financial aid; that it solved, if not completely, then partially the Ukrainian problem of pension and wage debts; that it made a bold attempt to reform one of the most corrupt sectors of the economy, the fuel and energy sector, shattering secret profit redistribution deals and capital flight schemes. Legal and legitimate return of funds to the state Treasury and transparent privatization of the largest industrial enterprises further laid the foundation for industrial growth and international economic ties of Ukraine. The resignation of Viktor Yushchenko's government showed that the oligarch entourage surrounding President Kuchma (and later Yushchenko himself as President and especially under President Yanukovich), created an elite characterized by temporary consensus on how to distribute state property to further individual and corporate interests.

34 The NFS, which initially consisted of seven parties: "Batkivshchyna" by Yulia Tymoshenko, "Sobor" by Anatoly Matvienko – Ukrainian Christian Democratic Party (UCDP) by Olesia Sergienko, Ukrainian Republican Party (URP) by Levko Lukyanenko, Ukrainian Conservative Republican Party (UCRP) by Stepan Khmara, Ukrainian Social Democratic Party (USDP) by Vasyl Onopenko, and Patriotic Party of Ukraine (PPU) by Nikolai Gaber. After the FNS was renamed Yulia Tymoshenko's Bloc (BYuT), it also included Oleg Soskin's Ukrainian National Conservative Party (UNKP).

35 It included 10 parties: the People's Movement of Ukraine, the Ukrainian People's Party, the Liberal Party of Ukraine, the Congress of Ukrainian Nationalists, the Christian Democratic Union, the Youth Party, the Reforms and Order Party, and others. In February 2002 this bloc was officially registered.

36 The Communist Party of Ukraine (CPU) – 20.01%; the block "For United Ukraine" (V. Litvin) – 11.79%, "For United Ukraine" – 11.79% and the block "For United Ukraine" (Yushchenko) - 10.89%. Lytvyn) - 11.79%; Yulia Tymoshenko's bloc – 7.25%; the Socialist Party of Ukraine (SPU) of Alexander Moroz – 6.87%; the Social Democratic Party of Ukraine (united) (SDPU/o/) of Viktor Medvedchuk – 6.27%.

37 The For United Ukraine bloc – in the south and east. Narodny Rukh – had its permanent electorate in western Ukraine.

38 In the Rada itself, the parties and blocs that won the elections formed their own factions. The faction "United Ukraine" had the largest number of MPs – 177. But this faction proved to be unviable and soon split up into six independent factions: "Party of Regions" – 52 deputies; "Labor Ukraine" – 31; "Party of Industrialists and Entrepreneurs" – 20; "Narodovlastiye" – 17; "Agrarii Ukrainy" ("Agrarian Party of Ukraine") – 17; faction "Democratic Initiative" – 15. "Our Ukraine" faction had 118 deputies, Communist Party of Ukraine – 64, Social Democratic Party of Ukraine (United) – 31, Bloc of Yulia Tymoshenko – 23, Socialist Party of Ukraine – 22. While the posts of speaker and deputy speakers were won by United Ukraine (Yeda) and the United Social Democrats, the leadership of the key parliamentary committees was taken over by Nashists (the name given to the members of the Nasha Ukraina faction).

Yushchenko and his supporters managed to win the parliamentary elections, but lost the negotiations on forming a parliamentary majority.

39 They were followed by Viktor Medvedchuk, Communist leader Petro Symonenko and Socialist leader Oleksandr Moroz. Yanukovich and Yushchenko were not inferior to each other. They came to the finish line practically together.

40 The first deputy chairman of the SBU.

41 The Party of Regions, the CPU, and the administration of President Kuchma.

42 Symptoms of dioxin poisoning are: acute pancreatitis, gastrointestinal pain, acute pain in the

back, and bleeding ulcers.

43 Prylipko.

44 The beginning of the recording of this phone conversation:
Klyuyev: Good afternoon.
Prilipko: Good afternoon.
Klyuyev: This, Klyuyev, is one short question... tell me the address of our central opponent.
Prilipko: From memory, Yaroslavskaya.
Klyuyev: Yaroslavskaya?! What's next?
Prilipko: One fraction of something there... Just a second, and I'll call you back.
Klyuyev: Well, call me back, please.
Prilipko: Hello.
Klyuyev: Hello.
Prilipko: Well, the biggest one is the one I called, Yaroslavskaya 1/3.
Klyuyev: Wait a minute. Yaroslavskaya...
Prilipko: There's a big 3-story building, and there are two Borychev Tok offices on Podol.
Klyuyev: Borichev Tok.
Prilipko: Yes, 8a and 22.
Klyuyev: And the main one where?
Prilipko: That's the first one I named, the very first one.

45 And they did! Chairman of the Central Electoral Commission, lawyer Sergei Kivalov, announced that according to preliminary data from the Central Electoral Commission, Viktor Yanukovich had won a convincing victory, gaining 49.42% against Yushchenko's 46.69%. The electoral geographic preferences remained the same: the center and west of Ukraine for Yushchenko, the southeast and the Crimea for Yanukovich.

46 As described in *The Age of Assassins: How Putin Poisons Democracy*, Felshtinsky and Pribylovsky.

47 The same Serhiy Klyuyev had organized the computer falsifications. At the governmental level, he was assisted by his brother Andriy Klyuyev, Deputy Prime Minister of the Government and Senior Advisor to Prime Minister Edward Prutnik, Head of the Presidential Administration Viktor Medvechuk, Senior Advisor to President Serhiy Lyovochkin, former advisor to Kuchma on elections Yuri Levenets, and computer specialist Zimin. Technical support was provided by the Ukrainian company Ukrtelecom, headed by Grigory Jackson. All this was done with the connivance of CEC head Sergey Kivalov.

48 Viktor Yushchenko's entire election campaign was orange. Orange ribbons, scarves, ties and hats were used as a distinctive sign of Yushchenko's supporters. His son patented the color orange, and the "street industry" sold orange in mass quantities to all comers. Yanukovych's supporters gathered under white and blue banners.

49 The Donetsk, Dnepropetrovsk, Zhitomir, Zaporizhzhia, Kirovograd, Luhansk, Mykolaiv, Odessa, Poltava, Sumy, Kharkiv, Kherson, Chernigov oblasts, the Crimean autonomy, and Sevastopol were represented at the Severodonetsk congress. Representatives of the Cherkasy and Zakarpattia oblasts did not attend the congress. According to the organizers, delegates from Cherkasy and Transcarpathian regions could not come to the congress for technical reasons.

50 The session elected the current governor of the oblast, Yevgeny Kushnarev, as chairman of the oblast executive committee. It was he who was charged with coordinating with Donetsk, Dnepropetrovsk, Zaporizhzhia, Lugansk, Odessa, Kherson, and Mykolaiv oblast councils, the Supreme Council of Crimea, and the Sevastopol City Council to create a southeastern autonomy when the political situation worsened.

51 The congress also issued an ultimatum that, if Yushchenko wins, the southeast will reserve the right to take adequate action to protect the rights of the citizens of its regions, up to and including

the creation of a southeastern Ukrainian autonomous republic.

52 As Yushchenko had filed a complaint declaring illegal the CEC, which on November 26 declared Yanukovich the winner of the second round and canceled the voting as falsified.

53 Nikolai Azarov was appointed as acting Prime Minister in his place.

54 Including the People's Movement of Ukraine and the Ukrainian People's Party. The main actors on the political scene of the Orange Revolution were undoubtedly Yushchenko and Tymoshenko, who complemented each other

55 Cousin Petro Poroshenko was appointed head of the National Security and Defense Council (CNSD). Oleg Rybachuk's cousin was appointed deputy Prime Minister for European integration. Kum Yuri Pavlenko - Minister of Family, Youth and Sports. In Kharkov, Victor Yushchenko's own nephew (son of his older brother Peter), Yaroslav Yushchenko, despite his young age and lack of any managerial experience, became deputy governor. Another cousin, Oleksandr Cherevko, was appointed head of the Cherkasy regional state administration. The famous Ukrainian singer Oksana Bilozir, who was close to Yushchenko's family and baptized one of Poroshenko's daughters, was appointed Minister of Culture. Yushchenko did not benefit from the scandal of his son Andrei, who drove around the capital in a fancy limousine with a cell phone worth several thousand dollars.

56 In fact, any government that comes to power begins by reducing the state apparatus by at least 10 percent, while increasing control or other functions of the state, which then leads to an increase in the very apparatus that originally needed to be reduced.

57 : 12 thousand hryvnias were paid for a first-born child, 25 thousand for the second, and 50 thousand for the third and each subsequent children. Under the banner "Heroic Mothers", families began to receive ten times the minimum standard of living. As a result, for the first time in Ukraine began to show an increase in the birth rate, and in 2009, over half a million children were born, the highest figure since independence.

58 Victor Pinchuk, Rinat Akhmetov.

59 Wishing to downsize the Security Service of Ukraine, separating the Special Communication and Information Security Service and the Foreign Intelligence Service into separate agencies, Yushchenko automatically increased their numbers by giving them a sizable budget, and encouraged the creation of new security academies. In addition to the academies of the Ministry of Internal Affairs and the SBU, the Foreign Intelligence Academy appeared.

60 Borys Tarasyuk, a, a supporter of NATO and European integration, was re-appointed as Foreign Minister.

61 Also, regional businessmen Boiko, and Lyovochkin.

62 If you look at the voting results in the Verkhovna Rada, it was the votes of the "regionalists" and "Nashists" in April 2006 that decided the parliamentary resolution on the lease of the shelf by "Venko".

63 . An especially fierce struggle was waged during the mass reprivatization of three thousand enterprises, privatized by the previous government through corrupt schemes. As a result, the program of reviewing the privatization decisions of the old authorities and the mass re-privatization of property was derailed.

64 The question of the re-privatization of other large enterprises owned by Rinat Akhmetov's and Victor Pinchuk's financial and industrial groups was left open. The latter were certainly not interested in revision of the privatization results.

65 It caused the resignation of Roman Zvarich, Minister of Justice of Ukrainian-American origin.

66 He also included in his statement: "first presidential aide Oleksandr Tretyakov, MP Mykola Martynenko and several of their partners are implementing a scenario of using power for their

own purposes..."

67 "I would like to hear at least one concrete fact about any of the names that were mentioned. If there are facts, we will investigate them. But no such fact has been named!"

68 He admitted only that he fought against the forcible seizure of the Nikopol Ferroalloy Plant: "I believe that Nikopol Ferroalloy Plant should be the property of a private entity. But this is my position as a representative of the government: I believe that the damage that the country suffered as a result of the reprivatization far exceeds the profits received.

69 "I understand that my tenure as Secretary of the National Security and Defense Council of Ukraine may be seen as an opportunity to put pressure on the investigation. In this regard, and to prevent speculative statements about the use of my official position to influence the conduct of a transparent and objective investigation, I have decided and yesterday submitted my resignation from the position of Secretary of the National Security and Defense Council of Ukraine to the President of Ukraine".

70 As well as, first presidential aide Oleksandr Tretyakov, head of the parliamentary faction "Our Ukraine" Mykola Martynenko and several other high-ranking officials.

71 "Ukrainian President Viktor Yushchenko, after months of increasingly unseemly disputes, fired his charismatic Prime Minister and appointed an interim guardian in her place.

Fired Prime Minister Yulia Tymoshenko has made no statement – yet. But she is bound to say something. Her rousing speeches were a major factor in the popular uprising that brought Mr. Yushchenko to power last fall, and she is sure to turn this weapon against the President and his new government, especially with elections scheduled for next March for the Ukrainian parliament.

This is a serious blow to the hopes and expectations for the future of Ukraine, as well as for reformers in Belarus and other former Soviet republics.

Perhaps these expectations were always unrealistic. People united in their desire to overthrow one government, as Ukrainians did with their many demonstrations, are not necessarily unanimous about what the next government should be, and the alliance between Mr. Yushchenko, formerly Prime Minister and the country's chief banker, and Ms. Tymoshenko, who made her fortune in the gas business, has always been precarious.

Mr. Yushchenko and Ms. Tymoshenko, fighting among themselves over control of lucrative sectors of the economy, over relations with Russia, and over how to deal with skyrocketing energy prices, have wasted the kinetic energy that has been generated in the streets of Kyiv. It seemed as if the government had no specific goal.

Having dismissed the government, Mr. Yushchenko claimed that its only goal was stability. But the Ukrainian demonstrators wanted change"

72 Nor Martynenko, and Tretyakov.

73 The charge was brought under Art. 205, Part 3 of the Criminal Code of Ukraine.

74 In the independent Ukraine he was the Chairman of the State Property Fund and the Minister of Economy in the Pustovoytenko government. When he became an MP, he took the post of Deputy Chairman of the Committee for Economic Policy at the Rada, and then in the administration of President Kuchma he was responsible for cooperation with the regions and implementation of administrative reforms. In Yushchenko's government (under President Kuchma) Yekhanurov served as First Deputy Prime Minister, and after the parliamentary elections of 2002, he again became Deputy and headed the Committee on Industrial Policy and Entrepreneurship. Since April 2005 he had been governor of Dnipropetrovsk Region.

75 Initially, the average price for Russian gas was $50 per 1,000 cubic meters. Gradually, during bilateral negotiations with each of the CIS countries, Russia began to increase the price to $100-115. For Belarus, as a member of the Union State, the price remained the same, and for the Baltic and Caucasian countries the prices were increased depending on the level of bilateral relations.

76 From Turkmenistan, Uzbekistan and Kazakhstan. Ukraine failed, however, to agree on direct gas supplies from Turkmenistan.

77 The previous elections were held under a mixed proportional-majoritarian system with a 4% election threshold. The 2006 parliamentary elections were held only under a proportional system, and parties or blocs had to pass a 3% threshold.

78 The Party of Regions, Yulia Tymoshenko's Bloc, the People's Union "Our Ukraine", the Socialist Party (SPU) and the Communist Party of Ukraine (CPU) were the main favorites, as always. They, in fact, got into the new parliament. The Party of Regions received 186 seats, Yulia Tymoshenko Bloc – 129, People's Union "Our Ukraine" (NSNU) – 81, SPU – 33, CPU – 21. As expected, the Regions gained support in seven regions of south-east Ukraine as well as in Crimea, taking the traditional electorate from the Communists; the Yulia Tymoshenko Bloc won in 12 central regions and Kyiv, while Our Ukraine won only in the western regions of the country.

79 The attempt to create an "orange coalition" lasted for three months, and by June 22 it was announced that it consisted of Tymoshenko Bloc, the NSNU and the SPU. However, there was no consensus within the coalition regarding the candidacy of the Speaker of the Parliament. On May 27, members of the Our Ukraine bloc faction decided to nominate Poroshenko for speaker of the Verkhovna Rada. On June 30, the deputy head of the SPU faction, Vasyl Tsushko, stated that his faction would support Poroshenko's candidacy for the position of the VRU head. But on July 6, SPU faction leader Oleksandr Moroz said that part of the SPU faction would not vote for Poroshenko and offered his candidacy instead. Poroshenko withdrew his candidacy for head of the Verkhovna Rada and urged SPU leader Oleksandr Moroz to follow his example. Moroz declined and the next day. On 7 June, he accepted the offer of the Party of Regions and Communists to form a coalition bloc with them in exchange for the promise of the Party of Regions and the Communist Party of Ukraine to support his candidacy in choosing the chairman of the Rada. The resulting coalition, which included the Party of Regions, the SPU and the CPU, was dubbed "anti-crisis. It had 240 mandates in parliament and powers under the new constitution.

80 The Communists signed "Universal" with reservations concerning the administrative-territorial structure of the country, the Ukrainian language, Ukraine's accession to NATO, and the free sale of land.

81 In exchange for creating a governing coalition and a mixed government of the Party of Regions, Socialists, Our Ukraine, and Communists, the Regions Party agreed not to oppose the declared course towards European integration and Ukraine's possible accession to NATO, but was not going to be an apologist for this policy. The opinion that Yushchenko was forced to sign the "Universal" with the Party of Regions due to current circumstances: the SPU quitting the "Orange Coalition" and Oleksandr Moroz switching to the side of the Regions and the Communists was deeply rooted in the public conscience.

82 Hrytsenko told the ambassador that he had held talks with oligarch Akhmetov (whom the ambassador called the "godfather of Yanukovich's party) about the attitude of the Party of Regions toward NATO.

83 In Hrytsenko's opinion (in which the Minister of Defense pressed the Ambassador) the coalition of Our Ukraine and the Party of Regions was quite possible, and if formed the PR would not try to revise Yushchenko's plans concerning Ukraine joining NATO (under the condition that Hrytsenko remains the Minister of Defense of Ukraine).

84 On creating a broad parliamentary coalition, during the formation of the government, the process of which dragged on for four and a half months.

85 However, the work of such a government was not successful, as many ministers disagreed with Prime Minister Yanukovich.

86 Against this background, Tymoshenko's bloc, "Our Ukraine" and the social movement "People's Self-Defense" fully supported Yushchenko and boycotted Rada sessions for more than two months, effectively paralyzing its work.

87 In preparation for the elections, Ukrainian political parties began to hold consultations with the goal of creating electoral blocs and developing a joint strategy.

88 The Party of Regions, Communists and Socialists went into the election independently. Yulia Tymoshenko's bloc included the Reforms and Order party, the Social Democratic Party and Batkivshchyna directly. The Our Ukraine – People's Self-Defense Bloc (NUNS) included ten political parties, including the civil party Pora, the Ukrainian People's Movement, the People's Party, the Republican Party, and the European Party.

89 But in the voting the Party of Regions again received the most seats (175), losing 11 seats compared to the previous election. Yulia Tymoshenko Bloc received 156 seats, adding 27 seats, and the Our Ukraine – People's Self-Defense bloc was in third place with 72 seats, having lost 9 deputies. The Communist Party traditionally relied on its "red electorate" and won 27 seats (6 more than before). The SPU, which had "proved" by shifting from one camp to another, did not make it into the parliament at all. Its place was taken by the bloc of Vladimir Litvin (former speaker of parliament), consisting of the People's and Labor parties. It won 20 seats. As a result of the agreement between Yushchenko and Tymoshenko, BYuT and NUNS, formed a coalition and managed to secure a majority of 228 seats (out of a total of 450 in the Rada) with the right to form a cabinet.

90 The Party of Regions together with the Communists formed a "constructive" opposition, and Litvin's bloc occupied a favorable position as a buffer between the ruling coalition and the opposition. The formation of a new government in December 2007 ended Ukraine's political crisis.

91 The roll call vote resulted in the election of Tymoshenko as Prime Minister, as nominated by the president. On the same day the parliament approved the new government composition, which included four deputy Prime Ministers and 22 ministers. The first deputy Prime Minister, as expected, was Oleksandr Turchynov. Virtually all of the ministers were representatives of the coalition – the Yulia Tymoshenko Bloc and the Our Ukraine-People's Self-Defense Bloc. The enforcement ministries – Defense (Yuri Yekhanurov), Internal Affairs (Yuri Lutsenko), and Foreign Affairs (Vladimir Ohryzko) joined the Government by the presidential quota, as advised by the Prime Minister. Unexpectedly, Yushchenko appointed Raisa Bohatyryova, a representative of the Party of Regions, as the Head of the National Security and Defense Council (CNSD). Apparently, he did it to counterbalance Ms. Tymoshenko, especially as a new Law on the Cabinet of Ministers was to be discussed in the Parliament that would have considerably broadened the powers of the President via the CNSD.

92 The Government submitted to the Parliament a draft law "On the State Budget of Ukraine for 2008 and Amendments to Some Legislative Acts of Ukraine," which was adopted in the second reading just before the New Year's Eve 2008. During the election campaign, this program was presented as an election program and was called "Ukrainian Breakthrough: Towards a Fair and Competitive Country". Many accused Ms. Tymoshenko of plagiarism, since the title was taken from a book by the former Prime Minister and former secretary of the National Security and Defence Council, Anatoliy Kinakh, with the same title. However, Anatoliy Kinakh did not take offense, calling it "constructive plagiarism.

93 At the same time, critics felt that the program suffered from a lack of specific deadlines for its implementation and lack of financial backing.

94 Although she failed to fulfill one of her populist commitments. She offered to pay out 1000 hryvnias to depositors of the former Soviet Savings Bank as compensation for the loss of their

savings due to the hyperinflation that had occurred in the Soviet Union. It is clear that the government's promise to pay the population about $200 per former depositor was received with enthusiasm by the population. But money for this program was allocated by the government and depositors were not paid. Over time, bank cards were issued to those who wished to do so, to which the money was to be transferred. But the money was never transferred to the cards.

In 2008, Tymoshenko was once again very enthusiastic about taking up her privatization review program. The list of companies proposed by the Cabinet of Ministers included such large industrial enterprises as the Odessa Port Plant and Ukrtelecom, which privatization had been opposed by Tymoshenko during her first administration. There were also plans to reprivatize the Lugansk Locomotive Plant. As before, Yushchenko tried to put the privatizations on hold and asked the government to do nothing until a law on the state privatization program was adopted and a coordinated approach by all branches of power to the privatization process was worked out. Generally agreeing with him, Tymoschenko introduced substantial amendments to the law. She formulated the gist of the amendments at a briefing at the Cabinet of Ministers on January 23, 2008: "We want the law to contain a provision that in case of failure to fulfill conditions of a privatization agreement, such privatization agreement will be terminated without refund of money paid for the enterprise.

95 During a meeting at the NATO headquarters in Brussels on January 18.

96 "The signing by Yushchenko, Tymoshenko, and Yatsenyuk of a letter of appeal to the NATO leadership essentially means the beginning of the procedure of Ukraine's accession to NATO... At the same time, neither parliament, nor the government, nor any other collegial bodies have considered this issue. Relying on the opinion of the absolute majority of Ukrainian citizens, our voters, we demand the revocation of the 'letter of three'. We appeal to the leadership of NATO with the fact that the 'letter of three' does not express the will of the Ukrainian people, is not a subject of political consensus, but brings additional tension to the Ukrainian society, which will inevitably lead to the worsening of relations of Ukraine with the North Atlantic Alliance. In this connection, the factions of the Party of Regions and the Communist Party of Ukraine have decided to block the work of the Ukrainian parliament, demanding that the signatories – Yushchenko, Tymoshenko and Yatsenyuk – withdraw the letter on Ukraine's accession to NATO. We also draw the attention of the Chairman of the Verkhovna Rada that when signing the letter, you went beyond the constitutional powers and the requirements of the Verkhovna Rada Regulations. In this regard, we ask you to withdraw your signature from this letter. Otherwise we will act adequately, proceeding from the legislation of our state".

97 Ukraine was never a full member, but did become an Associate Member of the CIS's Economic Union.

98 Negotiations with Vladimir Litvin's buffer bloc ensued, and they promise Litvin the post of Speaker of the Verkhovna Rada in exchange for membership in the "democratic alliance".

99 The agreement stipulated a step-by-step three-year transfer of Ukraine to market prices for Russian gas, on the one hand, and to Ukrainian tariffs for transit of this gas to Europe, on the other. In addition, the parties agreed on the joint export of free volumes of Russian gas from the Ukrainian underground storage facilities, which exceed the needs of the Ukrainian market.

100 Later, on January 19, 2009, Alexey Miller, chairman of the management board of Gazprom, admitted that there had been attempts to disrupt negotiations: "Yes, indeed, at the end of December [2008] the Prime Ministers of Russia and Ukraine came to an agreement and our companies were ready to negotiate the price of gas at USD 235 per 1,000 cubic meters on the condition of joint export operations from the territory of Ukraine. RosUkrEnergo then offered to buy gas for Ukraine at a price of $285. For the Russian side, such an offer was obviously advantageous. For the Ukrainian side it was not as obviously advantageous, because Ukraine had to buy gas from an intermediary company not at $235 dollars per 1000 cubic meters, but at a price higher

than $285.

101 Oleg Dubina.

102 Tymoshenko was far from indebted and already in mid-January 2009 openly declared in the press that "negotiations which have been successfully moving since October 2, 2008 on the provision of Ukraine with natural gas at a price of $235 for Ukrainian consumers and transit in the range of 1.7-1.8 [dollars per 1000 cubic meters per 100 km] – these negotiations were disrupted by the fact that, unfortunately, Ukrainian politicians tried to save RosUkrEnergo as a shady corrupt intermediary ... Negotiations between the two Prime Ministers and then between Naftogaz and Gazprom were ruined by those political forces in Ukraine who have received and plan to receive corrupt benefits from the work of RosUkrEnergo."

103 They continued the talks from the points that remained unresolved by December 31, 2008.

104 According to the Russian side it corresponded to the average European price, although the transit price for Russian gas through Slovakia and the Czech Republic at the time was $4, and through Germany €4 (around $6).

105 The attempt to reach an agreement with Yanukovich a nd the Party of Regions to form a political coalition was not a success for either Yushchenko or Tymoshenko. Firstly, the former "Orange" comrades-in-arms and partners could not find a common language. Secondly, Mr. Yanukovich, who by that time had a rather high rating in the country while Yushchenko's rating was at 3%, relied both on a powerful political party and a clan in Donetsk, whose main sponsor was the billionaire Rinat Akhmetov. So Mr. Yanukovich did not try to negotiate with anyone. It was clear that he would take power independently, however, not excluding possible alliances with "third force" parties, i.e. newcomer parties, with which he could cooperate in the future parliamentary elections in order to ensure a pro-presidential majority in parliament.

In June 2009, the Verkhovna Rada decided to hold the presidential election on October 25, 2009. But after President Yushchenko appealed this decision in the Constitutional Court, the Ukrainian parliament set a new election date of January 17, 2010. The elections were held, as before, by an absolute majority system. If someone did not win an absolute majority, there would be a second round, with the two candidates who received the most votes. In the second round, the winner will be whoever gets the most votes.

The election campaign started long before its formal announcement: political parties tried to resuscitate their disintegrated alliances and coalitions in order to get on the parliamentary bench. Eighteen officially registered candidates (15 men and three women) entered the presidential race. Ten candidates were self-nominated. The rest were from parties. Forty candidates were denied registration for various reasons. The average age of the candidates was 50 years old.

Prominent among the candidates were Viktor Yanukovich (Party of Regions), incumbent Prime Minister Yulia Tymoshenko (Fatherland party), incumbent President Viktor Yushchenko (self-nominated), Arseniy Yatsenyuk (Front for Change party), Serhiy Tihipko (Strong Ukraine) and Petro Symonenko (CPU). All the other candidates played more of a technical than political role, especially since voters had never heard of many of them. Conducted from June to December 2009, opinion polls showed that the undoubted leaders of the presidential race would be Viktor Yanukovich and Yulia Tymoshenko, whose preliminary rating fluctuated between 26%-30% for Yanukovich and 15-18% for Tymoshenko. The young and energetic Yatsenyuk, former speaker of the Verkhovna Rada and former foreign minister in Tymoshenko's government, came in third. Fourth place went to Sergei Tihipko, who proposed a moderate but sufficiently clear program. Petro Symonenko, the leader of the Ukrainian Communists, firmly established himself in fifth place with his constant pensioner-veteran electorate. Yushchenko, the incumbent President of Ukraine, settled for the sixth place.

106 The Communists, as always, were faithful to their Communist tradition of repeating the same program year after year without proposing ways to implement it.

Despite the existence of the programs supposed for the candidate, the average Ukrainian voter usually did not read these programs and voted not by reason, but by feeling, which told him to vote not so much "for" as "against". With this sensual-emotional approach to voting, only those candidates remained on the ballot who were least likely to be voted against.

107 International observers assessed the first round of the presidential election positively, considering that it was held according to all European canons with free competition of candidates and without serious violations.

108 Sergiy Tihipko got the third place in the presidential race with slightly more than 13% of the votes cast for him, and Arseniy Yatsenyuk got the fourth place (6.96%), which is almost twice as far (according to the preliminary opinion polls) from his closest competitor. Ukrainians for the first time made it clear that they are "fed up" with the same faces in politics and therefore every fifth voter in the country cast his vote for the new leaders – Tihipko and Yatsenyuk. The compromised politicians were left behind and had no influence on the election, while their parties split.

Yanukovich and Tymoshenko divided their electorate in the eastern and western regions according to the established electoral tradition. Yanukovich, with his pro-Russian rhetoric, was beyond the reach of his competitors in the southeastern regions of the country. The Kharkiv, Dnipropetrovsk and Zaporizhzhia oblasts, as well as Crimea, gave him more than 60% of the vote, while Donetsk and Luhansk oblasts gave him more than 75%. Even in the Transcarpathian region, Yanukovich managed to pick up 30% of the vote, thanks to the Ruthenians who inhabited that region and traditionally voted for pro-Russian candidates for parliament or for president.

Tymoshenko was supported by central and western regions of the country oriented toward the European vector of development. She won Viktor Yushchenko's votes in his own region, but she did not receive support in her home region of Dnipropetrovsk, gaining barely 15% of the vote. Her favorite "fiefdoms" were Volynsk (almost 54%), Vinnitsa (43%), Zhytomyr (32.6%), Chernihiv (42.7%) and Kyiv region with the capital. It is interesting to note that in places of detention, where prisoners participated in the elections, former convict Yanukovych did not have much success. Lady Y. got more than 50% there, while her rival Yanukovych got 25%.

109 The gap between Yanukovich and Tymoshenko after the first round was 10%, which required from the candidates to do their best to win the second round. With her former Orange Revolution allies and her numerous parliamentary coalitions siphoning off votes from her electorate, Tymoshenko appeared to have many chances to close the gap after the first round, and she might even win.

The second round of the presidential election was scheduled for February 7. As early as the third day after the first round, Tymoshenko tried to negotiate with her countryman Tihipko and his Strong Ukraine party, as well as with Yatsenyuk and his Front for Change, to have them support her candidacy by promising them top government positions if she won. Tihipko was promised the post of Prime Minister. Yatsenyuk was promised the same post.

However, the leaders of these parties, given the mood of their voters, who distanced themselves from both Tymoshenko and Yanukovich, did not make any promises to Tymoshenko. Viktor Yanukovich, in turn, did the same thing: he invited the leaders of the parties that failed to make it to the second round to vote for him, promising that if he became President he would dissolve parliament and call a snap election.

Mr. Yanukovich and his entourage understood that if Ms. Tymoshenko loses the presidential election, she will try to revenge herself in the parliamentary election. Therefore, one of the tasks he would have to accomplish as the new President was to neutralize and isolate Tymoshenko, her eternal foe on the political scene.

The second round of voting that took place on February 7, 2010, finally decided the winner in the presidential race in Ukraine.

10 The electoral geography of the candidates remained the same: the southeast and Crimea for ʾanukovich, and the center and west for Tymoshenko.

11 Since each candidate was associated with a certain color (white and blue for Yanukovich and range for Tymoshenko), some observers noticed not without irony that during the presidential ampaign of 2010 Ukraine was painted not in the traditional blue-yellow color, but in orange and lue.

12 Immediately after the election, he returned his real last name, which he had used in the 2012 arliamentary elections (unsuccessfully, however).

13 Tymoshenko refused to recognize the election results and filed a complaint with the Supreme ъdministrative Court (SAC) of Ukraine against the election results, insisting that more than 900 oter lists be compared to the state voter register, which would have delayed the recount for everal months. However, a few days later, apparently not believing her appeal to be successful, he withdrew her suit from the SAC, arguing that the court refused to consider evidence of lection fraud or question witnesses.

14 Recall that Tymoshenko's government was formed due to the presence of a parliamentary нajority formed by Yulia Tymoshenko's bloc (YTB) and "Our Ukraine – People's Self-Defense" (NUNS). But the coalition was gradually falling apart: the group "For Ukraine", which was part f NUNS, left the coalition back in September 2008. Vladimir Litvin's bloc left the coalition after ʾanukovich's victory in the 2010 presidential elections, anticipating that Tymoshenko was a "wild ard" and in exchange for Yanukovich's promise to keep him as speaker.

15 This decision served as a political signal to start repressions against Tymoshenko and her ssociates.

16 On May 17, Tymoshenko was summoned for questioning.

17 Azarov's government commissioned a Washington-based company Trout Cacheris, PLLC, нnown in the U.S. for the scandalous case of Monica Lewinsky, to conduct the audit. Two other rms were subcontracted: Akim Gump and the Kroll Inc. investigative agency, which had сeviously been hired by Kuchma's entourage in connection with the Gongadze case. The overnment had to pay $10 million of budget money for the audit, although Azarov later denied . The world's leading auditing companies have repeatedly stated that Trout Cacheris, PLLC, is ot in fact an auditor. Tymoshenko herself when she was Prime Minister regularly engaged Ernst t Young, a world-renowned accounting firm that everyone trusted, to audit the government. In оntrast, Dmitry Firtash, a well-known oligarch and Tymoshenko's competitor, was a regular ient of Akim Gump; Rinat Akhmetov also used the services of this law firm. The company ecame "famous" in Russia, where it unsuccessfully sought the gold of the Communist Party of нe Soviet Union, and then worked on the case of Yukos. In Ukraine, after working 86 days, the оmpany's lawyers earned from 1000 to 1500 dollars per hour.

.8 By U.S. companies, apparently.

9 And believed that the very fact that Ukraine received money from Japan should be considered er merit, not a crime

ъ0 In turn, Tymoshenko appealed to the reputable American law firm Covington & Burling and нe major auditing company BDO USA, which had branches in more than a hundred countries, ith a request to investigate the validity of the charges brought against her. The conclusions of нe American companies were in Tymoshenko's favor. In particular, U.S. lawyers pointed out that нe money received from the Kyoto Protocol was withdrawn from the accounts in December)10, while Tymoshenko's government had already resigned in March 2010.

ъ1 On 24 June 2011 the Prosecutor-General's Office of Ukraine indicted Tymoshenko under Part Article 365 of the Criminal Code of Ukraine: "Exceeding power or official authority, resulting in grave consequences", which carried a maximum of 10 years in prison. The accusation stated that "Prime Minister of Ukraine Tymoshenko, acting deliberately, in personal interests, being aware of groundless and unreasonable requirements of the Russian party at the negotiations, with her participation and participation of leaders of the Russian government, Gazprom OJSC and Naftogaz Ukraine ... decided to agree to the said conditions disadvantageous for Ukraine". Tymoshenko was also accused of exceeding her authority under the law "On the Cabinet of Ministers" to sign "government directives" on her own, after which Ukrainian Fuel and Energy Minister Oleg Dubina signed the agreements. The former Prime Minister was accused of causing $195 million in damages, with grave consequences for Naftogaz Ukrainy. Tymoshenko and her lawyers denied the charges and argued that an international audit of Naftogaz of Ukraine conducted in 2009 found no cost overruns and that the total cost of "gas consumed in 2009" was less than in 2008. Concerning the "directives of the Cabinet of Ministers," Tymoshenko countered that she did not sign any directives of the government, but signed a directive of the Prime Minister to the minister of fuel and energy who in turn instructed Naftogaz of Ukraine to sign the contract. And since the ministry headed by Dubina had the exclusive right to manage Naftohaz Ukrayiny, no government directives were needed to sign the contracts. For her part, Yulia Tymoshenko filed a counterclaim against Firtash's Swiss company RosUkrEnergo in a district court in Manhattan, New York, demanding that Ukraine return about 12 billion cubic meters of gas. The thing is that Naftogaz Ukraina bought this volume of gas based on the decision of the Stockholm arbitrage court (of June 8, 2010), where the Ukrainian party was represented by Minister Yuriy Boyko, who was related to RosUkrEnergo. However, the trial did not end, as Tymoshenko and Firtash, who had been summoned to New York as witnesses, did not appear in court.

122 The Russian side did not react in any way to this discussion in Ukraine. Meanwhile, in October 2008, Russian and Ukrainian Prime Ministers Vladimir Putin and Tymoshenko signed an intergovernmental memorandum on gas prices for 2009: USD 250 per 1,000 cubic meters. Yushchenko was extremely dissatisfied with this and demanded to stop negotiations and recall the Ukrainian delegation from Moscow. Miller's statement that Russia would not sign a new gas contract until Ukraine's debts to Russia were paid off was a formal reason for the recall.

In January 2009 in response to the demarche of the Ukrainian government Gazprom offered a new price for Russian gas to Ukraine: $400 for 1,000 cubic meters (taking into account the accumulated debt of RosUkrEnergo of $1.7 billion). Because of this, negotiations reached an impasse. However, as a result of long and complex consultations, Tymoshenko managed to find a mutually acceptable solution both for the price of gas and for the transit of Russian gas through Ukraine. In the end she even managed to lower the 2009 price to $232 per 1,000 cubic meters even though world gas prices were much higher.

123 Tymoshenko demanded that her case be merged with other cases, particularly those on customs and Naftogaz, or even be dismissed without consideration "as clearly falsified," but the court rejected her request. Then Tymoshenko gave a 40-minute speech in which she revealed many of the secrets about the gas agreements the Ukrainian government had concluded before her. She demanded that former Prime Ministers and even presidents who bought Russian gas at even higher prices be prosecuted.

124 A representative of the Institute of State and Law of Ukraine tried to explain to the court that the Prime Minister did not exceed her authority since she signed "the Prime Minister's directives" rather than "the directives of the Cabinet of Ministers. According to her status, Tymoshenko had the right to give instructions and assignments to Naftogaz of Ukraine as a structure subordinate to the Cabinet of Ministers of Ukraine, and thus she did not violate the law.

125 Under an addendum to the January 2009 contract signed by Tymoshenko, Russia made a concession on the gas price, agreeing to reduce it by 30%, but by no more than $100 per thousand cubic meters. Technically, it was not a price reduction but a waiver of certain fees that Ukrain

would not have to pay. However, in order to reduce the customs payments the Russian government had to decide, which was never adopted in the end. In addition, the agreement stated that the actual price of natural gas supplied in excess of 30bn cu.m. in 2010 and 40bn cu.m. annually, starting from 2011, was not subject to reduction. However, the actual price was not fixed in the document, so the parties could adjust this price in the future.

126 However, Yanukovich insisted that clause 6.6, which implied penalties for Ukraine, was removed from the gas contract of 2009, if it purchased gas for 6% less than the monthly supply volume.

127 In violation of diplomatic protocol, the addendum was signed only in Russian, not in Russian and Ukrainian, the official languages of both countries.

128 Including Krymsoda (chemical industry), Gaztek (gas distribution), Ukrrechflot and Inter Media Group

129 Already in February 2010, immediately after his election, Yanukovich created the National Anti-Corruption Committee, the Presidential Committee for Economic Reforms, and the Council of Regions to facilitate cooperation between the central government and local authorities.

130 For a start he had his party allied with the Communists and the Bloc of Litvin, as well as with disaffiliated deputies from Batkivshchyna and Our Ukraine, to form a ruling coalition called Stability and Reforms, which in effect led to the resignation of the then not yet arrested Tymoshenko's second government.

131 The most important thing Yanukovych managed to do was to cancel the political reform of 2004 and regain his authority as head of the executive branch. Following an appeal to the Constitutional Court of Ukraine by 252 deputies obedient to Yanukovych, the changes made to the Constitution in 2004 under Yushchenko were declared unconstitutional. This allowed the ruling majority to change the form of government in the country and return from a parliamentary-presidential republic to a presidential-parliamentary one. The balance of power was shifted in favor of the President, who also subordinated the executive power.

132 According to which some owners left and others came in... Under Yanukovich the ideal conditions for raiding were created. The whole system was organized in such a way that all the people involved readily tried to unlawfully expropriate the property.

133 Andrei Semididko: "The scale of the phenomenon went far beyond 'covering the needs' of the 'family' itself. Sometimes people 'worked' under the guise of 'family interests'... Often, when the relevant 'order' went down to the regional level, to a prosecutor or an official... Often, when the relevant 'order' was passed down to the regional level – to a prosecutor or an official... the amount of taxes doubled due to the personal appetite of the official. The 'family' was interested in quite public and large companies".

134 Although this term does not exist in the basic agreements with the EU.

135 Opponents of European integration frightened Ukrainians that Ukraine's leading industrial enterprises, and the country's entire economy, were bound to collapse because of the influx of European goods and its inability to compete with the European economy.

136 The European Union was based on "three pillars" – economy and social policy; international relations and security; and justice and home policy. The criteria adopted by the European Council in Copenhagen back in 1993 included, along with the above, the equal rights of citizens in government (from local government to national government); free elections with secret ballot; the right to form political parties without interference from the state; fair and equal access to a free press; freedom of trade union and individual opinion; legislative restriction of the executive; the independence of courts from the government and the rule of law as a safeguard against arbitrary rule. Finally, the most important criterion was the adaptation of Ukrainian national laws to

European norms. This was probably one of the most difficult and time-consuming processes to be monitored by the European Commission. Could Ukraine meet these conditions in a relatively short historical period? It could if it really wanted to. But so far – at the level of 2013 – the only criterion Ukraine met was geographical: it was in Europe.

137 This meant the following: support of domestic manufacturer and exemption from taxes at the initial stage; availability of state programs and funds for support of priority economic spheres (especially agriculture); manufacturer's right to decide what and how to produce; free pricing; free competition; restriction of monopolies; separation of power and business; competitiveness of domestic manufacturers against European ones; system of private deposit guarantees; civilized procedure of bankruptcy and privatization.

138 Ukraine had to participate in the ERM2 mechanism for at least two years and ensure the stability of its currency exchange rate relative to the euro.

139 Arseniy Yatsenyuk (Fatherland), Vitali Klitschko (UDAR), and Oleg Tyahnybok (Svoboda).

140 Lutsenko, the organizer of the rally, also spoke and opposition leaders Yatseniuk, Klitschko, and Tyahnybok, who now appear only together.

141 The protesters were divided into two Maidans – "party" (under party slogans) on Kyiv's European Square and "popular" on Independence Square. But after Yulia Tymoshenko called for the removal of party slogans, the two Maidans united into one.

142 But the battle for an agreement seemed won. It remained to wait a few days, when Yanukovich was expected to arrive in Vilnius for the signing.

143 By Ilham Aliyev, President of Azerbaijan, Serzh Sargsyan, President of Armenia, Georgy Margelashvili, Prime Minister of Moldova, Yuri Leanca, President of Ukraine, Viktor Yanukovich and Vladimir Makei, Foreign Minister of Belarus. All EU structures were represented at the highest level.

144 The agreement was simply not signed under pressure from Russia, although the short historical experience of independence should have demonstrated that foreign policy decisions concerning the economic prospects of the country should be taken by the leadership of the state without any external pressure. Nevertheless, summit participants called on post-Soviet states in eastern Europe and Transcaucasia for broader democratic and economic reforms, and also called on Russia, in the interests of European integration, to respect the choice of its neighbors.

145 After the EuroMaidan victory, Yarosh was appointed Deputy Secretary of National Security and Defense of Ukraine, and in March 2014 he was nominated as a candidate for the presidential election, remaining the outsider. The Right Sector and Maidan Self-Defense fighters then formed the National Guard of Ukraine, and on March 22, 2014, it was announced that the Right Sector had been reorganized from a social movement into a party based on the Ukrainian National Assembly party. Right Sector's political influence, however, remained weak. In the 2014 presidential election, fewer voters voted for Yarosh than for Vadim Rabinovich, a prominent Ukrainian businessman of Jewish origin.

146 Located in a trade union building on Nezalezhnosti Square, which was seized by insurgents.

147 With opposition leaders Arseniy Yatsenyuk, Vitali Klitschko, and Oleg Tyahnybok following behind the flag.

148 The opposition deputies, Petro Poroshenko and Oleksandra Kuzhel, called on the demonstrators not to give in to the provocations of the government-paid "titushkas". Later they appeared together with opposition leaders.

149 The leader of the Fatherland party, Oleksandr Turchynov.

150 David Zhvaniya, Inna Bogoslovskaya, Nikolai Rudkovsky, and Volodymyr Melnichenko.

151 The authorities accused those arrested of intending to seize power in an unconstitutional

manner.

152 As well as members of the Ukrainian Insurgent Army (UPA), as well as all Ukrainian nationalists who considered themselves followers of the OUN.

153 And on Roman Shukhevich.

154 Within UNA-UNSO (Ukrainian National Assembly – Ukrainian People's Self-Defense), which later split into smaller parties, also had nationalist leanings.

155 Threatening a policeman – 10 to 15 years in prison. threatening a policeman or other law enforcement officer – 7 years in prison

156 Violating the order of peaceful assemblies, for participating in them wearing helmets and masks, using fire and in uniform – arrest for 10 days; - distribution of extremist materials – imprisonment for 3 years; non-governmental organizations (NGOs) funded from abroad must pay income tax and be officially called "foreign agents. - associations that they take part in political activities and intend to influence the decisions of the authorities require a license.

157 Vadym Kolesnichenko, Party of Regions.

158 After the removal of Yanukovich, he was "successfully pushed" out of the presidential race. Politics is not a ring, where the strongest wins.

159 A no confidence voted was first tabled by the opposition in parliament after the disruption of the signing of the Ukraine-EU association agreement on November 25, 2013. However, the resolution did not receive the necessary votes because only opposition parties voted for it, while the Communists, Regions and independents voted against it. Speaking at the Rada before the vote, the Prime Minister promised radical personnel changes, stressing several times that the government would continue the course towards European integration, but it sounded more like a mockery than an excuse. The Communists proposed their own draft resolution on the resignation of the government, with which the opposition also agreed, but at the last moment the Communists withdrew their signatures, and the resolution was again defeated. It was obvious that the ruling party tried to save the situation by relying on the Communists and independent deputies, but further aggravation of the political situation in the country and renewed demonstrations after the New Year put the question of Azarov's government dismissal back on the agenda.

160 Along with Azarov, his government resigned. First Deputy Prime Minister Serhiy Arbuzov took over as Prime Minister.

161 He ended up on the sidelines of national politics.

162 Yatsenyuk (from the All-Ukrainian Batkivshchyna Union), V. Klitschko (from the UDAR party) and O. Tyahnybok (from the All-Ukrainian Freedom Union)

163 German Foreign Minister Frank Walter Steinmeier, Polish Foreign Minister Radoslaw Sikorski, Europe Director of the French Foreign Minister Eric Fournier, and Putin's envoy Vladimir Lukin.

164 Agreement to resolve the political crisis in Ukraine:
Concerned about the tragic loss of life in Ukraine, seeking an immediate end to the bloodshed, determined to pave the way for a political resolution of the crisis, we, the undersigned parties, have agreed on the following:

1. Within 48 hours of the signing of this agreement, a special law will be adopted, signed and promulgated which will restore the operation of the Constitution of Ukraine of 2004, as amended up to that time. The signatories declare their intention to form a coalition and form a government of national unity within 10 days thereafter.

2. Constitutional reform balancing the powers of the President, government and parliament will begin immediately and be completed in September 2014.

3. Presidential elections will be held immediately after the adoption of the new Constitution,

but no later than December 2014. New electoral legislation will be adopted and a new Central Election Commission will be formed on a proportional basis in accordance with OSCE and Venice Commission rules.

4. The investigation of the recent violence will be carried out under the joint monitoring of the authorities, the opposition and the Council of Europe.

5. The authorities will not declare a state of emergency. The authorities and the opposition will refrain from the use of force.

The Verkhovna Rada of Ukraine will adopt a third law on exemption, which will apply to the same offenses as the law of February 17, 2014.

Both sides will make serious efforts to normalize life in towns and villages by vacating administrative and public buildings and unblocking streets, squares and squares.

Illegal weapons must be surrendered to the authorities of the Ministry of Internal Affairs of Ukraine within 24 hours of the entry into force of the above-mentioned special law (paragraph 1 of this Agreement).

After the specified period, all cases of illegal carrying and storage of weapons are subject to the current legislation of Ukraine. Opposition and government forces will step back from the positions of confrontation. The authorities will use the forces of law and order exclusively for physical protection of the buildings of the authorities.

6. The Ministers for Foreign Affairs of France, Germany, Poland and the Special Representative of the President of the Russian Federation call for an immediate end to all violence and confrontation.

Kyiv, 21 February 2014

From the government: President of Ukraine Viktor Yanukovich

From the opposition: Vitali Klitschko, leader of the UDAR party, Arseniy Yatsenyuk, leader of the Batkivshchyna (Fatherland) party, and Oleg Tyahnybok, leader of the Svoboda (Freedom) party.

Witnesses: From the European Union: Federal Minister of Foreign Affairs of the Federal Republic of Germany Frank Walter Steinmeier, Foreign Minister of the Republic of Poland Radoslaw Sikorski and Head of the Continental Europe Department of the French Ministry of Foreign Affairs Eric Fournier.

165 Ihor Kaletnik.

166 Their country residences were later vandalized by a furious mob.

167 With the formation of the government, the triple opposition (or as it was called "three-in-one") has virtually disintegrated. Representatives of Vitali Klitschko's UDAR party were left without ministerial portfolios, although Klitschko's "group of influence" included Defense Minister Admiral Igor Tenyukh, Foreign Minister Andrei Deshchytsia and Security Service Chairman Valentyn Nalyvaychenko. Klitschko himself said that his party would focus on preparations for the presidential election, so he would not participate in the formation of the government.

168 And Tymoshenko flew to Germany for treatment.

169 Vadym Kolesnichenko and Oleg Tsarev of the national deputies also attended the congress.

170 Speaker and Acting President Turchinov then signed a decree at the Rada appointing Yatsenyuk as Prime Minister and asking him to sit in the government box.

171 A new government was urgently formed, 21 people. Sixteen members of the government represented western Ukraine. Three were from the southeast. Four members of the government were natives of Russia. Representatives of the Party of Regions, the Communist Party and the Udar Party were not included in the government.

172 Four of them were members of Svoboda, and the rest were non-party. There was also the

"quota" of the Maidan. Ministers of Culture, Sports, Education, and Health. Yulia Tymoshenko managed to lobby her candidates: Speaker of Parliament Oleksandr Turchinov, Prime Minister Arseniy Yatsenyuk, Interior Minister Arsen Avakov, and Energy Minister Yuriy Prodan. Arseniy Yatsenyuk himself created his own lobby from the ministers of economy and justice, economic development and the chairman of the National Bank. Petro Poroshenko (one of the informal leaders of the opposition) managed to promote "his" Deputy Prime Ministers Vitaliy Yarema and Volodymyr Groysman into the government, whom he can count on in case he wins the presidential election. Despite the fact that Vitaly Klitschko refused to participate in the government, he had his "power bloc" under his influence: Defense Minister Admiral Tenyukh (despite the fact that he was a member of Freedom), Foreign Minister Andriy Deshchytsia; SBU Chairman Valentyn Nalyvaychenko.

173 Half of this wealth belonged to MPs V. Novinsky, P. Poroshenko, K. Zhivago and S. Tihipko.

174 "The Donets" experienced their renaissance three times – under Yefim Zvyagilsky (Prime Minister of Ukraine), Vadimir Shcherban and Viktor Yanukovich.

175 Among the Donetsk people were, in particular, Prime Minister E. Zvyagilsky and Deputy Prime Minister Valentina Landik, owner of the prosperous refrigerator plant Nord; the coal and energy ministries were headed by Viktor Tulub from the Donetsk people.

176 At one time the leader of the Ukrainian Communist Party, P. Symonenko, was the secretary of the Donetsk Regional Committee of the Komsomol. After the departure of Zviagilsky (who took for himself one of the most profitable mines in Donbass – the Zasyadko mine). By the mid-1990s, the interests of the Donbass citizens in the government were lobbied by their namesake Yevgeny Shcherban (owner of a network of gas stations in the region, as well as the corporations "Aton", "Amest" and "Gefest"; member of the Ukrainian parliament in the mid-1990s) and Vladimir Shcherban – then head of the Donetsk Regional Council and the Donetsk Regional State Administration. They tried to subdue the so-called metallurgical barons, which explains a whole series of murders in the region, including Yevhen Shcherban himself.

Vladimir Shcherban was forced out of Donbass by the metallurgical and coal barons. At first, he was forced to make do with the post of Sumy governor; then he left Ukraine. The death of E. Shcherban and V. Shcherban's departure for another region coincided with the rise of the Dnipropetrivsk clan, headed by Pavel Lazarenko and his loyal assistant Yulia Tymoshenko, who managed to spread their influence in Donbas.

177 Volodymyr Rybak, the former mayor of Donetsk and an old friend of Yefim Zvyagilsky, became speaker of the parliament; Andriy Klyuyev was appointed First Deputy Prime Minister; and Nikolai Azarov, a native of Russia, was appointed by the Prime Minister as Chairman of the Party of Regions.

178 The founder of the financial-industrial empire "System Capital Management" (SCM) (100% of shares of which belonged to Akhmetov) was also the owner and President of the Donetsk soccer club "Shakhtar". His SCM, which has a turnover of about $24 billion and a net profit of about $2 billion, controls various sectors of the Ukrainian economy. To understand the scale and spheres of influence of Akhmetov's structures in Ukraine, let's dwell on the most important of them. In the mining and metallurgy sector SCM, through its subsidiary Metinvest Holding, unites 24 enterprises based in Ukraine, Europe and the USA, with a management company registered in the Netherlands. The holding (where Akhmetov's partner is Russian-born billionaire Vadim Novinsky) controls a number of mining and processing plants in Krivoy Rog, producing pellets and iron-ore concentrate for Akhmetov's plants Zaporizhstal, the Mariupol Metallurgical Plant (MMK), Azovstal and the EnaKyivo Metallurgical Plant. His empire also includes Krasnodon Coal, Avdiivka Coke Plant, Khartsyzsk Pipe Plant and the Danube Shipping Company.

Rinat Akhmetov's empire is a group of Donetsk clans that includes several well-known politicians and businessmen: Rinat Akhmetov himself, Boris Kolesnikov, the Klyuyev brothers,

Yuri Ivanishchenko, known as Yura EnaKyivsky, and the "Yanukovich family. As the main sponsors of the Party of Regions, Akhmetov and his partners installed Viktor Yanukovich as president. There is also constant rivalry within Akhmetov's group of partners, which certainly affects the redistribution of business within Akhmetov's empire and the situation in the Party. Ukraine's energy sector is dominated by the Donbass Fuel and Energy Company (DTEK). It is a vertically integrated company that creates a production chain from coal mining and preparation to electricity generation and distribution. There are 29 mines: Pavlogradugol, Dobropolyeugol, Komsomolets Donbassa, Sverdlovanthracite, Rovenkianthracite, Belozerska mine and others. Coal enrichment is carried out by 12 coal enrichment plants. Donetskoblenergo, Kyivenergo, Dniproenergo and Krymenergo generate and distribute electricity. DTEK's enterprises, which employ about 140,000 people, are located in Donetsk, Dnipropetrovsk, Zaporizhzhia, Lugansk, Lviv, Ivano-Frankivsk and Vinnitsa regions, in Crimea, Kyiv and the Rostov region of Russia. One of Akhmetov's latest acquisitions was his $1 billion purchase of the United Coal Company (UCC), a US coal mining company. Akhmetov owns three banks in Ukraine: the First Ukrainian International Bank (FUMB); Renaissance Credit Bank and Dongorbank, as well as two insurance companies belonging to ASKA Group. The oligarch has also paid attention to the media space. In 2013, he bought the former state-owned company Ukrtelecom, and his media group "Ukraine" controls the TV channels "Ukraine", "Donbass", "34", "UFO-TV", the channels "Football-1" and "Football-2". Together with the founder of Ukrainian Media Holding, Kharkiv businessman Boris Lozhkin, Akhmetov founded Internet holding Digital Ventures, which includes a number of Ukrainian newspapers and magazines, as well as a network of modern business centers and five-star hotels in Kyiv and Donetsk. That is why it is not surprising that in practice Rinat Akhmetov can invade any of the Ukrainian industries and establish his own rules of the game there.

179 A man from the Donetsk land, born in Mariupol, he received a trade education. Later he graduated from the Donetsk Academy of Management. Kolesnikov started from trading activities, then turned to political activities, becoming the chairman of the Donetsk Regional Council, a leader of the Party of Regions and a member of the Verkhovna Rada.

180 The European Football Championship, which was also held in Ukraine. In a short period of time all the infrastructure of the European Football Championship was built under his leadership. His managerial skills were appreciated by FIFA managers

181 His fortune according to the magazine "Focus" amounted to 292.5 million dollars in 2011, and Kolesnikov himself considered this figure greatly understated, because he invested more than $ 200 million in livestock and $ 250 million in the construction of a new confectionery factory "Konti-Russ" in Kursk (Russia). Experts of the magazine "Korrespondent" as of 2011 counted his assets at 448 million dollars, giving Kolesnikov in their rating "Golden Hundred" the 28th place. Kolesnikov controlled ZAO Production Association "Konti" (confectionery); ZAO "Yug"; "Konti" Group; he also had interests in the subsidiary (DP) "Konti-Invest".

182 Also Igor Kolomoysky and Victor Pinchuk.

183 After Pshonka, Zakharchenko, Yakymenko, and Oleksandr Klymenko, the Minister of Revenues and Levies, who was also the head of the Ukrainian Customs Service, were appointed to these top government positions, it

184 Just as meaningless was the question of whether or not Khodorkovsky had committed crimes under Russian criminal law.

185 Vladimir Scherbitsky – first secretary of the Communist Party of Ukraine, Valentina Shevchenko and Alexei Vatchenko, who at different times headed the Ukrainian Supreme Soviet in the Soviet times, were from Dnepropetrovsk.

186 After independence was declared, Leonid Kuchma, General Director of Yuzhmash, became

Prime Minister of the country, and the business of the Dnepropetrovsk people flourished. Being a Komsomol member Alexander Turchinov – head of Propaganda and agitation Department of Komsomol Dnepropetrovsk regional committee – helped Sergey Tihipko (both studied at Dnepropetrovsk metallurgical institute), a young and energetic Moldavian guy from the village of Draganesti in Lazov district of Moldavian SSR, to become the first secretary of the Dnepropetrovsk regional Komsomol committee.

187 The fact that S. Tihipko moved to Dniepropetrovsk and joined the Dniepropetrovsk clan is not surprising, since his father, Leonid Tihipko, was the secretary of the Dniepropetrovsk City Committee of the Communist Party of Ukraine. It is clear that with the help of his father, S. Tihipko was able to establish and lead a financial empire, the "PrivatBank" group, which became the financial pillar of the Dnepropetrovsk clan of Ukraine.

188 Lazarenko included in his team Sergei Tihipko, who became Deputy Prime Minister, and Yulia Tymoshenko, who headed United Energy Systems of Ukraine.

189 But Kuchma himself had grown weary of Lazarenko's growing influence by this time and in July 1997 sent him out of office

190 Further fate of Lazarenko became a cautionary example for businessmen-politicians in conflict with the authorities, and for the rulers who were planning to get rid of their rival politicians-businessmen. On February 9, 1999, the Prosecutor General of Ukraine demanded that the Verkhovna Rada deprive Lazarenko of parliamentary immunity; on February 15, under threat of arrest, Lazarenko left Ukraine. On February 17, 310 deputies out of 450 voted for depriving Lazarenko of parliamentary immunity and gave their approval for his arrest. On February 20, at the request of the Ukrainian authorities, Lazarenko was detained at the airport in New York, but applied for political asylum to the US authorities. Instead of asylum, Lazarenko was charged in 2000 with extortion, money laundering and fraud. The amount of funds transferred by Lazarenko to the United States was estimated at $114 million, and US prosecutors demanded that Lazarenko be imprisoned for up to 18 years and fined $66 million. Lazarenko was jailed.

191 Lazarenko owned real estate in California, and for this reason his trial was held in San Francisco. In 2006 all the money in his accounts (approximately $477 million) were frozen. All these years, his lawyers had been filing appeal after appeal. When these options were exhausted, Lazarenko was placed in a US federal prison.

192 For Kuchma, Lazarenko posed a threat even in custody. Ukrainian authorities repeatedly asked the US for Lazarenko's extradition, but the US side refused, citing the lack of an extradition treaty between Ukraine and the US In March 2006, Mr Lazarenko was elected to the Dnipropetrovsk regional council by Hromada in absentee voting in the Ukrainian local elections. But the Central Election Commission of Ukraine refused to register him as a candidate for deputy, and Hromada refused to take part in the 2007 parliamentary elections. In October 2012, Lazarenko asked to run in the next elections to the Rada from a US prison. He was denied registration again, but not because of the crimes he had committed, but because he had not lived in Ukraine for the past five years.

On November 1, 2012, Lazarenko was transferred from a federal prison to an immigration prison. US authorities deemed his sentence exhausted, but reserved the right to determine whether, as a former criminal, he could continue to be in the country. Lazarenko was placed in an immigration prison near the town of Adelanto, California. He was allowed 30-minute visits from relatives through a glass window, without the right to receive parcels. True, Lazarenko himself could order groceries and personal items, except video games. At the same time, his California home, valued at $6.6 million, was confiscated in connection with earlier fraud and money laundering charges against him. His immigration hearing was scheduled for May 2013.

193 The Dnepropetrovsk clan, like the Donetsk clan before it, split up into several groups.

Kuchma's "presidential team" included Oleg Dubina (First Deputy Prime Minister), Ivan Kirilenko (Minister of Agrarian Policy), Yuri Smirnov (Minister of Internal Affairs), Valery Pustovoytenko (Prime Minister and Minister of Transportation), Ivan Sakhan (Minister of Labor and Social Policy), Alexander Shlapak (Minister of Economy), and Vladimir Yatsuba (State Secretary of the Cabinet of Ministers). Vitaly Boyko, Chairman of the Supreme Court of Ukraine, joined the "seven" from December 1994. However, now we can see them together only on social parties and at soccer matches.

The former Head of the Security Service of Ukraine Leonid Derkach and his son Andrey did not keep any special positions in the business. Andrei Derkach retained some positions in the media sphere. He actively lobbied the interests of Russian companies in Ukraine together with the billionaire and former presidential candidate Vadym Rabinovych. In particular, they helped Roman Abramovich and Oleg Deripaska's Siberian Aluminum to take over the Nikolayev Alumina Refinery.

Leonid Kuchma, the former President, stayed afloat primarily because his son-in-law Victor Pinchuk controlled gas sales and rolled pipes in Ukraine. His concern "Interpipe" controlled a number of tube-rolling plants in the Dnieper region and enterprises of the iron and steel industry. "Interpipe also owned controlling stakes in Nikopol Ferroalloy Plant and a number of ore-dressing and processing plants. As well as the oligarchs should, Pinchuk also controlled a part of the media market (the Kyivstar cellular operator and the Fakty newspaper). The largest east European company, Krivororozhstal, purchased with the help of his father-in-law, was however lost during Yushchenko's presidency and under Tymoshenko, the head of the Tymoshenko government.

Due to the former President's connections, Pinchuk carried out the most important business forums in Yalta, where he invited not only the largest international companies and media holdings, but also prominent world politicians. Clearly, no other Ukrainian oligarch could afford this. Pinchuk's group had close ties to the Russian pro-Kremlin Alfa Group run by Mikhail Fridman and Petr Aven and to the Mogilev Metallurgical Plant in Belarus. Against President Kuchma, Tymoshenko provoked a number of political scandals and led the Our Ukraine opposition that was formally led by Viktor Yushchenko.

194 There was a reason for this: gas contracts with Russia at exorbitant prices. Then everything was in the hands of Ukrainian justice, which, as always, did its job. As a result, Yulia Tymoshenko was sentenced to seven years in prison, and her

195 Another Dnipropetrovsk group was the Privat Group, led by Igor Kolomoysky, Gennady Bogolyubov, and Alexei Martynov. Under Yanukovich, it managed not only to hold but also to strengthen its position. The group included not only the bank bearing the same name but more than 100 enterprises in Ukraine and abroad. Having started from selling office equipment and importing sneakers and phones, the group gradually started to buy the assets of metallurgical, ferroalloy and oil-refining companies. Thanks to the connections of Igor Kolomoysky, the Surkis brothers and Victor Medvedchuk, Privat Group bought 40% of Ukrnafta shares and appointed its own man to head it. In addition, the group became the owner of the Prykarpatneft company. Kolomoisky's joke motto "I don't pay taxes and don't pay debts" became the motto of the whole group. The group even managed the seemingly impossible – to take away the Kremenchug oil refinery from the Russians.

After the opposition came to power, part of which was financed by the group, Igor Kolomoysky offered himself as governor of Dnepropetrovsk Region in order to restore order and calmness there, which he managed to do partially, and by this Kolomoysky guaranteed himself and his group the opportunity to continue influencing the future of Ukrainian politics.

196 Khadzhi Giray I was supposedly born in the city of Lida (Belarus), so the Belarusians can rightfully claim the Crimea as well.

197 During the reign of Selim Girei I (1671-1678), the Crimean Khanate fought together with the Turks, first against Poland, then against Russia. But the war with Russia was unsuccessful, and after the unsuccessful siege of Chiguirin in 1677 Selim Giray was deprived of the Khan's throne and exiled to the island of Rhodes, and in his place Murad Giray I (1678-1683) was put, who had to continue the war with the Russians. In 1678 Chigirin was taken, and in 1684 Selim Giray I ascended the khan's throne again, first until 1691, then from 1692 to 1699, and finally for the fourth time in 1703-1704.

After the battle of Poltava in 1709, in 1710, between the Crimean khan Devlet Giray II, Ivan Mazepa's successor Pilip Orlik and the Cossacks there was signed a treaty on the struggle of Ukraine for liberation from the Moscow dominion. The Crimean Khan promised to facilitate separation of the Left-bank Ukraine from the Moscow state and its joining to the Right-bank Ukraine in order to recreate a single independent Ukrainian state. But although Russia is now a direct threat to the Crimean Khanate, unsuccessful Prut campaign of Peter in 1711 slowed down at least a quarter of a century Russian intentions to seize the Crimea and move on Azov.

During the Russian-Turkish war of 1735-1739, when the Crimean Khanate was forced to fight on the side of Turkey against Persia, the Russian army, taking advantage of this, in 1736 ruined the capital of the Crimean Khanate, Bakhchisarai, by killing the local population. A year later, the Russian army re-entered the Crimea and devastated it, which was a national catastrophe for the khanate. Khan Mengli Giray (1725-1730; 1736-1741) planned to take revenge on Russia, but his campaign against Russia in 1738 ended unsuccessfully.

In 1768 the Crimean Khanate took part in the war against Russia on the side of Turkey. The main goal of the war for Russia was to get an access to the Black Sea. Turkey expected to get Podolia and Volhynia, to expand its possessions in the Northern Black Sea and the Caucasus, to capture Astrakhan and establish a protectorate over the Polish-Lithuanian Commonwealth. In the course of the war the Russian army under the command of Peter Rumyantsev and Alexander Suvorov defeated the Turkish troops in the battles of Largo, Cahul and Kozluga, and the Mediterranean squadron of the Russian fleet under the command of Alexei Orlov and Grigory Spiridov defeated the Turkish fleet in the Battle of Chios and at Chesme.

There were few supporters of Russia in Crimea, so "elected" in the Kuban pro-Russian Shagin Giray (commander of the Kuban horde) was entrenched with the help of Russian troops and Nogai in Bakhchisarai as the Crimean Khan, who became the last khan in the history of the Crimea. Wishing to strengthen the Russian influence in Crimea, Suvorov, who at that time commanded the Russian troops in Crimea, moved to Azov province against their will a part of the Christian population: including Greeks to Mariupol, and Armenians to Nakhichevan, having built the so-called Dnieper protective line against attacks of Crimean Tatars, consisting of seven fortresses, that stretched from Dnieper to Sea of Azov.

198 This was done in the years 1782-1783. Catherine's manifesto issued in 1783 annexed the Crimean Khanate and the Taman Peninsula to the Russian Empire, and Shagin Giray, who abdicated the throne, settled initially in Taman and then in Voronezh and Kaluga. After emigrating to the Ottoman Empire in 1787, Shagin Giray was exiled to Rhodes Island and then executed by order of the Turkish Sultan Abdul-Hamid I. In 1791, under the terms of the Peace of Jassy, Turkey was forced to recognize the annexation of the Crimea.

199 Russia negotiated with Ukraine, including the Crimean territories, but the presence of German troops in Ukraine delayed Soviet plans to seize the peninsula indefinitely.

200 the southern Front of the Red Army under the general command of M.V. Frunze launched a general assault, which goal was to take Perekop and Chongar and break into the Crimea. The offensive involved units of the 1st and 2nd Cavalry Armies, as well as the 51st Division of Vasily Blucher and the army of Nestor Makhno. The remnants of the White units, about 100 thousand people, were evacuated from the Crimea to Constantinople. And Wrangel's Crimean evacuation

has long been in military history an example of exemplary maritime evacuation of the army: all the ports were in absolute order, and everyone who wished was able to get on the steamships. And General Wrangel, before leaving Russia, personally bypassed all Russian ports on a destroyer to make sure that the steamships carrying soldiers and refugees were ready to put to the open sea.

201 The RSFSR.

202 Minutes № 49 approved the draft decree of the Presidium of the Supreme Soviet of the USSR on the transfer of the Crimean region from the RSFSR to the Ukrainian SSR.

203 On February 19, 1954, the Decree of the Presidium of the Supreme Soviet of the USSR (presided by Kliment Voroshilov) on the transfer of the Crimea from the RSFSR to the Ukrainian SSR was adopted. However, before the meeting of the Presidium of the Supreme Soviet of the USSR a meeting of the Presidium of the Supreme Soviet of the RSFSR was held where the decision was made "unanimously" and the First Secretary of the Regional Committee of the Party of the Crimea was dismissed and transferred to Moscow "for promotion" as Deputy Minister of Agriculture of the RSFSR. Later the Law of the USSR from April 26, 1954, about the cession of the Crimea region from the RSFSR to the Ukrainian SSR, was passed. None of these documents was signed by Khrushchev.

At the nearest 5th session of the Supreme Soviet of the RSFSR of the 3rd convocation on June 2, 1954, delegates voted unanimously to bring the Russian Constitution in line with the all-union one; the law "On introducing changes and additions to the Article 14 of the Constitution (Fundamental Law) of the RSFSR" was published, and all questions on the legality of the deed of ceding the Crimea region in terms of the Soviet legislation were closed. We should not assume that this was the only transfer of the territory of one Soviet republic to another. We have already mentioned the seizure of the Taganrog District in favor of Russia in 1925. But besides that, the Karelian ASSR was transferred to the Karelian-Finnish SSR; the Moldavian ASSR, which was part of the Ukraine, was transferred to the newly formed Moldavian SSR. The mechanisms were the same: the consent to change of the borders and administrative-territorial division was received at the 3rd session of the RSFSR Supreme Soviet of the 1st convocation on June 2, 1940. If we admit the right of the Soviet leadership to revise the borders within the USSR, it should be noted that from the legal point of view, the transfer of the Crimean peninsula from the RSFSR to the Ukrainian SSR in 1954 was made in accordance to its laws.

204 Just a few days after the resolution of May 1, the Supreme Soviet of the RSFSR made an appeal to the Supreme Soviet of Ukraine, in which, noting the problem of statehood of Crimea, it assured Ukrainians of a fraternal attitude and peaceful intentions towards them:

"Now in Russia there is a broadening and strengthening of public opinion about taking effective measures to protect the state interests of the Russian Federation, there are demands for legal assessment of the decisions related to the transfer of Crimea by Russia to Ukraine. In bringing this issue to the meeting of the Supreme Soviet of the Russian Federation today, we are by no means pursuing the task of making any territorial claims against Ukraine or the fraternal Ukrainian people. The task is different – to speak about the real, extremely unfavourable state of affairs in the Commonwealth itself. To draw public attention of each of the CIS countries to the real policy of their governments, whose activities often do not take into account the aspirations of all peoples to live in peace and harmony with the peoples of the former Soviet Union. It is in the interests of the peoples to strengthen the Commonwealth in every possible way and develop international processes.

Remaining committed to the principle of the inviolability of the borders existing within the CIS, including those between the Russian Federation and Ukraine, Russia intends to adhere strictly to the fundamental principles of the UN Charter, the CSCE, as well as the provisions of the Minsk Agreement on the establishment of the CIS and the Alma-Ata Declaration.

The Supreme Council of the Russian Federation proceeds from the assumption that the dialogue on this issue should develop in a civilized manner, lead to the search for mutual under-standing, and not to the aggravation of relations within the Commonwealth and the undermining of its foundations. At this moment all those who cherish the ideals of democracy and justice need to show wisdom, responsibility and restraint in relation to Crimea, ensure strict observance of the rights of the entire population of Crimea, including the Crimean Tatar people.

The Supreme Soviet of the Russian Federation appeals to the President of Ukraine and the Supreme Soviet of Ukraine to refrain from any actions aimed at suppressing the free will of the population of Crimea, which, in accordance with international norms, has the full right to determine its own destiny.

On behalf of the Russian peoples, the Supreme Soviet of Russia confirms its friendly feelings to the peoples of fraternal Ukraine and expresses the hope that our voice will be heard and that all questions of Russian-Ukrainian relations will be resolved peacefully through political negotia-tions with a view to reaching fair agreements that meet the interests of the parties and promote peace and harmony. The Supreme Soviet hopes that the same approach will be shown by Ukraine and its higher authorities."

205 The Law On Abolishment of Constitution and Some Laws of Autonomous Republic of Crimea.

206 See *The Age of Assassins* by Yuri Felshtinsky and Vladimir Prybilovsky.

207 But now they did not need to speak Portuguese or Spanish.

208 The work of the Trilateral Contact Group in 2014-2015 resulted in the preparation of a whole set of Minsk Agreements: a Protocol (September 5, 2014), a Memorandum (September 19, 2014), a Set of Measures to Implement the Minsk Agreements (February 12, 2015) and a Declaration to Support the Set of Measures to Implement the Minsk Agreements (February 15, 2015). On the Ukrainian side, the Protocol of September 5 was signed by former Ukrainian President Leonid Kuchma, who was authorized to represent the country at the talks; on the Russian side, by Ambassador Extraordinary and Plenipotentiary of the Russian Federation to Ukraine Mikhail Zurabov; on the OSCE side, by Swiss diplomat Heidi Tagliavini; on the LPR and DPR side, by their heads Igor Plotnitsky and Alexander Zakharchenko

209 An example is included as an Appendix to this book.

210 The same thing, only now without Czechoslovakia, was be repeated in 1939 during the Soviet government's talks with France and Britain concerning a pact of mutual assistance in the event of German aggression. The Soviet Union was again ready to sign a treaty with France and Britain, but on the condition that Poland agree to let Soviet troops to pass through its territory.

INDEX